First World War
and Army of Occupation
War Diary
France, Belgium and Germany

60 DIVISION
179 Infantry Brigade
London Regiment
2/13 Battalion
8 September 1915 - 30 November 1916

WO95/3030/3

The Naval & Military Press Ltd
www.nmarchive.com
Published in association with The National Archives

Published by

The Naval & Military Press Ltd

Unit 10 Ridgewood Industrial Park,

Uckfield, East Sussex,

TN22 5QE England

Tel: +44 (0) 1825 749494

www.naval-military-press.com

www.nmarchive.com

This diary has been reprinted in facsimile from the original. Any imperfections are inevitably reproduced and the quality may fall short of modern type and cartographic standards.

© **Crown Copyright**
Images reproduced by permission of The National Archives, London, England, 2015.

Contents

Document type	Place/Title	Date From	Date To
Heading	WO95/3030/3		
Heading	60 Division 179 Brigade 2/13 London Regt 1915 Sep-1916 May		
War Diary	Saffron Walden	08/09/1915	10/09/1915
War Diary	Quendon	23/09/1915	23/09/1915
War Diary	St. Chishall	27/09/1915	27/09/1915
War Diary	S Walden	05/10/1915	26/10/1915
War Diary	Sawbridge Worth	10/11/1915	19/11/1915
Heading	War Diary Of 2/13th Battalion London Regiment From 1st December 1915 To 31st December 1915 Volume 1		
War Diary	Sawbridge Worth	01/12/1915	06/12/1915
War Diary	Bps Stortford	06/12/1915	06/12/1915
War Diary	Sawbridgeworth	07/12/1915	13/12/1915
War Diary	Bps Stortford	13/12/1915	13/12/1915
War Diary	Sawbridgeworth	14/12/1915	16/12/1915
War Diary	Bps Stortford	16/12/1915	16/12/1915
War Diary	Sawbridgeworth	17/12/1915	31/12/1915
War Diary	Bps Stortford	31/12/1915	31/12/1915
Miscellaneous	British Museum Newspaper Library		
Heading	Appendix I Battalion Exercises.		
Operation(al) Order(s)	2/13th Battalion London Regiment Operation Order No 1	01/12/1915	01/12/1915
Miscellaneous	Appendix I (B) 2/13th Battalion. London Regiment.	06/12/1915	06/12/1915
Miscellaneous	Appendix I (C) 2/13th Battalion. London Regiment.		
Miscellaneous	Appendix I (D) 2/13th Battalion. London Regiment.		
Miscellaneous	Appendix I (E) 2/13th. Battalion. London Regiment.	29/12/1915	29/12/1915
Heading	Appendix 2 Brigade Exercises.		
Miscellaneous	Appendix 2 179th Infantry Brigade.	07/12/1915	07/12/1915
Heading	War Diary Of 2/13th Battalion London Regiment From 1st January 1916to 31st January 1916 Volume 1		
War Diary	Bishops Stortford	01/01/1916	01/01/1916
War Diary	Sawbridgeworth	01/01/1916	03/01/1916
War Diary	Bishops Stortford	03/01/1916	03/01/1916
War Diary	Sawbridgeworth	03/01/1916	05/01/1916
War Diary	Bps Stortford	05/01/1916	05/01/1916
War Diary	Sawbridgeworth	05/01/1916	10/01/1916
War Diary	Bps Stortford	12/01/1916	12/01/1916
War Diary	Sawbridgeworth	13/01/1916	13/01/1916
War Diary	Bps Stortford	13/01/1916	13/01/1916
War Diary	Sawbridgeworth	13/01/1916	14/01/1916
War Diary	Bps Stortford	14/01/1916	14/01/1916
War Diary	Sawbridgeworth	15/01/1916	22/01/1916
War Diary	Sutton Veny	23/01/1916	31/01/1916
Heading	War Diary 2/13th Battalion London Regiment From Feb 1. 1916 To Feb 29. 1916		
War Diary	Sutton Veny	01/11/1916	29/11/1916
Heading	War Diary 2/XIII Bn London Regiment From 1/3/16 To 31/3/16		
War Diary	No 8 Camp Sutton Veny	01/11/1916	30/11/1916

Heading	War Diary Appendix From 1st March To 31st March 1916		
Miscellaneous	A No 1	02/03/1916	02/03/1916
Miscellaneous	179th Infantry Brigade	11/03/1916	11/03/1916
Miscellaneous	Syllabus of Training		
Miscellaneous	Outpost Scheme		
Miscellaneous	Appendix A N2	18/03/1916	18/03/1916
Miscellaneous	Appendix No 3 179th Infantry Brigade.	25/03/1916	25/03/1916
Miscellaneous	Appendix A No 4 179th Infantry Brigade.	01/04/1916	01/04/1916
Miscellaneous	Programme Of Training For Week Commencing	27/03/1916	27/03/1916
Heading	War Diary 2/13th Battalion London Regiment From 1.4.16 To 30.4.16		
War Diary	No 8 Camp Sutton Veny	01/04/1916	29/04/1916
War Diary	Warminster Station	29/04/1916	29/04/1916
War Diary	No 8 Camp Sutton Veny	29/04/1916	29/04/1916
War Diary	Warminster Station	29/04/1916	29/04/1916
War Diary	Neyland	29/10/1916	29/10/1916
War Diary	No 8 Camp Sutton Veny	28/10/1916	30/10/1916
War Diary	Neyland	30/04/1916	30/04/1916
War Diary	S S Snowdon	30/04/1916	30/04/1916
Heading	War Diary Appendix From 1st April To 30th April 1916 Sutton Veny No 8 Camp		
Miscellaneous	Appendix No 1		
Miscellaneous	Programme Of Training For Week Commencing	03/04/1916	03/04/1916
Miscellaneous	Programme Of Training For Week Ending 8th April 1916	08/04/1916	08/04/1916
Miscellaneous	Weekly Programme Of Traning For Machine Gun Sections	03/04/1916	03/04/1916
Miscellaneous	A Form Messages And Signals.		
Miscellaneous	Appendix No 2		
Miscellaneous	Programme Of Training For Week Commencing	10/04/1916	10/04/1916
Miscellaneous	Programme Of Training For Week Ending 15th April 1916	15/04/1916	15/04/1916
Miscellaneous	Appendix No-3		
Miscellaneous	Programme Of Training For Week Commencing	17/04/1916	17/04/1916
Miscellaneous	Programme Of Training For Week Ending April 22nd 1916	22/04/1916	22/04/1916
Miscellaneous	Syllabus Of Training	13/04/1916	13/04/1916
Miscellaneous	A Form Messages And Signals.		
Miscellaneous	Appendix No-4		
Miscellaneous	Programme Of Training For Week Commencing	24/04/1916	24/04/1916
Miscellaneous	Programme Of Training For Week Ending 29th April 1916	29/04/1916	29/04/1916
Miscellaneous	Lewis Guns	10/05/1916	10/05/1916
Miscellaneous	179th Infantry Brigade Orders By Colonel E.W. Baird Commanding	29/04/1916	29/04/1916
Miscellaneous	2/13th Battalion L.R.	30/04/1916	30/04/1916
Miscellaneous	A Form Messages And Signals.		
Miscellaneous	Appendix No-5		
Heading	War Diary Appendix From 1st May-31st May 2/13th Bn London Regt		
Heading	2/13th Battalion London Regiment From 010516 To 310516		
War Diary	SS. Snowdon	01/05/1916	01/05/1916
War Diary	Queenstown	02/05/1916	02/05/1916
War Diary	Tota Park Camp	02/05/1916	06/05/1916

War Diary	Ballin Collic Barracks	07/05/1916	07/05/1916
War Diary	Coachford	07/05/1916	08/05/1916
War Diary	Macroom	08/05/1916	09/05/1916
War Diary	Hillstrek	09/05/1916	10/05/1916
War Diary	Macroom	10/05/1916	11/05/1916
War Diary	Hill Street	11/05/1916	12/05/1916
War Diary	Rosslare	12/05/1916	12/05/1916
War Diary	Hill Street	12/05/1916	12/05/1916
War Diary	Rosslare Harbour	12/05/1916	13/05/1916
War Diary	SS Connaught	13/05/1916	13/05/1916
War Diary	Fishguard	13/05/1916	14/05/1916
War Diary	Warminster	14/05/1916	14/05/1916
War Diary	Long Bridge Deverill No 12 Cam	14/05/1916	14/05/1916
War Diary	Warminster	14/05/1916	14/05/1916
War Diary	Longbridge Deveill No 12 Camp	14/05/1916	14/05/1916
War Diary	Sutton Veny No 18 Camp	03/05/1916	12/05/1916
War Diary	Longbridge Deverill No 12 Camp	13/05/1916	31/05/1916
Miscellaneous	Appendix No 1		
Miscellaneous	Disembarking Orders by Colonel M.W. Baird Commanding	02/05/1916	02/05/1916
Miscellaneous	179th Infantry Brigade Orders By Colonel E.W. Baird Commanding	02/05/1916	02/05/1916
Miscellaneous	Orders For Slatty Bridge Guard	03/05/1916	03/05/1916
Miscellaneous	Emergency Alarm	03/05/1916	03/05/1916
Miscellaneous	179th Infantry Brigade Orders By Colonel E.W. Baird Commanding	03/05/1916	03/05/1916
Miscellaneous	179th Infantry Brigade Orders By Colonel E.W. Baird Commanding	04/05/1916	04/05/1916
Miscellaneous	179th Infantry Brigade Orders By Colonel E.W. Baird Commanding	06/05/1916	06/05/1916
Miscellaneous	179th Infantry Brigade Orders By Colonel E.W. Baird Commanding	07/05/1916	07/05/1916
Miscellaneous	Orders For Main Gate Guard	08/05/1916	08/05/1916
Miscellaneous	Major Thorp Nov		
Miscellaneous	179th Infantry Brigade Orders By Colonel E.W. Baird Commanding	08/05/1916	08/05/1916
Miscellaneous	179th Infantry Brigade Orders By Colonel E.W. Baird Commanding	09/05/1916	09/05/1916
Miscellaneous	179th Infantry Brigade Orders By Colonel E.W. Baird Commanding	10/05/1916	10/05/1916
Miscellaneous	Appendix No 2		
Miscellaneous	Programme Of Training	20/05/1916	20/05/1916
Miscellaneous	Syllabus Of Training	11/05/1916	11/05/1916
Miscellaneous	Programme Of Training	22/05/1916	22/05/1916
Miscellaneous	Programme Of Training	27/05/1916	27/05/1916
Miscellaneous	Lewis Gun Course	20/05/1916	20/05/1916
Miscellaneous	Trench Scheme	24/05/1916	24/05/1916
Map	Sutton Veny Trenches		
Miscellaneous	A Form Messages And Signals.		
Miscellaneous	Appendix No 4		
Miscellaneous	Programme Of Training For Week Commencing	29/05/1916	29/05/1916
Miscellaneous	Programme Of Training For Week Ending 3rd June 1916	03/06/1916	03/06/1916
Heading	2-13th Bn London Regt 1915 Sep-1916 Nov		
Heading	War Diary 2/13th Bn London R From 1st June 1916 To 30th June 1916 Vol 1		

War Diary	Longbridge Deverill	01/06/1916	21/06/1916
War Diary	Southampton	21/06/1916	21/06/1916
War Diary	Le Havre	22/06/1916	23/06/1916
War Diary	Station	23/06/1916	23/06/1916
War Diary	Houvin	23/06/1916	23/06/1916
War Diary	Monts en Tournois	24/06/1916	24/06/1916
War Diary	Penin	24/06/1916	25/06/1916
War Diary	Ecoivres	25/06/1916	27/06/1916
War Diary	Neuville St Vaaste	27/06/1916	30/06/1916
Miscellaneous	Appendix A 2/13th. Battalion London Regiment.		
Heading	War Diary 2/13th Battalion London Regiment July 1 1916 To July 31 1916		
War Diary	Neuville St-Vaaste	01/07/1916	05/07/1916
War Diary	Bray Huts	06/07/1916	06/07/1916
War Diary	Maison Blanche	07/07/1916	12/07/1916
War Diary	Boyau Des Abris	13/07/1916	15/07/1916
War Diary	Bray Huts	16/07/1916	19/07/1916
War Diary	Boyau Des Abris	20/07/1916	27/07/1916
War Diary	Maison Blanche	28/07/1916	31/07/1916
Heading	War Diary Of 2/13th Battalion London Regiment From 1st August 1916 To 31st August 1916 Vol III		
War Diary	Maison Blanche	01/08/1916	03/08/1916
War Diary	Boyau Des Abris	04/08/1916	11/08/1916
War Diary	Bray	12/08/1916	18/08/1916
War Diary	Boyau Des Abris	20/08/1916	26/08/1916
War Diary	Maison Blanche	27/08/1916	31/08/1916
Miscellaneous	Appendix A		
Miscellaneous	Raid By 2/13th London Regt	06/05/1916	06/05/1916
Miscellaneous	Special Arrangement		
Miscellaneous	Duties Of Groups		
Miscellaneous	Artillery And T.M Programme (Provisional)		
Map	Map		
Miscellaneous	Map Reference	07/08/1916	07/08/1916
Miscellaneous	Appendix A		
Miscellaneous	Report By Lieut W Read	08/08/1916	08/08/1916
Miscellaneous	Advanced Headquarters 179th Infantry Brigade	01/09/1916	01/09/1916
Operation(al) Order(s)	179th Infantry Brigade Operation Order No 6.		
Map	Map		
Miscellaneous	Trench Mortar Programme		
Miscellaneous	Appendix C		
Miscellaneous	Time Table Of Operation	11/08/1916	11/08/1916
Heading	War Diary Of 2/13th London Regt. From September 1st To September 30th 1916 Volume 4		
War Diary	Boyau Des Abris	01/09/1916	06/09/1916
War Diary	Bray	07/09/1916	11/09/1916
War Diary	Boyau Des Abris	13/09/1916	18/09/1916
War Diary	Maison Blanche	19/09/1916	23/09/1916
War Diary	Boyau Des Abris	25/09/1916	30/09/1916
Miscellaneous	Appendix I		
Heading	War Diary 2/13th Bn L.R. Confidential Vol 5 From 1st October-31st October 1916		
War Diary	Boyau Des Abris	01/10/1916	01/10/1916
War Diary	Bray	03/10/1916	07/10/1916
War Diary	Boyau Des Abris	08/10/1916	13/10/1916
War Diary	Maison Blanche	14/10/1916	19/10/1916
War Diary	Boyau Des Abris	20/10/1916	24/10/1916

Type	Description	From	To
Miscellaneous	Appendix No I		
War Diary	Bois Des Alleux	26/10/1916	26/10/1916
War Diary	Savy	27/10/1916	27/10/1916
War Diary	Buneville	28/10/1916	28/10/1916
War Diary	Noeux	29/10/1916	29/10/1916
War Diary	Proville	30/10/1916	31/10/1916
Miscellaneous	Particulars Of Casualties		
Miscellaneous	Roll Of Draft To Be Attached To Your Coy		
Miscellaneous	Appendix 2		
Miscellaneous	Officer Commanding 2/13th Battalion London Regiment	12/10/1916	12/10/1916
Heading	2/13th Battalion London Regt. War Diary for November 1916 Vol 6		
War Diary	Prouville	01/11/1916	03/11/1916
War Diary	Vauchelle-Les-Quesnoy	04/11/1916	14/11/1916
War Diary	Longrre-Le-Corps-Sant	14/11/1916	14/11/1916
War Diary	Marseilles	18/11/1916	20/11/1916
War Diary	Malta	22/11/1916	27/11/1916
War Diary	Salonika	30/11/1916	30/11/1916
Miscellaneous	No. 7 Infantry Base Depot.		

WO 95/3030/3

60 DIVISION

179 BRIGADE

2/13 LONDON REGT

1915 SEP — 1916 MAY

2902

Army Form C. 2118.

WAR DIARY
or
INTELLIGENCE SUMMARY.
(Erase heading not required.)

2/3 LOND

Instructions regarding War Diaries and Intelligence Summaries are contained in F. S. Regs., Part II. and the Staff Manual respectively. Title pages will be prepared in manuscript.

Hour, Date, Place	Summary of Events and Information	Remarks and references to Appendices
11.45 p.m., 8 Sept. 1915, Lappare Hadleer	Zeppelin arrived over Camp from S.W. — Stayed from 4 to 5 minutes and departed N.E.	
about 9.45 a.m., 10 "	Anti aircraft practice, single Brigades (Composite Battalion V 2/13 & 2/14)	
" 7 a.m., 23 " Reindon	Sound alarm practice, to Signalers by S.O.C.	
" 8.30 a.m., 27 " Gt. Chishall	Exercise of Brigade + Outpost scheme with Rearguard action.	

W J M Keary M.J.A.
Commanding 2/13 & 14th London Regt.

Army Form C. 2118.

WAR DIARY
or
INTELLIGENCE SUMMARY.
(Erase heading not required.)

Instructions regarding War Diaries and Intelligence Summaries are contained in F. S. Regs., Part II. and the Staff Manual respectively. Title pages will be prepared in manuscript.

Hour, Date, Place	Summary of Events and Information	Remarks and references to Appendices
5 a.m. 5th Oct. 1915, S. Welbury	⎫	
8 " " " "	⎬ 4 days' TuR & Tactical Exercises.	
12 " " " "	⎭	
14 " " " "	Artillery Tactical Scheme.	
8.45 a.m. 19 " " "	⎫	
22 " " " "	⎬ 4 days' TuR & Tactical Exercises.	
8.45 a.m. 26 " " "	Move to Tonbridge Wells by Route March	

W.M. Rose
Lt. Col.
Comdg. 2/13th Bn. London Regt.

Army Form C. 2118.

WAR DIARY
or
INTELLIGENCE SUMMARY.
(Erase heading not required.)

Instructions regarding War Diaries and Intelligence Summaries are contained in F. S. Regs., Part II. and the Staff Manual respectively. Title pages will be prepared in manuscript.

Date, Place	Summary of Events and Information	Remarks and references to Appendices
November 10th, 1915. SAWBRIDGEWORTH	Band struck off disbanded and musicians returned to duty. (Central Force Order.)	copy
November 19th, 1915. SAWBRIDGEWORTH	Inspection of Battalion by Brigadier.	copy

W.J.McLean M.N.
Cmdg. 2/13th Bn. London Regt.

CONFIDENTIAL.

WAR DIARY.
of
2/13th Battalion London Regiment

from

1st December 1915 to 31st December 1915.

Volume 1.

Army Form C. 2118.

WAR DIARY
or
INTELLIGENCE SUMMARY.
(Erase heading not required.)

2/10th BATTALION LONDON REGIMENT.

Instructions regarding War Diaries and Intelligence Summaries are contained in F.S. Regs., Part II. and the Staff Manual respectively. Title pages will be prepared in manuscript.

Hour, Date, Place	Summary of Events and Information	Remarks and references to Appendices
8.55 a.m. 1.12.15. SAWBRIDGEWORTH	Battalion Drill (Ceremonial)	wagon
8.55 a.m. 2.12.15. "	Company's Practicing Transport entraining practice at HARLOW STATION (day & night)	wagon appendix 1.(a)
8.55 a.m. 3.12.15. "	Battalion practicing retirement from a position as a Rearguard. Eight men transferred to 105th Provisional Battalion. "GEORGE V." Public House LONDON ROAD placed out of Bounds	wagon authority Medical Board authority major
9 a.m. 4.12.15. "	Inspection of Feet, Heads, Kits + Billets. Lecture to Battalion Brushes by Captain F.R. RADICE	wagon
8.55 a.m. 5.12.15. "	Church Parade	wagon
8.55 a.m. 6.12.15. "	Defence of the Village of HATFIELD HEATH. The Machine Gun Section Lieut. L.F. BAKER, 2 N.C.O.'s, + 12. Men went to BISHOPS STORTFORD	wagon Appendix 1. (b)
" BPS STORTFORD	Lecture by Captain CABUCHE See: Lieut: G.T. NIGHTINGALE Commissioned Corps of Musketry at BISLEY.	
8.45 a.m. 7.12.15. SAWBRIDGEWORTH	Brigade Concentration March	wagon Appendix 2.

(1.)

Army Form C. 2118.

WAR DIARY
or
INTELLIGENCE SUMMARY.
(Erase heading not required.)

2/13th BATTALION LONDON REGIMENT.

Instructions regarding War Diaries and Intelligence Summaries are contained in F. S. Regs., Part II. and the Staff Manual respectively. Title pages will be prepared in manuscript.

Hour, Date, Place		Summary of Events and Information	Remarks and references to Appendices
8.55 a.m.	8.12.15. SAWBRIDGEWORTH.	Visual Training for all Officers under Assistant Adjutant for Musketry. Company Drill under Company Sergeant Majors. Captain BROCKHURST and I.N.C.O. to attend 3rd Army Trench Fighting School Course at KELVEDON	nil
8.55 a.m.	9.12.15 "	Battalion practising the Attack	nil
4.30 p.m.	10.12.15 "	Night Concentration March	nil
9 a.m.	11.12.15 "	Foot, Head, Kit & Blanket Inspection	nil
9.15 a.m.	12.12.15 "	Church Parade	nil
8.55 a.m.	13.12.15 "	Training in Street Fighting in Billeting Area. Battalion Bombers practising under Lieut. ROSEVEAR	nil
5 p.m.	" BPs STORTFORD.	Lecture by Commandant of the Divisional Machine Gun Section at Brigade Headquarters	nil
8.55 a.m.	14.12.15. SAWBRIDGEWORTH.	Battalion Route March. Captain G.W. COLLIER appointed Divisional Instructor in Bombing. Captain A.C. HERNE detailed to attend District Court Martial at BISHOPS STORTFORD.	nil
8.55 a.m.	15.12.15 "	Battalion Close Order Drill. Defence of a River (without Troops)	nil appendix 1.(C)

(2.)

WAR DIARY
or
INTELLIGENCE SUMMARY.

(Erase heading not required.)

2/13th BATTALION LONDON REGIMENT.

Army Form C. 2118.

Hour, Date, Place		Summary of Events and Information	Remarks and references to Appendices
8.55.a.m.	16.12.15. SAWBRIDGEWORTH.	Training in Escort of Battalion Convoy (one Platoon as Enemy)	nil
		Lieut. F.R. ROSEYEAR, 3. N.C.O's and 14 men attended Divisional Bombing School "ALSA LODGE" STANSTED	
3.15.p.m.	BPS: STORTFORD	Lecture on Trench Fighting by Captain PALMER at the "DRILL HALL" B.	nil
9.a.m.	17.12.15 SAWBRIDGEWORTH	Companies Close Order Drill	nil
		Board of Officers:- President Captain A.C. HERNE Members Captains C.E. BROCKHURST and R.P. GLADSTONE, to check Stores in possession of Battalion	
9.a.m.	18.12.15.	Inspection of Kits, Feet, + Billets	nil
9.15.a.m.	19.12.15.	Church Parade	nil
10.a.m.	20.12.15	Inspection by G.O.C. 60th (London) Division.	nil
8.55.a.m.	21.12.15	Handling of Tactical Units in the Field by Platoon Commanders and N.C.O's	nil
		The ADJUTANT:- Captain's R.P.M. SLADE and C.E. BROCKHURST and Sec: Lieut: K. RIVINGTON visited School of Instruction in Military Engineering at ONGAR	
8.55.a.m.	22.12.15	Battalion Close Order Drill	nil
		Reconnaissance of Defensive Position	Appendix I. (a)

(3.)

Army Form C. 2118.

WAR DIARY
or
INTELLIGENCE SUMMARY.

2/13th BATTALION LONDON REGIMENT

(Erase heading not required.)

Instructions regarding War Diaries and Intelligence Summaries are contained in F.S. Regs., Part II. and the Staff Manual respectively. Title pages will be prepared in manuscript.

Hour, Date, Place			Summary of Events and Information	Remarks and references to Appendices
8.55 a.m.	23/12/15	SAWBRIDGEWORTH	Battalion Route March	
9 a.m.	24/12/15	"	Inspection of Kits, Feet, & Billets	
11 a.m.	25.12.15	"	Church Parade	
9.15 a.m.	26.12.15	"	Church Parade	
	27.12.15	"	General Holiday	
			Sec. Lieut: F.R. STOCKWELL & 17 N.C.O's & men (Battalion Bombers) attend Divisional Bombing School at STANSTED	
			Lieut-Col: W.R.J. McLEAN. T.D. assumed temporary Command of the 179th Infantry Brigade during the absence on duty of the Brigadier	
8.55 a.m.	28/12/15	"	Battalion Concentration Route March. Companies Concentrate on Battalion	
8.55 a.m.	29.12.15	"	Battalion Close Order drill	
8.55 a.m.	30.12.15	"	Reconnaissance of a Village (Officers)	appendix 1.(2)
			Battalion practising attack & clearing village, reconnoitred previous day	
8.55 a.m.	31.12.15	"	Platoon Commanders exercised in handling Platoons	
			Handling of Tactical Units in the Field by Platoon Commanders	
8.15 p.m.	"	BPS: STORTFORD	Lecture by Captain PALMER at the "DRILL HALL"	

W.R.J. McLean
Lieutenant Colonel
Commanding 2/13th Battalion London Regiment.

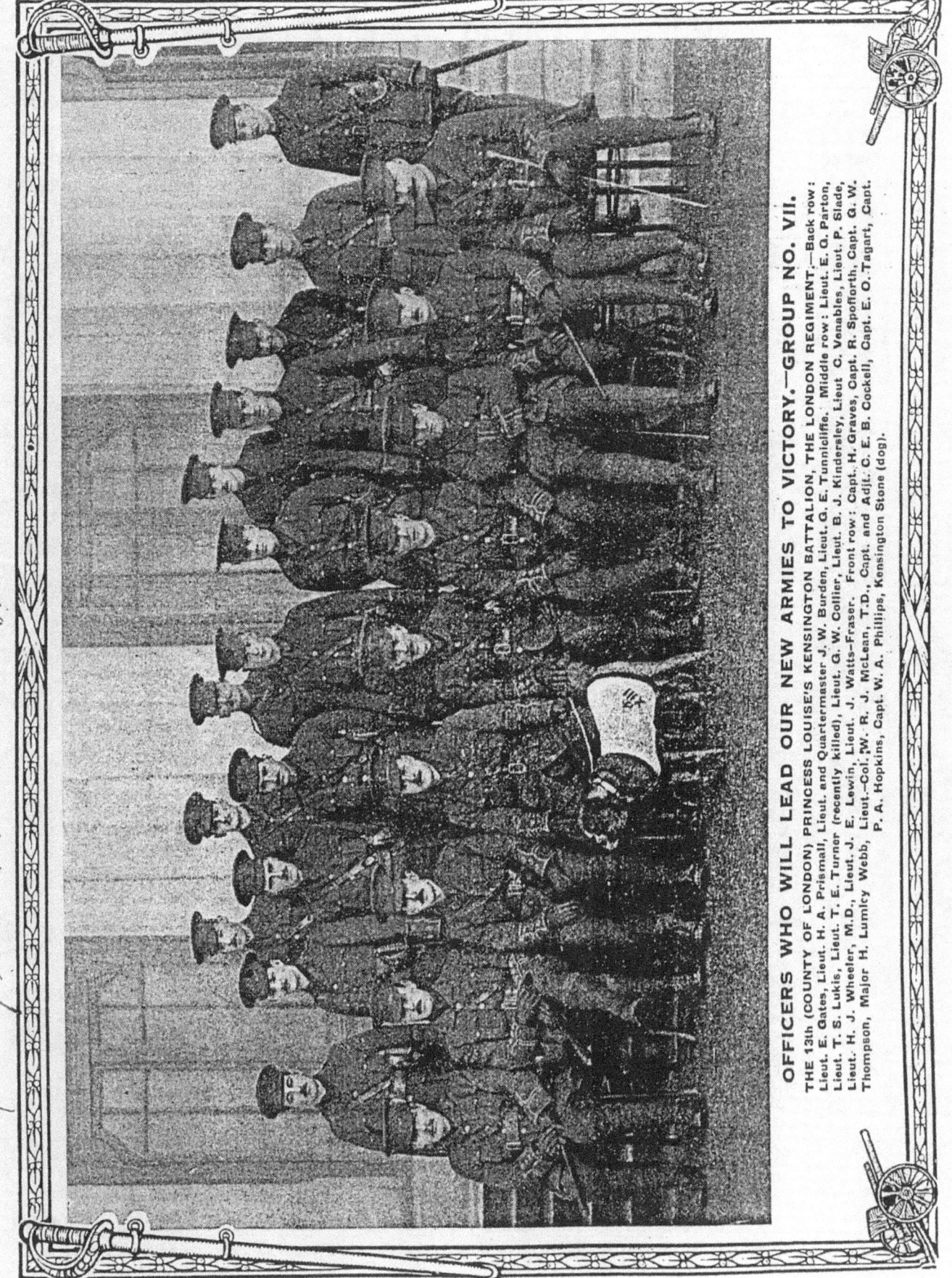

OFFICERS WHO WILL LEAD OUR NEW ARMIES TO VICTORY.—GROUP NO. VII.

THE 13th (COUNTY OF LONDON) PRINCESS LOUISE'S KENSINGTON BATTALION, THE LONDON REGIMENT.—Back row: Lieut. E. Gates, Lieut. H. A. Prismall, Lieut. and Quartermaster J. W. Burden, Lieut. G. E. Tunnicliffe. Middle row: Lieut. E. G. Parton, Lieut. T. S. Lukis, Lieut. T. E. Turner (recently killed), Lieut. G. W. Collier, Lieut. B. J. Kindersley, Lieut. C. Venables, Lieut. P. Slade, Lieut. H. J. Wheeler, M.D., Lieut. J. E. Lewin, Lieut. J. Watts-Fraser. Front row: Capt. H. Graves, Capt. R. Spofforth, Capt. G. W. Thompson, Major H. Lumley Webb, Lieut.-Col. W. R. J. McLean, T.D., Capt. and Adjt. C. E. B. Cockell, Capt. E. O. Tagart, Capt. P. A. Hopkins, Capt. W. A. Phillips, Kensington Stone (dog).

FIGHTERS FOR THE FREEDOM OF EUROPE: XXI.—OFFICERS OF THE 2/13TH LONDON REGIMENT (PRINCESS LOUISE'S KENSINGTON BATTALION).

In the Back Row (standing) are (reading from left to right): 2nd Lieut. L. F. Baker, 2nd Lieut. B. H. Wood, 2nd Lieut. E. Hignett, Lieut. G. L. D. Hall, 2nd Lieut. C. T. Foster, Lieut. B. J. F. C. Kindersley, Lieut. C. F. Brookhurst, Lieut. C. Venables, Lieut. C. E. Tunnicliffe, 2nd Lieut. C. W. Hill. Seated in the Middle Row (again reading from left to right) are: Lieut. G. W. Collier, Capt. W. E. David-Devis, Capt. W. A. Phillips, Major P. A. Hopkins, Lieut.-Col. W. R. J. McLean, A.D., Capt. and Adjt. C. E. B Cockell, Capt. A. C. Herne, Capt. P. P. M. Slade, Capt. J. E. L Higgins. In the Front Row, sitting on the ground (as before, reading from left to right), are: 2nd Lieut. F. W. Heath, 2nd Lieut. G. V. Thompson, 2nd Lieut. F. R. Rosevear, Lieut. S. W. Caldbeck. The Hon. Colonel of the Princess Louise's Kensington Battalion is Major-Gen. Sir A. E. Turner, K.C.B., Colonel-Commandant of the Royal Artillery. The badge of the battalion displays the heraldic arms of the royal borough, and the Corps' motto is "Quid nobis ardui." The "Kensingtons" have the honour of inscribing "South Africa, 1900-2" on their colours, commemorating the work of the 1st Battalion.—[Photo. by Bassano.]

FIGHTERS FOR THE FREEDOM OF EUROPE: XXI.—N.C.O.'S OF THE 2/13TH LONDON REGIMENT (PRINCESS LOUISE'S KENSINGTON BATTALION).

In the Back Row (reading from left to right), standing on a raised platform, are: Cpl. Barnet, Lce-Cpl. Simons, Lce-Cpl. Smith, Cpl. Lumley, Cpl. Hardy, Cpl. A. Martin, Lce-Cpl. Elliott, Cpl. Jackson, Cpl. C. Miller, Cpl. Pearce, Lce-Cpl. Whyman, Cpl. Tottman, Lce-Cpl. Dwyer. In the Second Row, standing on the ground (left to right), are: Sgt. Porters, Sgt. Winfield, Sgt. Moody, Sgt. Reardon, Sgt. Acres, Sgt. Westwood, Sgt. Frapwell, Sgt. Scammell, Sgt. Sellers, Sgt. Dawes, Sgt. Barnes, Sgt. Moss. In the Third Row from the top (left to right, and seated), are: Sgt. Cory, Co.-Q.M.S. Knapton, Co.-Q.M.S. Fozard, Co.-Sgt.-Major Lystor, Co.-Sgt.-Major Murray, Regt.-Sgt.-Major Cattermole, Regt.-Q.M.S. Bailey, Co.-Sgt.-Major Hellawell, Co.-Sgt.-Major Gulland, Co.-Q.M.S. Chant. In the Front Row (reading as before) are, sitting on the ground: Cpl. Blakey, Lce-Cpl. Parkes, Lce-Cpl. Taylor, Cpl. Stone, Cpl. Cusiack, Lce-Cpl. Castle, Lce-Cpl. Davies, Lewington. The 1st Battalion is one of the London Territorial regiments. It was in existence several years before Lord Haldane's reorganisation scheme. It has been at the Front, and brilliantly distinguished itself, particularly in the Ypres fighting.—[Photo. by Bassano.]

48—THE ILLUSTRATED WAR NEWS, AUG. 25, 1915.—[PART 55]

SAFFRON WALDEN 1915.

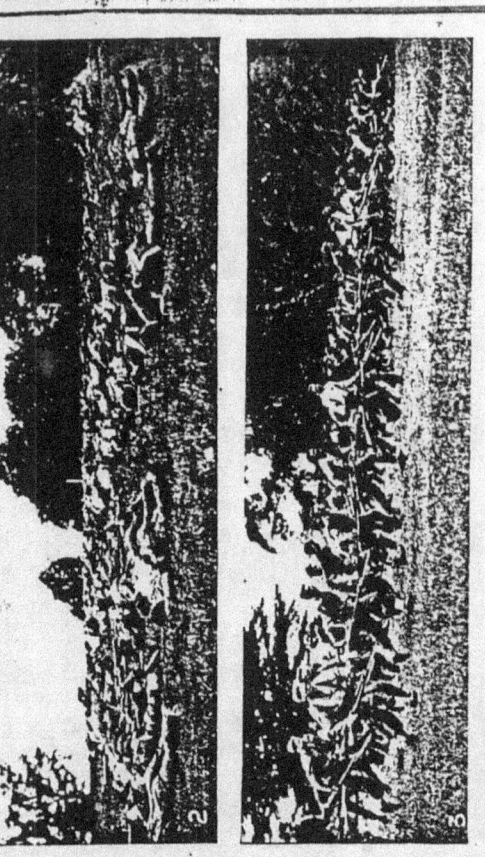

FIGHTERS FOR THE FREEDOM OF EUROPE: XXI.—THE 2/13TH LONDON REGIMENT (PRINCESS LOUISE'S KENSINGTON BATTALION) UNDER TRAINING.

In the first photograph we see part of the Transport Section of the 2/13th "Kensingtons" on the road, accompanying the battalion on a field day during its training for the front. In the second, companies of the battalion are shown at battle-practice, lying down in the open before making an attack, as in action, while the artillery are firing over their heads to clear the way for the coming onset. The third photograph shows the beginning of a charge with the bayonet. Photograph No. 4 shows part of a company defending a line of hedge with musketry. Photograph No. 5 shows another piece of practical training: First Aid being rendered during "action" to a man told off to assume, for the moment, the rôle of a wounded man.—[Photos. by Sport and General.]

LONDON: Published Weekly at the Office, 172, Strand, in the Parish of St. Clement Danes, London, by THE ILLUSTRATED LONDON NEWS AND SKETCH, LTD., 172, Strand, aforesaid; and Printed by THE ILLUSTRATED LONDON NEWS AND SKETCH, LTD., Milford Lane, W.C.—WEDNESDAY, AUG. 25, 1915.

British Museum Newspaper Library

APPENDIX 1.
BATTALION EXERCISES.

2/13th. Battalion London Regiment.

OPERATION ORDER No. 1

by

O. C. W H I T E   F O R C E.

Appendix 1.(A)

RED HOUSE,
SAWBRIDGEWORTH.
1.12.1915.

Reference:- ½" Training Sheet No.29.

Information.	1.	The 2/13th. Battalion will escort a convoy tomorrow from SAWBRIDGEWORTH to HADHAM CROSS. The convoy will proceed via STORTFORD ROAD - TRIMS GREEN - GREEN TYE. The enemy's main body are reliably reported to be at CHESHUNT and its mounted troops are in the neighbourhood of STANSTED. Our main body is at HATFIELD BROAD OAK.
Starting Point.	2.	The starting point will be the WHITE LION INN.
Convoy. Transport Officer. 2/13th. Battn.	3.	The convoy will consist of 4 wagons.
Distribution of Escort	4.	Advanced guard: main body: rear guard.
Advanced Guard. O.C. No.1 Coy. 2/13th. Battn. No.1 Coy. 2/13th. Battn.	5.	Will proceed as in route for convoy and will report obstacles delaying march and reconnoitre cover near road and select site for halts.
Main Body. O.C. No.3 Coy. 2/13th. Battn. 2/13th. Battn. (less 2 Coys.).	6.	Will march via ROOK END - SACOMBE ASH - PERR GREEN. Will pass starting point at 9.15 a.m.
Rear Guard. O.C. No.4 Coy. 2/13th. Battn. No.4 Coy. 2/13th. Battn.	7.	Will follow ½ mile in rear of Main Body.
Reports.	8.	Reports will be sent to head of Main Body.

L S David-Davis

Captain & S.O.,

WHITE FORCE.

Handed at 9 p.m. :-
No. 2 copy to O.C. Transport.
 " 3 "   " O.C. No.1 Company.
 " 4 "   " O.C. Advanced Guard.
 " 5 "   " O.C. Main Body.
 " 6 "   " O.C. Rear Guard.
 " 7 "   retained for Operation File Order.
 " 8 "   WAR DIARY.

Appendix I(B)

2/13th Battalion. London Regiment.
(Princess Louise's Kensington Bn).

Scheme for the Defence of the village of Hatfield Heath.
Monday, 6th December 1915.

Reference:-
Ord. Survey. Sheet No. 29.
½" - 1 mile.

General Idea.

A White Force, estimated strength one Brigade, is credibly reported at GREAT DUNMOW, and marching at 8.30.a.m. on 6th December, on SAWBRIDGEWORTH.

A Brown Force - the 179th Infantry Brigade - is ordered to actively intercept its advance on the line LITTLE HALLINGBURY - HATFIELD HEATH - WHITE RODING.

Special Idea.

BROWN.

The O.C., 179th Infantry Brigade, orders the 2/13th Battalion to occupy and defend HATFIELD HEATH: the 2/15th and 2/16th Battalions being on right and left flanks respectively, with the 2/14th Battalion in Reserve at the K in COWICKS.

appendix 1.(c)

2/13th BATTALION LONDON REGIMENT

SCHEME for Defence of River line.
(without troops)

Reference - Ordnance Survey Sheet No. 29   ½" 1 mile.

GENERAL IDEA.

A White detached force strength 1 Brigade is halted at MUCH HADHAM on the night 14/15 December 1915. The Commander receiving information that a hostile force Brown estimated strength 2 Battalions is advancing from the Eastward determines to oppose the passage of the River Stort.

SPECIAL IDEA.

The 2/13th Battalion is detailed to prevent the passage of the River Stort at SAWBRIDGEWORTH

2/13th Battalion London Regiment.

SCHEME FOR DEFENSIVE RECONNAISANCE

Reference. Ord. Survey.
Sheet 29 - ½" - mile.

GENERAL IDEA

A White Force consisting of 2 Infantry Battalions and 1 Battery R.F.A is credibly reported to be advancing South West on SAWBRIDGEWORTH and to be halted on the night of 21/22 December 1915 at GREAT BARDFIELD.

A Brown Force - the 179th Infantry Brigade with 1 Battery R. F. A. is halted at EASTWICK.

SPECIAL IDEA

The O. C. 179th Infantry Brigade detaches the 2/13th Battalion and R. F. A. Battery under O. C. 2/13th Battalion and orders him to move at dawn on the 22nd December and to hold the line HATFIELD HEATH - HALLINGBURY.

NOTE. Officers will be taken over the ground and will work in two groups. Each group will prepare :-

1. Reconnaissance Report.
2. An Appreciation.
3. Operation Orders as for O. C. Detached Force.
4. Panorama Sketches from position taken up.
5. Plans.
6. Range Cards.

Appendix I.(E)

2/13th. Battalion London Regiment.

Tactical Scheme for December 29th, 1915.
Attack on and Clearing a Village.

Reference Ordnance Survey Sheet – ½" to 1 mile.

GENERAL IDEA.

A BROWN Force – the 179th. Infantry Brigade – is moving from HARLOW to BISHOP'S STORTFORD with the 2/13th. Battn. as its advanced Guard. When approaching SAWBRIDGEWORTH information is received that a WHITE detached column is holding the village of LITTLE HALLINGBURY.

SPECIAL IDEA.

The Officer Commanding BROWN FORCE orders the Officer Commanding Advanced Guard to attack and disperse WHITE Column.

APPENDIX 2.
BRIGADE EXERCISES.

Appendix 2.

179th Infantry Brigade.

CONCENTRATION MARCH.

Tuesday, 7th December, 1915.

Reference:- Ord. Survey Training Sheet No. 29.   BISHOP'S STORTFORD.
            1 inch - 2 miles.   4th December, 1915.

The 179th Infantry Brigade will concentrate on LITTLE HADHAM - WIDFORD Road facing SOUTH - head of column at road junction WEST of C in HADHAM CROSS. at 12 o'clock noon on Tuesday, 7th December, 1915, in the following order:-

        2/15th Battalion.
        2/13th Battalion.
        2/14th Battalion.

Companies will concentrate to Battalions at the following points.

2/13th Battalion concentration point - Road bend WEST of first T in THORLEY STREET.
2/14th Battalion concentration point - Cross roads SOUTH of O in STANDON.
2/15th Battalion concentration point - Road junction EAST of Point 182 on BARWICK - HADHAM CROSS Road.

Transport *fully loaded* will accompany battalions, sufficient being left behind to deal with supplies.

A haversack ration will be carried.

                BY ORDER.

                B. LEVETT.

          CAPTAIN & BRIGADE MAJOR.

            179th Infantry Brigade.

179 BDE

CONFIDENTIAL.

WAR DIARY.

of 2/13th Battalion London Regiment.

From 1st January 1916 to 31st January 1916.

Volume 1.

Army Form C. 2118.

WAR DIARY
or
INTELLIGENCE SUMMARY.
(Erase heading not required.)

2/13th BATTALION LONDON REGIMENT.

Instructions regarding War Diaries and Intelligence Summaries are contained in F.S. Regs., Part II. and the Staff Manual respectively. Title pages will be prepared in manuscript.

Hour, Date, Place	Summary of Events and Information	Remarks and references to Appendices
1.1.16 BISHOPS STORTFORD.	Lieut: Col: W.R.J. McLEAN, T.D. will continue to Command the 179th Infantry Brigade until the return to duty of Colonel F. W. BAIRD.	(PH) authority (Brigade orders No1 of 1.1.16.)
" SAWBRIDGEWORTH.	Major G. THOMPSON, second in command, remains in command of 2/13th Battalion during the absence of Lieut Col: W.R.J. McLEAN, T.D. at Brigade Headquarters.	(PH) " O.C. Brigade
" "	Major P.H. HOPKINS appointed Acting Adjutant during absence in rear of Captain N.E. DAVID-DEVILS.	(PH) " O.C. Battalion
9 a.m. "	Companies in their areas; Kit & Foot Inspection, Physical Training, Bayonet fighting and Musketry.	
" "	Received instructions from Brigade to detail 2 Officers & 2 N.C.O.t attend a Rifle Range finding Course (1st and 3rd Strand) at Bde: STRATFORD. Commencing Monday 3rd inst — 2nd Lieut W.A. EBDON & 2nd Lieut H.G. CLARK No. 2459 Sergt: COLEMAN H.T. & No 2329 Corp: WATTS W.G. Selected.	(PH) Authority (Bde: Minute No 2124 dated 31.12.15.)
" "	Received further orders to hand over, for the use of the "9th Rifles Coonol", 2nd Lieut MILLER 2/1/6 Rn: Ken: R14: The officer in Charge — the two "BANK & STROUD" Range finders in charge of the Battalion.	
2.30 pm "	Party of Bombers detailed in Battalion Orders No 296 had 1.(Appx.3) dated 24.12.15 returned from STANSTED Bombing Course — —	(PH) " Division 6.12.15.

(1)

Army Form C. 2118.

WAR DIARY
or
INTELLIGENCE SUMMARY.
(Erase heading not required.)

2/13th BATTALION LONDON REGIMENT

Instructions regarding War Diaries and Intelligence Summaries are contained in F. S. Regs., Part II. and the Staff Manual respectively. Title pages will be prepared in manuscript.

Hour, Date, Place	Summary of Events and Information	Remarks and references to Appendices
1.1.16 (Sat.) SAWBRIDGEWORTH		
11.30 a.m. "	Armourer Sergeant sent by D.A.D.O.S. 60th LONDON Divn visited Q.M. Stores. Inspected & passed as satisfactory 20 Rifles '303. Three Rifles returned to O.C. 3/3rd Field Coy. R.E. — — — —	(P.H.) Authority/Bde: 2046 (of 22.12.15)
" "	The following men were selected to attend a Saddlery Course (18 Exam) at BISHOPS STORTFORD on Monday next. — 3/- No 3241 Driver HODGSON J.C. & No 2903 Pte: DELCHAR R.D.	(P.H.) Bde. minute No 5. of 1.1.16.
" "	Report upon Billeting Accommodation in SAWBRIDGEWORTH called for by A.A. & Q.M.G. Division — + reply sent by Battalion Billeting Officer Captain GLADSTONE — — — —	(P.H.) Appendix 1. Authority A/2040/1 of 1.1.16. Bryant (?) 4. of 1.1.16.
7 p.m. "	Telephone message from Brigade Hdqrs: requesting names of selected Officers to be used in by 10 a.m. tomorrow — for attendance at Young Officers Class at GIDEA PARK. — —	(P.H.)
" "	Programme of forthcoming weeks training received from Bde: Hdqrs.	(P.H.)
12.43 a.m. 2.1.16.	Received over telephone "TRIAL ALARM" (Brigade time 12.40) and replied in writing to Brigade that message was received (1 a.m.). — —	(P.H.)
11.0 a.m. "		(P.H.)
8.55 a.m. "	Battalion Parade — — — — — — — —	(P.H.)
9.15 a.m. "	Church Parade — — — — — — — —	(P.H.)

(2)

Army Form C. 2118.

WAR DIARY
or
INTELLIGENCE SUMMARY

(Erase heading not required.)

2/17th BATTALION LONDON REGIMENT.

Instructions regarding War Diaries and Intelligence Summaries are contained in F.S. Regs., Part II. and the Staff Manual respectively. Title pages will be prepared in manuscript.

Hour, Date, Place		Summary of Events and Information	Remarks and references to Appendices
10.30 a.m.	2/1/16 SAWBRIDGEWORTH	1 Passed Batt: Hdqrs: name of officer selected to attend Young Officers class at IDEA PARK. 2/Lieut: F.R. STOCKWELL — This message to be confirmed in writing —	(P.H.)
5.57 p.m.	"	1 Sergeant & 1 man left for Bde=Hdqrs: with No 2. Range finder, Barn & Stand, for use on Range finding Course at BISHOPS STORTFORD commencing 9 a.m. tomorrow —	Authority (Bde=minute No 21267 of 31/12/15) (P.H.)
"	"	2/Lieut: W.A. EBDON & 2/Lieut: H.G. CLARK left for BISHOPS STORTFORD & Report at Bde=Office for instructions in Tomorrows Range finding Course. These officers to billet at MULLETTS, 2/14 F Batt: R.F.A. whilst attending the Course	(Bde: Order No 1. 1/1/16) (P.H.)
8.14 a.m.	3-1-16 "	No 2329. Corporal WATTS. W.S. & No 2459 Corporal COLEMAN. H.T. left for BISHOPS STORTFORD Range finding Course — Barn & Stand — to be attached to 2/14 Bn: for R.F. Rations — These men not having returned from Xmas leave at 11 p.m. last evening were unable to Report at Bde: Hdqrs: as per Bde: minute — Bn Hdqr: concerned.	(P.H.)
8.55 a.m.	"	Battalion Parade. — Company Close order Drill including marching in points under Company Commanders	(P.H.) Bde: programme
11. am	BISHOPS STORTFORD	"	(P.H.)
4.45 p.m.	"	No 4392 Pte: PARSONS. D.N. DCoy: reported at 7Bde: Hdqrs: as G.M.P.	(P.H.)
5. pm	"	No 3241. Driver HODGSON T.E. B Coy: & No 2903 Pte: DELCHAR R.D. B Coy: reported at Technical Institute for Saddlery Course (12 lessons) these men to return to Batt: each evening	(P.H.)
"	"	3rd Lecture by Captain PEMBERTON at WHARF HOUSE. Lectures not given returns being in leave	(P.H.)
"	SAWBRIDGEWORTH	No 4392 Pte: PARSONS. D.N. DCoy: returned from BISHOPS STORTFORD having been rejected as G.M.P.	(P.H.)
2 p.m.	"	Captain & adjutant W.E. DAVID-DAVIS returned from leave —	(P.H.) (P.H.)

Army Form C. 2118.

WAR DIARY
or
INTELLIGENCE SUMMARY.

(Erase heading not required.)

2/13th BATTALION LONDON REGIMENT.

Instructions regarding War Diaries and Intelligence Summaries are contained in F. S. Regs., Part II. and the Staff Manual respectively. Title pages will be prepared in manuscript.

Hour, Date, Place	Summary of Events and Information	Remarks and references to Appendices
8.55 am. 4.1.16. SAWBRIDGEWORTH	Battalion Parade — Route March 15 miles — Adv: Hanks Rear Guards	(P.H.)
8.15 p.m. " "	C.Os lecture to officers upon the Essentials for training	(P.H.)
6.55 am. 5.1.16 "	Battalion Parade — 8th Close order drill under Adjutant	W.O.D.
" " " "	Officers' Tour: — Preparation & Reports and Operation Order WALLBURY CAMP	W.O.D.
3.15 P.M " " B/SSTORTFORD	Lecture on Drill by Lt-Colonel W.R.T. McLEAN T.D.	W.O.D.
12.30 P.M " " SAWBRIDGEWORTH	Telegram from CAMBRIDGE HOSPITAL without date 8.1420 A/L CODRY 136 and is struck off the Strength accordingly. Appointment — Mr S.H. GREEN Assistant Adjutant & Musketry v/c Capt T.P.H. SLADE	W.O.D. Appx. apendix 2.
8.55 am. 6.1.16 SAWBRIDGEWORTH	Battalion Parade: Return of a farm	W.O.D.
10.30 am. " "	Examination & Nomm (3rd Bombers) Bd. Bombing M. Nude Capt. T.R. RADICE	W.O.D.
" " " "	Examination & B.S. Musketry in standard 4, Bd. Musketry M. charge Capt. MUNRO	W.O.D.
5 P.M " "	Strength NZ 2199 Common Sergeant 3 3 Yrs. A.O.C. reports for duty and	W.O.D. Outdraft A.O. Order 5-1-16.
" " " "	Taken on the Strength on Posn 7.1.16. L.A.O.C. Orders 5.1.16.	W.O.D.
8.55 am. 7.1.16 " "	Battalion Parade.	W.O.D.
" " " "	Rehearsal Ceremonial Drill PISHIOBURY PARK	W.O.D.
12.10 P.M " "	Lt. ALLISTON M.O.B. W.D. inspects meat certifies all correct	W.O.D.

(4)

Army Form C. 2118.

WAR DIARY
or
INTELLIGENCE SUMMARY.
(Erase heading not required.)

2/1st Battalion Hertfordshire Regiment

Instructions regarding War Diaries and Intelligence Summaries are contained in F.S. Regs., Part II. and the Staff Manual respectively. Title pages will be prepared in manuscript.

Hour, Date, Place	Summary of Events and Information	Remarks and references to Appendices
3.15 pm 7.1.16 SAWBRIDGEWORTH	Lecture to officers on ceremonial Drill. Strength — 3492 Pte BEALES. B. Transferred to M.T.A.S.C. GROVE PARK. Stations: Hadham M.G. 5.1.16	WSD—0 WSD—0 - authority - 179ⁿ 13 de memo Ref M54-5.1.16
8.55 am 8.1.16 " "	Battalion Parade. Ceremonial Drill PISHIOBURY PARK	WD—0
11.30 am " "	Kit + Foot Inspection.	ﾓED—0
8.55 am 9.1.16 " "	Church Parade.	WD—0
8.55 am 10.1.16 " "	Battalion Parade. Ceremonial Drill. PISHIOBURY PARK. one riding horse from Turnament. Orders on Strength. Reprimended No 2. Div. Machine Gun Course: HADHAM HALL	WSD—0 WSD—0 WSD—0 - authority - Bde Letter Reg No 69/2 - 9.1.16
10.20 am " "	6 men sent to Divisional Machine Gun Course. Telegram ﾗ﹅ Wire — 100 men and 3 officers warned for Hertfordshire this unit	WSD—0
11.1.16 " "	2.30 Bn. Bn. Inspection by H.R.H. Princess LOUISE DUCHESS of ARGYLL. Lt. L.F. BAZER reports for duty from ﾃ﹅ line Sent Lt R. HILL taken by ambulance to hospital ELSENHAM HALL Battalion Parade.	DS D—0 WD—0 WD—0
12.1.16 " "	Training: A + B Cos filling in trenches, C+D Cos physical drill. e.t.f 160 men (DRAFT) received from ﾃ﹅ line	WOD—0 WSD—0

(5)

WAR DIARY
or
INTELLIGENCE SUMMARY.

(Erase heading not required.) 2/1? Battalion London Regiment

Army Form C. 2118.

Hour, Date, Place	Summary of Events and Information	Remarks and references to Appendices
5.30. P.M. 12.1.16. BPS STORTFORD	Lecture: Physical Training: Major CAMPBELL ASSISTANT INSTRUCTOR OF GYMNASIA	MSO-J
7.40. a.m. 13.1.16 SAWBRIDGEWORTH	4 officers & 235 men filling in trenches. Bde Bombing School HADHAM HALL	MSO-J
8.45 a.m. " " "	Recruit Training under Lt THOMPSON until further orders.	MSO-J MSJ-J
8.55 a.m. " " "	B° Bombing School under Sect EBDON.	MSO-J
" " " " "	Remainder of B° : fatigue duties.	
11 a.m. " " BPS STORTFORD	Inspection of transport horses by D.A.D. Remounts	MSO-J
6. P.M. " " SAWBRIDGEWORTH	Sect N. READ reported for duty from W.O.	MSO-J
8.55. a.m. 14.1.16. " "	Battalion Parade.	MSO-J
" " " "	Filling B° Instructional Trenches	MSO-J
10. a.m. " " "	Inspection of C°: Bombs by Lt Col NASH. ROYAL SCOTS	MSO-J
2. P.M. " " BPS STORTFORD	4 officers attended Bde Riding School	MSO-J
8.55. a.m. 15.1.16 SAWBRIDGEWORTH	Battalion Parade.	MSO-J
" " " "	Training: filling in B° instructional trenches. Kitland for inspection	MSO-J
" " " "	Sect N READ the acting Signalling officer during absence of Sect R. HALL	MSO-J
8.55 a.m. 16.1.16 " "	Church Parade	MSO-J

(6)

Army Form C. 2118.

WAR DIARY
or
INTELLIGENCE SUMMARY.
(Erase heading not required.)

2/3 Battalion London Regiment

Instructions regarding War Diaries and Intelligence Summaries are contained in F.S. Regs., Part II. and the Staff Manual respectively. Title pages will be prepared in manuscript.

Hour, Date, Place	Summary of Events and Information	Remarks and references to Appendices
7.40 A.M. 17.1.16. SAWBRIDGEWORTH. HADHAM HALL	4 officers and 250 men filling in trenches at Bde Bombing School at—	W.P.D-0
8.15 P.M. " " "	Lecture to officers on Operation Orders	W.P.D-0 / W.S.O-1
8.55 A.M. 18.1.16. " "	Battalion Parade. Training Route march with Scheme.	W.P.D-0 / W.S.O-1
" " " " "	Inspection by G.O.C. Bde and A.D.M.S. of draft	W.P.D-0
" " " " "	Inspection of 1st line transport by Bde	W.S.O-1
" " " " "	Review of H.Q. Section (Service) under 2nd Lt Q. Lancaster to duty from Bde. Course of Instruction at B'SHOP STORTFORD	W.P.D-0
3.30 P.M. " " "	Court of Enquiry— Dilapidations. President Major P. HOPKINS members. Capts A.C. Heron – P.P.M. Slade – C.F. BROCKHURST	W.P.D-0
" " " " "	Lt. F.R. Rusevear— Capt R.P. GLADSTONE attended as Witness officer	
8.55 A.M. 19.1.16 " " "	B'm Parade. Training — Platoon & Company.	W.P.D-0 / W.S.O-1
3. P.M. " " "	Bde Ridney School for Officers attended by C.O.	W.S.O-1

(7)

Army Form C. 2118.

WAR DIARY
or
INTELLIGENCE SUMMARY.
(Erase heading not required.)

2/1st Battalion London Regiment

Instructions regarding War Diaries and Intelligence Summaries are contained in F.S. Regs., Part II and the Staff Manual respectively. Title pages will be prepared in manuscript.

Hour, Date, Place	Summary of Events and Information	Remarks and references to Appendices
A.M.		
6.55. 20.1.16. SAWBRIDGEWORTH	Battalion Parade cancelled owing to bad weather	WSD-1
10. " " "	Parade of Companies under Company arrangements	WSD-1
8.10 " " "	An advance Party consisting of Capt. R.P. Gladstone Sec. Lt. R. Rivington 3 N.C.O.s and 17 men proceed to No. 8 Camp SUTTON VENY via BPs STORTFORD.	WSD-1 Authority Bde Orders No. 216 dated 19.1.16.
P.M.		
6.15 " " "	Lecture to officers on the "MOVE" entraining and detraining.	WSD-1
A.M.		
8.30 21 " "	General fatigues	WSD-1
	A Rear Party and Salvage Corps remained at SAWBRIDGEWORTH of 3 N.C.O.s and 16 men under Capt. R.P. GLADSTONE	WSD-1 Authority Bde Orders No. 16. dated 19.1.16.
A.M.		
2.15. 22.1.16 " "	Right Half Battalion under Major HOPKINS entrained at HARLOW STN for WARMINSTER and proceeded by route march to No. 8 CAMP SUTTON VENY	WSD-1 do:
4.15 " " "	Left Half Battalion under C.O. ditto ditto	WSD-1
11. A.M. "	Battalion in Quarters No. 8 CAMP SUTTON VENY	WSD-1
10. A.M. 23.1.16. SUTTON VENY	Church Parade. General fatigues	WSD-1

(6)

Army Form C. 2118.

WAR DIARY
or
INTELLIGENCE SUMMARY.
(Erase heading not required.)

7/13 Battalion London Regiment

Hour, Date, Place	Summary of Events and Information	Remarks and references to Appendices
AH		
9.30. 24.1.16. SUTTON VENY No. 6 CAMP	Battalion Parade. — Battalion-in-waiting General fatigue	WSD
	Strength 3359. Pt WHIDDON from 24.1.16.	WSD
	HAND SALISBURY for 24.1.16. Lecture to officers on march discipline	Authority Telegram TERRECOFF dated 21.1.16.
8.55. 25.1.16. " "	Battalion Parade. Training Route march	WSD
	1 Machine gun on loan from 2/14" B" L.R.	WSD
	Lecture to officers on Camp duties	WSD
8.30. 26.1.16. " "	Battalion Parade. Inspection by G.O.C. SALISBURY TRAINING CENTRE	WSD
8.55. 27.1.16. " "	Battalion Parade Training: Platoon and Company Training	WSD
2.P.M. " " "	Practised Fire Alarm. Strength. Sec.W. BYLES.E.M.B. transferred from 3/13 B" L.R. re- Posted for duty	WSD
	(Lt.L. Plant 2118/10/16 dog' Xmas leave, being struck off the strength B The Division reported for duty.	WSD - authority L.D. 3780/A 21.1.16. WSD - authority D.O. No. 19 Pt. II para 10 - 22.1.16

Army Form C. 2118.

WAR DIARY
or
INTELLIGENCE SUMMARY.
(Erase heading not required.)

2/15 Battalion London Regiment

Hour, Date, Place	Summary of Events and Information	Remarks and references to Appendices
A.M.		
9.55. 28.1.16. SUTTON VENY N°8 CAMP	Battalion Parade. Training. Route march with Sherns.	(LCD) MVD appendix 2
P.M.		
2.30. " " "	Inspection of lines by G.O.C. 60th (London) Division	(LCD)
5.30 " " "	Return from SAWBRIDGEWORTH of Rear Party and Salvage Corps under Capt. R.P. GLADSTONE	(LCD)
6.15 " " "	Lecture to officers on military administration.	(LCD)
A.M.		
9.55. 29. 1.16 " " "	Co. Parade. Training. Physical Drill Bayonet fighting Saluting. Tour and Kit Inspection.	(LCD) (LCD)
	Instruction of the hired by MLCo.	
	Strength: Capt. The Rev. C.R. HARDINGE C.F. reports for duty	(LCD) — authority D.O. N° 31. Part II June 31.1.16
	Pte. SHEARS 3129 + Pt. WALL 2877 transferred from 105 P.B.S.	(LCD) — authority W.O. B.M. 176/ [T.T.T.]
	reports for duty	

(10)

Army Form C. 2118.

WAR DIARY
or
INTELLIGENCE SUMMARY.

(Erase heading not required.)

2/15 Battalion London Regiment

Hour, Date, Place	Summary of Events and Information	Remarks and references to Appendices
9.45. 30.1.16 SUTTON VENY N°5 CAMP	Church Parade	WCSO
	M.I. RANGE moves to attend a Junior Officers' Course commencing on 31.1.16 at S.t ALBANS.	W.S.2 authority — 179th Bde minute 26.1.16.
8.55. 31.1.16 " "	Battalion Parade.	W.O.O.
P.H. " " "	Inspection by Field Marshal VISCOUNT FRENCH	
6.15. " " "	Lecture to officer on Bombing.	W.O.O

W. H. Meredith
Commanding
2/15 Bgn London Regt.

(11)

CONFIDENTIAL.

WAR DIARY.

2/13th Battalion. London Regiment.

From Feb: 1. 1916 —————— To Feb: 29. 1. 1916.

Army Form C. 2118.

WAR DIARY
or
INTELLIGENCE SUMMARY.
(Erase heading not required.)

2/13th Battalion London Regiment

Hour, Date, Place	Summary of Events and Information	Remarks and references to Appendices
9am 1.ii.16. N°8 Camp SUTTON VENY	Early morning parade by Platoons, etc. Programme of Training carried out as per Divisional Programme for the week. Appendix N° 1A	WPD→ appendix N° 1A
H 9.15.	Lecture to officers Battalion Orders Order Drill by C.O.	WPD→
H 9.30. 2.ii.16 "	Programme as per Appendix N° 1. 2/Lt WAFBDON and CH 2220 EYLES P.A attend a Bombing Class at SUTTON VENY 3662 " WAFBDON and CH 2220 EYLES taken on sheep Dip, Terminatus & enters 12.ii.16. 9 miles from LARKHILL	read WPD 2 { authority Div L.S 429/1 H.92.2 { 1.ii.16 outlined, 13 de L 256/2. 1.ii.16 WPD→
H " "	Lt-Col. NASH lectures to officers on "Military Law"	WPD→
H 9.30 3. ii. 16 "	Programme as per Appendix N° 1 2955 Pte SEXTON } Transferred to 105' Prov. B° 3662 " LESSITER 2372 " JOHNSON	WPD→ authority TF Record Office Letters: Reg N° 13/264. 27.i.16 13/265 29.i.16
H 9.0. 4. ii. 16 "	Programme as per Appendix. N° 1A	WPD→ WPD→
H 9.15. " "	Lecture to Officers Infantry in Attack by CAPTAIN HERNE	WPD→ authority Bde. O. N° 30 31. 4. ii. 16
H 9.5 5. ii. 16 "	Programme as per Bde order.	WPD→ WPD→
H " 6. ii. 16 "	Church Parade.	
" 7. ii. 16 "	Programme as per appendix N° 1A	
H " " "	Lecture to officers "Infantry in Defence" by MAJOR THOMPSON	WPD→

Army Form C. 2118.

2/XIII Bn LONDON REGIMENT

WAR DIARY
or
INTELLIGENCE SUMMARY.

(Erase heading not required.)

Instructions regarding War Diaries and Intelligence Summaries are contained in F.S. Regs., Part II and the Staff Manual respectively. Title pages will be prepared in manuscript.

Hour, Date, Place	Summary of Events and Information	Remarks and references to Appendices
8.ii.16 No 8 Camp SUTTON VENY 1.30	Programme as per Appendix No 1A	W.D.D.
H. 15.	Sec. Lt TE DUFFY 1st LANCS. ROYAL FUSILIERS attached for light duty.	W.D.D. authority D.O. 10.ii.16. § 86.
m. 30	Lecture to Officers "Protection" by the ADJUTANT.	W.D.D.
9.ii.16	Programme as per Appendix No 1.D	W.D.D.
10.ii.16	" "	W.D.D.
H. 30	Court of Enquiry. President MAJOR G. THOMPSON members CAPT MCHEIRNE & Lt F.R. ROSEVEAR adjourned until next day	W.S.I.D. authority C.O.
11.ii.16 H. 30	Programme as per Appendix No 1b	W.S.I.D.
m. 02	Court of Enquiry [assembled 10.ii.16] finds on 9 men guilty of the attempt having been desertion.	W.D.D. authority Appendix 2 B.O. Order No 29. 16.ii 16. Pt II § 4 and 13°
15.	Lecture to Officers. "Outposts" by the ADJUTANT.	W.D.D. Orders No 33. 22.2.16 Pt II § 3
12.ii.16 H. 05	Programme as per Appendix No 1. B.d. Order.	W.D.D. authority Bd. Order. No 36 § 1. 11.ii.16

(2)

Army Form C. 2118.

WAR DIARY
or
INTELLIGENCE SUMMARY.
(Erase heading not required.)

2/13th Bn LONDON REGIMENT

Instructions regarding War Diaries and Intelligence Summaries are contained in F.S. Regs., Part II and the Staff Manual respectively. Title pages will be prepared in manuscript.

Hour, Date, Place	Summary of Events and Information	Remarks and references to Appendices
M. 13.ii.16 N° 6 Camp SUTTON VENY 30	Church Parade	W S D-2
00 14.ii.16	Programme as per Appendix N° 1A	W S D-2
	2nd Lt ALANCASTER and Sergt H. SMITH proceed to HAYLING ISLAND to attend Lewis Machine Gun Course.	W S D-2
	Lt. G.V. THOMPSON, 2nd Lt E.W. PHILLIPS and CORPORAL BOOTH proceed to HAYLING ISLAND to attend a rifle course.	authority D.O. 9.ii.16. § 76 W S D-2
M. 15	Lecture to Officers "Advanced Guards" by Major HOPKINS	W . D-2
M. 00 15.ii.16	Programme as per Appendix N° 1A	W C D-2
	3961 Pte GRAVESTOCK attached to ammunition park	W S D-2 authority W.O. L 19/Gen/AF 5415 (A.G.1)
	2nd Lt H. READ and 2/CORPORAL HOSKING allowed Signalling + Telephone Course at SUTTON VENY	W S D-2 authority Bde. L 362.17.ii.16.
15 M. 30 16.ii.16	Lecture to Officers "Musketry" by 2/Lt PREEN	W C D-2
	Divisional Scheme : Appendix N° 1A	W S D-2
	Scheme cancelled owing to weather.	W S D-2
00	Programme as per Appendix N° 1A	W S D-2

(3)

Army Form C. 2118.

WAR DIARY
or
INTELLIGENCE SUMMARY.
(Erase heading not required.)

2/13 Bn L.R.

Hour, Date, Place	Summary of Events and Information	Remarks and references to Appendices
12.11.16 18th C Camp SUTTON VENY	Divisional Scheme Appendix No 1A	W.D.0
13.11.16	Programme as per Appendix N. 1A	W.D.0
14.11.16	Inspection of Transport by Major General LANDON QMG SERVICES M.0	W.D.0
	303 Musketry Practice (10 rounds) C.C.	W.D.0 authority Bde.O. N° 40 S.4. 18.11.16
19.11.16	Programme as per Bde Orders ~~ ~~	W.D.0
	4572 Pte TRINDELL V.S. released for munition work	W.D.0 authority W.O.L. 19/ (Gen. N° 5415/5581) released
	11 men struck off the Strength and transferred to 105 Prov: Bⁿ	W.D.0 authority O.C.Records letter 13/4144.12.11.16
	3395 Pte HOLE. H. Struck off the Strength and transferred to 105 Prov Bⁿ	W.D.0 authority O.C.Records letter 13/4145.12.11.16
20.11.16	Church Parade.	W.D.0
	4081 Pte G.GROVE proceeds ballers course of cookery at WEYMOUTH	W.D.0 authority Bde 2. 264 14.11.16

(4)

Army Form C. 2118.

WAR DIARY
or
INTELLIGENCE SUMMARY.

2/13th Bn LONDON REGIMENT

(Erase heading not required.)

Instructions regarding War Diaries and Intelligence Summaries are contained in F.S. Regs., Part II and the Staff Manual respectively. Title pages will be prepared in manuscript.

Hour, Date, Place	Summary of Events and Information	Remarks and references to Appendices
21.11.16 No 8 Coy SUTTON VENY	Programme as per appendix No 1ª	Orders
A.M.	303 Musketry	WSO-1
9.40	Inspection of arms by Lt. Colonel J. Shropshire & Beaumont. S. Commands.	WSO-2
	4065 Corporal BROOMHALL attended Officers Mess Cookery Course at GREENWICH	WSO-2. Authority S.C. Telegram T.6367 - 19.11.16
	3716 Pte WINTER. R. and 2691 Pte LOTT. C. attend School of Cookery at BETHNAL GREEN	WSO-2 Authority DIV. L. 9/499/1 15.11.16
	au with his Services	WSO-2 Authority S.T.C. Order No 93.
	Return to officer i/c Sect. T.E. DUFFY on BOMBING	WSO-6
22.11.16	Programme as per appendix No 1ª	WSO-7
9.0 A.M.	Outpost Scheme (day) to have norm as per appendix No 1ª	W/0-3
11.0	303 Musketry	WSO-5
2.0 P.M.	ALLEZ-ALLEZ Scheme at Bn. HQ & Majors THOMSON and HOPKINS & Capt HERNE	WSO-1
2.15	Lecture to officers "Night Outposts" by Major HOPKINS	WSO-2 Authority Od. O. No 45
	Captain RUSSELL. MUNSTER FUSILIERS. } attached for light duty.	WSO-2 Authority SS.22.11.16
	2/Lt ALLEN. ²/₇ ROYAL WARWICK REGT. }	

(5)

Army Form C. 2118.

WAR DIARY
or
INTELLIGENCE SUMMARY.   2/13th Bn LONDON REGIMENT.

(Erase heading not required.)

Hour, Date, Place	Summary of Events and Information	Remarks and references to Appendices
9.H 9.30 23.11.16 Nr Camp SUTTON VENY	Programme as per appendix N° 1ᴬ	N° 20-3
	303 Huddle to 300 M.G.G and one	40.0.1. authent Bd. O. N°45 §2. 22.11.16.
	3142 Pt MACDONALD, 3676 Pt JONES, 4042 Pt NUTLEY struck of strength	L.80 4 authent. T. F O.C Records L. 13/269. 14.11.16
	and transferred to 105' Prov. Bn	H 20-3
24.11.16	Programme as per appendix N° 1ᴬ	N° 20-1
	Battalion route march cancelled owing to state of weather	H 20-1
	Lecture to Officers by Capt. RUSSELL	H 23-1
25.11.16	Programme as per appendix N° 1ᴬ	
	303 Musketry for remainder of men and over the have not yet fired	H 20-1 authent. Bdo O N° 47 §4. 24.11.16
15	Inspection of Signalling Section by CAPTAIN FLADGATE	H 20-1
	ALLEZ-ALLEZ Scheme for officers under MAJR R THOMPSON	H 18-1
26.11.16	Programme as per Bde orders	H 20-1 outlines Bd. O. N° 98 §1. 25.11.16
	Pt DINES 3673 transferred from 165 Prov. Bn	H 20-1 authent. TF. O.C Records Re N° 1009/k 19.11.16

(6)

WAR DIARY
or
INTELLIGENCE SUMMARY. 2/13 Bn. L.R.

(Erase heading not required.)

Army Form C. 2118.

Hour, Date, Place	Summary of Events and Information	Remarks and references to Appendices
9.30 a.m. 27.11.16. HQ Camp, SUTTON VENY	Church Parade	W.S.D-1
	2nd Lt W.A. EBDON paraded on a General Church at CLAPHAM COMMON commencing 28.11.16.	W.O.O- authority D.O. S/144 28.11.16.
28.11.16	Programme as per Appendix No 1.ª	W.S.D-1
	3152 Pte A.T. MAGSON transferred to the A.C. for munition work.	W.S.D-1 authority W.O. 19/Gen/5415 (A.G.1) RELEASES. 4.11.16.
29.11.16	Lecture to officers by C.O. "estimated order drill"	W.S.D-1
	Programme as per Appendix No. 1.ª	W.S.D-1
2.15 p.m.	Digging party 120 NCOs & men under Capt. BROCKHURST	W.S.D-1
" "	2 N.C.O. & men under Lt ROSEVEAR	W.S.D-1

Suttonbury
3.3.16

(Signature)
LM.

(7) Comdg. 2/13 A.R. London Regt.

CONFIDENTIAL
WAR DIARY.

From 1.3.16 to 31.3.16.

CONFIDENTIAL
WAR DIARY
2/XIII Bn London Regiment.

From 1. 3. 16 to 31. 3. 16.

Army Form C. 2118.

WAR DIARY
or
INTELLIGENCE SUMMARY. 2/13ᵘ Bⁿ London Regiment
(Erase heading not required.)

Instructions regarding War Diaries and Intelligence Summaries are contained in F.S. Regs., Part II and the Staff Manual respectively. Title pages will be prepared in manuscript.

Hour, Date, Place			Summary of Events and Information	Remarks and references to Appendices
1.iii.16	M&S Comp	SUTTON VENY	routine as per divisional programme appendix A N°1	N⁰ D→0
.55	—		Battalion Route march	N⁰ D→0
8.—	—		.303 Musketry Pl 1ᴬ and 2ᴬ.	N⁰ D→0
.M	—			
2.iii.16	—		routine as per appendix A N°1	N⁰ D→0
.55	—		routine as per appendix A N°1	N⁰ D→0
.—	—		Lewis gun course of 2 NCOs and 2 men for nine working days.	L⁰ D→0
.M	—		Lecture by MAJOR HOPKINS to Officers: "Discipline"	N⁰ D→0
.15	—		2ⁿᵈ Lt B. TEMPLE attached from 'I' GLOUCESTERS for light duty from 29.ii.16	I⁰ D→0
.M 3.iii.16	—		routine as per appendix A N°1	N⁰ D→0
—	—		"	N⁰ D→0
H	—		Lecture by CAPTAIN C.A. BOULTON. DIV. STAFF = "Protection"	N⁰ D→0
.—	—		" MAJOR HOPKINS to Officers = "NIGHT WORK"	N⁰ D→0
.M 4.iii.16	—		routine as per Bde orders.	N⁰ D→0 authority Bde orders N° 54 S 1. 3.iii.16

(1)

Army Form C. 2118.

WAR DIARY
or
INTELLIGENCE SUMMARY.
(Erase heading not required.)

2/13th Bn LONDON REGIMENT

Instructions regarding War Diaries and Intelligence Summaries are contained in F.S. Regs., Part II. and the Staff Manual respectively. Title pages will be prepared in manuscript.

Hour, Date, Place	Summary of Events and Information	Remarks and references to Appendices
5.iii.16 N°5 Camp SUTTON VENY	Church Parade	W.D.=D
	3153 Pte HANCE transferred 2/2nd London Bde R.F.A.	W.D.=D authority T.F. Rec.
6.iii.16	routine as per appendix A N°2	W.D.=D letter 13/566
—	"	W.D.=D
—	Divisional Bombing School 4 S² N.C.Os. and men	W.D.=D U.D.=D
—	lecture to Officers by C.O. Close order Drill	U.D.=D
7.iii.16	routine as per appendix A N°2 morning outposts cancelled owing to weather.	U.D.=D U.D.=D U.D.=D
	MAJOR G. THOMPSON returned from tour of inspection from FRANCE	
	lecture to officers by Sec/Lt A. LANCASTER on LEWIS GUN	
8.iii.16	routine as per appendix A N°2	U.D.=D
—	" route march cancelled owing to weather.	U.D.=D
	Ref/ LONDON GAZETTE 29.ii.16. T.F. RES. Lt-Col. W.R.T. McLEAN T.D. from LONDON REGT. return Lt-Col. dated 2.iii.16 The services of Lt-Col. W.R.T. McLEAN T.D. 2/XIII Bn L.R. are the referred with and including WEDNESDAY 8.iii.16 on the pointer of handing over to MAJOR G. THOMPSON 2/A.III Bn L.R. now absent on leave. MAJOR S. THOMPSON Assumes Command and a/L 9.iii.16. (2)	W.D.=D authority 60 (LONDON) DIV.2 9.iii.16

Army Form C. 2118.

WAR DIARY
or
INTELLIGENCE SUMMARY.   2/13th Bn LONDON REGIMENT

(Erase heading not required.)

Instructions regarding War Diaries and Intelligence Summaries are contained in F. S. Regs., Part II. and the Staff Manual respectively. Title pages will be prepared in manuscript.

Hour, Date, Place	Summary of Events and Information	Remarks and references to Appendices
9.iii.16. M° Coy SUTTONVENY	routine order per appendix A N°2	WCD-D
" "	" "	WCD-D
10.iii.16	hostile toy/liceer. see A LANCASTER & LEWIS GUN	WCD-D
"	routine as per appendix A N°2.	WCD-D
"	"	WCD-D
11.iii.16	routine as per Bde order	WCD-D artillery Bde Orders N° 60. S1. 10.iii.16.
12.iii.16	Church Parade	WCD-D
13.iii.16	routine as per appendix A N°2	WCD-D
"	"	WCD-D
	II Division bombing course. 52 N.C.o. and men	WCD-D
	Recruits on (1/1 march under Lt S.H. GREEN	WCD-D
	LEWIS MACHINE GUN course under Bde. M.G. officer. 1 N.C.O. and six men	WCD-D artillery T.F. Roc. L 13/567 7.iii.16
	3754 Pt SPARKES transferred to 2/XIII Bn L.R. (3)	

(73089) W4141—463. 400,000. 9/14. H.&J.Ltd. Forms/C. 2118/10.

Army Form C. 2118.

WAR DIARY
or
INTELLIGENCE SUMMARY.
(Erase heading not required.)

2/13ᵗʰ Bⁿ LONDON REGIMENT

Hour, Date, Place	Summary of Events and Information	Remarks and references to Appendices
3.iii.16 Nᵒ 6 Camp SUTTON VENY	arrival of draft of 204 N. Cos and men from 104 and 105 Prov Bⁿˢ	W.D=2
4.iii.16	Bde Orders. entries on for appendix A Nᵒ 2	W.D=2
		W.D=2
15	CAPT GLADSTONE L' RANGE. Sent L.S. STOCKWELL + SNUTE alias a class of instruction in FIRE DIRECTION & MAJOR KIRR- PATRICK Lieutenants 18.iii.16	} WED=2 arrival Bde Orders Nᵒ 61 § 1 which
15	CAPT BROCKHURST attends courses of instruction at R.H. Coley, CHAGFORD MAJOR P. THOMPSON lectures & officers on the Organization with Front	W.D=2 arrival B.O. 8.159. 3.iii.16
		W.D=2
	1952 STAFF SERJT BRISTOLL transferred to 105 Prov Bⁿ wef After from 11.iii.16	W.D=2 arrival 17/65). 11.iii.16
15.iii.16	} entries on to appendix A Nᵒ 2 sent month	W.D=2
		W.D=2
	draft from 2ᵗʰ Bⁿ 2ᴬ 363. O.H.C.	W.D=2
	Proposition of draft to G.O.C. relative to Bde Help Full Sub-Altens	W.D=2

(4)

WAR DIARY or INTELLIGENCE SUMMARY.

Army Form C. 2118.

2/13th Bn London Regiment

Hour, Date, Place	Summary of Events and Information	Remarks and references to Appendices
16.iii.16 H.Q. Camp Sutton Veny	} routine as per Appendix A No 2	WD⇒
	24/12 Cpl TIMPANY attached LNL & Cadet Bn LICHFIELD Barrack LICHFIELD with effect from 14.iii.16.	WD⇒ authority W.O.L. SD 601 (SDS) 4.iii.16
	On enlistment L/Cpl CATTERALL allowed a 2 days Corps class. Seen by Captain WEYMOUTH.	WD⇒ authority Bde Ltr S43/2 11.iii.16 WD⇒ authority O.R.
	1 NCO and 11 men transferred to 105 Prov Bn.	T.F. Recd 13/707 9.iii.16
	Between 4 officers & Major THUM 250 w. Range Disposition —	WD⇒
17.iii.16	} routine as per appendix A No 2	WD⇒
		WD B-2
		} WD⇒
	Reveille alarm. Recd 9.15 am. Warn known 10.25 am. 1942 Pte CRAPP transferred to 105 Prov Bn with effect from	
18.iii.16	3.iii.16. and attached to 4 Officer Cadet Bn Oxford sent to return to Bde Orders.	WD⇒ authority Bde Orders 14.iii.16. §1. 17.iii.16
	4945 Pte BAILEY released for trade training. Sent. from C Base 23 Heeley Bridge Ironworks SHEFFIELD. Shewing showing	WD⇒ authority W.O.119/Gen 809 5415 (A.G.L.2 Class) 2.iii.16

(5)

Army Form C. 2118.

WAR DIARY
or
INTELLIGENCE SUMMARY.   2/13th Bn London Regiment

(Erase heading not required.)

Instructions regarding War Diaries and Intelligence Summaries are contained in F.S. Regs., Part II. and the Staff Manual respectively. Title pages will be prepared in manuscript.

Hour, Date, Place	Summary of Events and Information	Remarks and references to Appendices
19.iii.16 M&S Camp SUTTON VENY	Church Parade	WD&A
20.iii.16	routine as per appendix A No 3	WD&A
	2 Coys (A.B) Q.H.C. 303	
	2nd Lt S.O. SHAVE reported for duty from the 3rd Lon.	WD&A outfit Bn letter 6742. 20.iii.16
	Lecture to officers by Major THOMPSON "Fire discipline"	WD&A
21.iii.16	routine as per appendix A No 3	WD&A
		DCD&A
	Lecture to officers by the ADJUTANT "military reminiscences"	
22.iii.16	routine as per appendix A No 3 with rifle exercises more technical	WD&A
	Inspection of Draft (200 NCOs and men) from Prov. Bn. by LORD FRENCH 7.h.	LCD&A
23.iii.16	routine as per appendix A No 3.	WD&A
	2262 Pte ANDERSON K released from military service to NATIONAL GAS ENGINE Co Ltd NEWTON-LE-WILLOWS ASHTON-UNDER-LYNE	WD&A outfit N.C.L 19 Reg/M/101 release 20.iii.16
	handover to A.C. with effect from 22.iii.16	

(6)

Army Form C. 2118.

WAR DIARY
or
INTELLIGENCE SUMMARY.   1/13th Bn London Regiment

(Erase heading not required.)

Instructions regarding War Diaries and Intelligence Summaries are contained in F.S. Regs., Part II. and the Staff Manual respectively. Title pages will be prepared in manuscript.

Hour, Date, Place	Summary of Events and Information	Remarks and references to Appendices
24.III.16 No 4 Camp Sutton Veny	Routine as per Appendix A No 3	1/13 D=2
	Lecture by officer to Major Hopkins "Rear Guards"	1/13 D=2
25.III.16	Routine as per appendix A No 3	1/13 D=2
26.III.16	Church Parade	1/13 D=2
27.III.16	Routine as per appendix A No 4	1/13 D=2
	2nd Lt Rivington allowed leave London Corner HAYLING ISLAND 2.O.S 219 15.III.16	
28.III.16	Routine as per appendix A No 4	1/13 D=2
	Lecture to officer by Major Thompson "Wounded over seen"	1/13 D=2
29.III.16	Routine as per appendix A No 4	1/13 D=2
30.III.16	Routine as per appendix A No 4	1/13 D=2
	Army Instructions for 10/ Pour G. War Office 8th 25.III.16	1/13 D=2 accident 19.O.E.9/ 14/260 (A.S.1) 9.III.16

Army Form C. 2118.

WAR DIARY
or
INTELLIGENCE SUMMARY.
(Erase heading not required.)

2/13th B.n London Regiment

Hour, Date, Place	Summary of Events and Information	Remarks and references to Appendices
31st/1st N° Camp Sutton Veny	Routine as per appendix A N° 4	APX=A
	Initial t-Officer 4 NA 502 C Thompson to outposts	APX=D

Geo. Thompson Major
Commanding 2/13th Bn Lon. Regt

10th April 1916

WAR DIARY

APPENDIX

CONFIDENTIAL.

From 1st MARCH — to 31st MARCH. 1916

SUTTON VENY.   2/XIII Bn LONDON REGIMENT.

General Officer Commanding,
180th Infantry Brigade.

Officer Commanding,
179th Infantry Brigade,
181st Infantry Brigade.

During the sixth and seventh weeks of training which will commence on Monday, March 6th, the following Training is to be carried out. A copy of Programme issued by Brigades should be submitted to this Office by 6 p.m. on Sunday

RECRUITS AND TRAINED SOLDIERS.

(a) Route marching will be carried out one day in each week. A company should be detailed as advanced guard and one as a rearguard for each route march. Day out-posts schemes may be combined with the route march if considered desirable. Whistle calls, as laid down in this Office Circular Memorandum No. 33 of 23rd December, 1915, are to be practised on these and all other marches.
(b) Officers Commanding Battalions will practise the whole Battalion in close order or extended order drill on one day in each week.
(c) Digging will be continued as for the fifth week in accordance with this Office Letter G/404/17 of 24th February, 1916. The following working parties and tools will be detailed from each Brigade:-

	Morning.			Afternoon.		
	Men.	Picks.	Shovels.	Men.	Picks.	Shovels.
Mar 6th	110	72	48	140	84	56
" 7th	140	84	56	120	72	48
" 8th	80	48	32	130	108	72
" 9th	180	108	72	80	48	32
" 10th	100	60	40	150	96	64

The hours for digging will be the same as hitherto

RECRUITS.
The Syllabus of Training as laid down for the sixth and seventh weeks in W.O. Pamphlet O/Gen.No./5757 (M.T.2) dated 23rd December, 1915, is to be followed generally as far as time permits. Trench Warfare and Grenade Training will be carried out at a later stage. Musketry and Miniature Range practices are to be continued.

TRAINED MEN.
(a) The training of the class now under instruction in the Lewis Gun will be continued. The training of detachments will be commenced during the seventh week.
(b) The training of Grenadiers will commence on Monday, 6th instant, as per instructions issued in this Office G/470/1, dated 2nd March, 1916.
(c) All Battalions who have not carried out their day and night outposts schemes owing to weather, which were due to be held during the fourth and fifth weeks, will do so during these weeks.
(d) Drill under Company and Platoon Commanders will be continued, as before, on all days other than one in each week when Battalions are at the disposal of Battalion Commanders for drill.

Lieut: Colonel, General Staff,
60th (London) Division.

Sutton Veny,
2nd March, 1916.

179th. Infantry Brigade.

PROGRAMME OF TRAINING FOR WEEK ENDING SATURDAY, MARCH 11th. 1916.

UNIT.	MONDAY.	TUESDAY.	WEDNESDAY.	THURSDAY.	FRIDAY.	SATURDAY.	REMARKS.
2/13th. Battn. L.R.	Digging 120 O.R. Picks 72 Shovels 48. 9.30 a.m. to 12.30 p.m.	Route March.	Night Outpost Scheme.	Digging 80 O.R. 48 Picks 32 Shovels 2 p.m. - 4.30 p.m. Drill (morning)	Digging 100 O.R. 60 Picks 40 Shovels 9.30 a.m. - 12.30 p.m.		
2/14th. Battn. L.R.	Digging 140 O.R. 84 Picks 56 Shovels. 2 p.m. to 4.30 p.m. Drill (morning)	Route March.	Range Fatigue 100 O.R. 9.30 a.m. to 12.30 p.m.	Digging 180 O.R. 108 Picks. 72 Shovels. 9.30 a.m. - 12.30 p.m.		Kit Inspection, etc.	DRILL – As laid down in Divisional week Syllabus for Recruits and trained men, para (b) Time and place to be notified to Brigade Headquarters. RANGE FATIGUE:- Special Orders will be issued later.
2/15th. Battn. L.R.	Route March.	Digging 140 O.R. 84 Picks. 56 Shovels. 9.30 a.m. to 12.30 p.m.	Digging 180 O.R. 108 Picks. 72 Shovels. 2 p.m. to 4.30 p.m. Drill (morning).		Range Fatigue. 100 O.R. 9.30 a.m. to 12.30 p.m.		
2/16th. Battn. L.R.	Route March.	Digging 120 O.R. 72 Picks. 48 Shovels. 2 p.m. to 4.30 p.m. Drill (morning).	Digging 80 O.R. 48 Picks. 32 Shovels. 9.30 a.m. to 12.30 p.m.	Recruits Musketry. (Range).	Digging 160 O.R. 96 Picks. 64 Shovels. 2 p.m. to 4.30 p.m.		

Syllabus of Training.

Officer Commanding,
179th Infantry Brigade,
180th Infantry Brigade,
181st Infantry Brigade.

During the fourth and fifth weeks of training, which will commence on MONDAY Feb 21st, the following training is to be carried out, and a copy of Programmes issued by Brigades should be submitted to this Office.

1. RECRUITS. The Syllabus of Training as laid down for the fourth and fifth weeks, issued under War Office Letter 9/Gen No. /5757 (M.T.2), dated 23rd December, 1915, is to be followed generally.

(a) Musketry and Miniature Range practices are to be carried out in accordance with the memorandum issued on the subject on 9th February, 1916.
(b) In the digging (to be done during the fifth week) special attention is to be paid to the quick organisation of working parties, e.g. distribution of tools, allotment of tasks, placing of equipment and rifles so that they can be easily used in case of necessity, etc. Before commencing to dig, a covering party is always to be put out, as if under service conditions. This covering party can, later on, be withdrawn, so that all men shall have digging instruction
(c) Brigade Commanders will call on the C.R.E. to provide instructors to show the correct method of using the pick and shovel before the actual digging commences.
(d) Recruits will route march with their Battalions.

2. TRAINED MEN. (a) The Programme issued from this Office for the third week should be, generally, continued. Artillery formations and extensions therefrom are to be carried out by Battalions.
The passing of messages is to be practised constantly.
(b) Route marching will be carried out on one day in each week as was done during the first two weeks' training. During these marches and all other marches, the calls on the whistle, as laid down in this Office Circular Memorandum, No. 33 of 28th December, 1915, are to be practised.
(c) A day Outpost Scheme and a night Outpost Scheme is to be carried out by each Battalion during the fortnight. In order that the available ground may be used to the best advantage, the general outline of the scheme for each Brigade is attached. The night Outpost Scheme should be rehearsed by daylight so that no error may escape notice and no time wasted when the scheme is carried out by night.
Units should leave camps at 6 p.m. and be back in camp not later than 9.20 p.m.
Lectures on Outposts will be given in each Battalion.
An "Allez Allez" scheme mostly on Outposts will be carried out by the G.S.O.1 for the Officers of each Brigade as under:
    180th Inf. Bde.   Feb. 21st   5 p.m.
    179th Inf. Bde.   Feb. 22nd   5 p.m.
    181st Inf. Bde.   Feb. 23rd   5 p.m.
Details as regards the schemes have already been communicated verbally to Brigade Commanders.
(d) The firing of the 10 rounds, allowed before commencing the General Musketry Course, is to be continued.

(sd) C.A. BOLTON, Captain, G.S.
For Lt:Colonel, Gen: Staff 60th Ln:Dv:

OUTPOST SCHEME.

The general tactical idea for each Brigade should be on the following lines:-

(1) 179th. Infantry Brigade is halted in LONGBRIDGE DEVERILL with one Battalion on outposts between the LONGBRIDGE DEVERILL - MAIDEN BRADLEY and the LONGBRIDGE DEVERILL - MONKTON DEVERILL roads (both inclusive). The enemy is coming from the S.W. and is about 10 miles distant.

179th Infantry Brigade.   PROGRAMME OF TRAINING FOR WEEK ENDING 18TH MARCH, 1916.

UNIT.	MONDAY.	TUESDAY.	WEDNESDAY.	THURSDAY.	FRIDAY.	SAT.	REMARKS.
2/13th Bn. L.R.	100 Other Ranks Range Fatigue. 9 a.m.-12.30 p.m. 15 Officers, 28 Other Ranks, Gas Lecture 10.30 a.m. Recruits, Night Field Work.	Digging 80 Other Ranks. 2.0 p.m. - 4.30 p.m.	Route March.	Digging, 160 Other Ranks. 9.30 a.m. - 12.30 p.m.		KIT INSPECTION, ETC.	DIGGING. The parties for digging on Tuesday, 14th inst. will be found from recruits/trained to bear arms. insufficiently. GAS LECTURES. Lectures will be held in Y.M.C.A. Hut, No. 4 Camp.
2/14th Bn. L.R.	Route March.	Digging 160 Other Ranks. 9.30 a.m. - 12.30 p.m.	100 Other Ranks, Range Fatigue. 9.0 a.m.-12.30 p.m. 15 officers 28 O.R. Gas Lecture 10.30 a.m. Recruits, Night Field Work.	Digging, 80 Other Ranks. 2.0 - 4.30 p.m.	Digging 160 Other Ranks, 9.30 a.m. - 12.30 p.m.		
2/15th Bn. L.R.	105 Other Ranks, Musketry Range, 2.0 p.m. Digging, 80 Other Ranks. 2.0 - 4.30 p.m.		Digging, 160 O.R. 9.30 am.-12.30 pm 15 Off., 28 O.R. Gas Lecture 2.30 p.m. Recruits, Night Field Work.	Route March.	100 O.R., Range Fatigue. 9.a.m. -12.30 p.m. Digging, 80 Other Ranks. 2.0-4.30 p.m.		
2/16th Bn. L.R.	Digging, 160 O.R. 9.30 a.m.-12.30 p.m. 15 Officers, 28 Other Ranks, Gas Lecture, 2.30 p.m.		Digging 80 O.R. 2.0-4.30 p.m.	100 O.R. Range Fatigue, 9 a.m. -12.30 p.m. Recruits, Night Field Work.	Route March.		
BRIGADE.		Brigade Exercise.	Lecture by Bde. Major to all Capts. and Subs. 2/13th and 2/14th in 2/14th Lines 5.30 p.m.	Recruits Musketry, 1A and 2A 9.a.m. -12.30 p.m. and 2. p.m. -4.30 p.m.	Lecture by B. Major to all Capts.& Subs 2/15th and 2/16th in 2/16th Lines 5.30 p.m.		W.N.HERBERT. MAJOR. Brigade Major. 179th Inf. Bde.

Appendix No 3

179th Infantry Brigade.   PROGRAMME OF TRAINING for week ending Saturday, 25th March, 1916.

UNIT.	MONDAY.	TUESDAY.	WEDNESDAY.	THURSDAY.	FRIDAY.	SATURDAY.	REMARKS.
2/13th Bn. L.R.	2 Coys. G.M.C.	2 Coys. G.M.C. 50 O.R.Digging 9.30 a.m. - 12.30 p.m. Bn. Grenadiers Parade 7.15 a.m.	2 Coys. G.M.C. Night Work.	2 Coys. G.M.C. 50 O.R.Digging. 2 - 4.30 p.m.	2 Coys. G.M.C. Bn. Grenadiers Parade 7.15 a.m.	2 Coys G.M.C.	GRENADIERS. A new party of Grenadiers will commence training on Monday, 20th inst. The Grenadiers recently trained will parade twice during week as shown, under Brigade Bombing Officer, who will arrange with Battalion Grenade Officers as to place of parade. NIGHT WORK. Night work is scheduled once for each Battalion, this is only to avoid Battalions clashing in Training Area.
2/14th Bn. L.R.	2 Coys. G.M.C. Night Work.	2 Coys. G.M.C. 50 O.R. Digging. 2. - 4.30 p.m. Bn. Grenadiers Parade 7.15 a.m.	2 Coys. G.M.C.	2 Coys. G.M.C. 50 O.R.Digging. 9.30 a.m. - 12.30 p.m.	2 Coys. G.M.C. Bn. Grenadiers Parade 7.15 a.m.	2 Coys G.M.C.	
2/15th Bn. L.R.	50 O.R.Digging. 2.0 - 4.30 p.m.	Route March.	50 O.R.Digging 9.30 a.m. - 12.30 p.m. Bn. Grenadiers Parade 7.15 a.m.	Battn. Drill. Night Work.	50 O.R.Digging. 2 - 4.30 p.m.	Bn. Grenadiers Parade 7.15 a.m.	
2/16th Bn. L.R.	50 O.R.Digging. 9.30 a.m. - 12.30 p.m.	Battn. Drill. Night Work.	Bn. Grenadiers Parade 7.15 a.m. 50 O.R.Digging 2 - 4.30 p.m.	Route March.	50 O.R.Digging 9.30 a.m. - 12.30 p.m.	Bn. Grenadiers Parade 7.15 a.m.	
BRIGADE.	Conference of C.O's, Brigade Headquarters, 4.0 p.m.						

W.N.HERBERT.
MAJOR.
BRIGADE MAJOR.
179th Infantry Brigade.

179th Infantry Brigade.   Appendix A to

PROGRAMME OF TRAINING FOR WEEK ENDING 1st April, 1916.

UNIT.	MONDAY.	TUESDAY.	WEDNESDAY.	THURSDAY.	FRIDAY.	SATURDAY.	REMARKS.
2/13th Bn. L.R.	2 Companies G.M.C.	2 Companies G.M.C.	2 Companies G.M.C.	50 Other Ranks Digging. 9.30 a.m. - 12.30 p.m. Route March.	50 Other Ranks Digging. 2 - 4.30 p.m. Night Field Work.		
2/14th Bn. L.R.	2 Companies G.M.C.	2 Companies G.M.C.	2 Companies G.M.C.	50 Other Ranks Digging. 2 - 4.30 p.m. Night Field Work.	50 Other Ranks Digging. 9.30 a.m. - 12.30 p.m. Route March.	2 Companies G.M.C.	KIT INSPECTION, ETC.
2/15th Bn. L.R.	50 Other Ranks Digging. 9.30 a.m. - 12.30 p.m. Night Field Work.	Route March. 50 Other Ranks Digging. 2 - 4.30 p.m.	50 Other Ranks Digging. 9.30 a.m. - 12.30 p.m.	2 Companies G.M.C.	2 Companies G.M.C.	2 Companies G.M.C.	
2/16th Bn. L.R.	50 Other Ranks Digging. 2 - 4.30 p.m.	50 Other Ranks Digging. 9.30 a.m. - 12.30 p.m. Night Field Work.	Route March. 50 Other Ranks Digginf. 2 - 4.30 p.m.	2 Companies G.M.C.	2 Companies G.M.C.	2 Companies G.M.C.	
BRIGADE.					Conference of C.O's 4.0 p.m.		

W.N.HERBERT.
MAJOR.
Brigade Major.
179th Infantry Brigade.

Programme of Training for Week Commencing 27.3.1916.   2/13th Battalion London Regiment.

Company.	Monday.	Tuesday.	Wednesday.	Thursday.	Friday.	Saturday.	Remarks.
A	G. M. C. Physical Training. Bayonet Fighting.	G. M. C. Phys. Training. Bayonet Fighting.	G. M. C. Phys. Training; Bayonet Fighting.	13 other Ranks digging, 9.30 a.m. to 12.30 p.m. Route March.	Phys. Training. Bayonet Fighting; Bn. Close Order Drill; 13 Other Ranks digging; Night Field Work.	Kit Inspection, etc.	Battalion field is situate 400 yards West of No. 8 Camp.
B	ditto.	ditto.	ditto.	ditto.	ditto.	ditto.	
C	Phys. Training; Baynt. Fighting; Musketry Instrn.; Lecture; Close & Extended Order Drill.	Phys. Training; Baynt. Fighting; Lecture; Artillery Formations. Musketry Instruction	Phys. Training; Bayonet Fighting; Musketry Instruction; Lecture; Close & Extended Order Drill.	ditto.	ditto.	ditto.	
D	ditto.	ditto.	ditto.	ditto.	ditto.	ditto.	
Specialists.							
Signallers.	G. Telephonic Work on Range.	M.	C.	Route March.	Co. Signallers will train with Bn. Signallers. ditto.		
Machine and Lewis Gun Section.	G.	M.	C.	School of Instruction.			
Grenadiers.	Brigade School of Instruction for the Week.						
Scouts.	G.	M.	C.	With Companies for Remainder of Week.			

W. David Davis
Captain & Adjutant. 2/13 London Regt

CONFIDENTIAL

WAR DIARY

From 1.4.16   To   30.4.16

2/13ᵗʰ Battalion
London Regiment.

WAR DIARY
or
INTELLIGENCE SUMMARY. 2/13ᵗʰ Bⁿ L.R.

Army Form C. 2118.

(Erase heading not required.)

Instructions regarding War Diaries and Intelligence Summaries are contained in F.S. Regs., Part II. and the Staff Manual respectively. Title pages will be prepared in manuscript.

Hour, Date, Place	Summary of Events and Information	Remarks and references to Appendices
1.IV.16 M⁴⁵ Camp SUTTON VENY	Aweite	
	Routine: Physical Drill. Bayonet fighting Close order Drill. Kit inspection	MED.D
5.55	2nd Lt H.G. CLARK to opposite Transport Office vice Lt S.W. CALDBECK	M.D.D
	Lt S.W. CALDBECK returns to A Coy for duty	M.D.D
am 2.IV.16	Church Parade.	ALD-D
	MAJOR C.H. MACKENZIE reports for duty as O.C. 13ᵗʰ	ALD-D
	3 horses taken off strength. A.D.V.S. 65 (Lon) Div. 1.IV.16.	MED-D
3.IV.16	Routine as laid in programme training Appendix 1	MEN-D
am	Health & moral kept very excellent.	MED-D
am 4.IV.16	Routine as per appendix 1. recruits weeks	MED-D
	Pte SALVATERI discharged & immediate app.	MED-D authority T.F.R.C. letter 13/9357
	3 horses transferred to Signal Coy R.E. 60 (Lond) Division } 4 mares ... VET HOSPITAL BULFORD.	MED-D A.D.V.S. 60 (Lond) Div.
	Sgt. L.B. HAWKES pressed on bar for Sgt. Farrier L Reserv. 13ᵗʰ	MED-D
5.IV.16	Routine as per appendix 1.	DI.80
	MAJOR C.H. MACKENZIE assumes command of the 13ᵗʰ	MED-D authority A.A. O. 1820 P.92 5.IV.16
	Pte BASS 3097 discharged.	MED-D authority T.F.R.S 347/(16)

Army Form C. 2118.

WAR DIARY
or
INTELLIGENCE SUMMARY.
(Erase heading not required.)

2/13th Bn LONDON REGIMENT.

Hour, Date, Place	Summary of Events and Information	Remarks and references to Appendices
6.3.16. R & Camp SUTTON VENY.	Routine as per Appendix 1	AF2118
	#Capt LANGTON 3179 transfers London Electrical Engineers	AF2118 T.F. Res. L. 13/1004 31.III.16
7.III.16	Routine as per Appendix 1	AF2118
-15.	Pte Eric Olsson grounded as per appendix 1	AF2118 ailment. Bd.
.38	Bn wix Wigtown transport arrived upon arrival at destination a Bd.	AF2118
	Elections took place. Weather unsettled.	
	2 NCO's and 3 men Transferred to 107 Prov. B⁹. unfit for G. Service	AF2118 auth T.F Res L.13/983 20.III.16
	1 man Transferred to 101 Prov. (B⁹ information Coy)	AF2118 auth T.F Res L.13/977 22.III.16
	2 N.C.O.'s and 3 men (attached from 11 (B⁹. L.R) unfit for G. Service returned to	AF2118 auth T.F Res L.13/983 30.III.16
	their unit 10th Bn 13⁹.	
	2 men (attached from 2/5 (3rd LR) and 4 men (attached from HAC) unfit [ ]	AF2118 auth T.F Res L.13/982 30.III.16
	G. Service returned to their unit 101 Prov. B⁹.	
	2b G.I.H.E.A.T (attached from HAC) Struck off Strength [ ] No 7 Officer	
	cadet B⁹	AF2118 auth WO L. S.D.60 (3 b 3)

WAR DIARY
~~INTELLIGENCE SUMMARY~~
(Erase heading not required.)

2/13th (3rd) LONDON REGIMENT

Army Form C. 2118.

Hour, Date, Place	Summary of Events and Information	Remarks and references to Appendices
6.iii.16 N.d. Camp ROTTEN VENN	Routine as per appendix 1	W.D.S
	L/ BAKER and Corporal RING obtains a Leave for Course at HAYLING ISLAND	W.D.S auth. Div. order. 219. 18.iii.16
	Corporal KNIGHT (attached from 2/15 B.LR) struck off strength	D.D.A auth: W.O.L A/Book Yeo./181 (I.T.3)
	Posted L/ No 2 g/Wen Rodrel Squad on Quality School KILDARE	
	Pte OWENS (attached from 2/15 (3rd-L.R) Cases Fit attaches released & hold with SOPWORTH AVIATION Co.	W.D.S auth: W.O.L 19/Gen.No/ 5415 (A.G.S)
9.iv.16	Reveille	W.D.S
	Church Parade	W.D.S
	Major C.H. MacKENZIE reads out attacks men W.O. Telegram	W.D.S
	2. Cancellation of transfer of N.C.O's and men from 60 (Lon) Division	W.D.S
5am 10.iv.16	Routine as per appendix 2	W.D.S
	R.H.C. of C and D Coys.	W.D.S
	Recruit (illegible) from in time of 12.i.16. are returned to C.P. on brand orders.	W.D.S

(3)

Army Form C. 2118.

WAR DIARY
or
INTELLIGENCE SUMMARY.
(Erase heading not required.)

2/13. B. L.R.

Instructions regarding War Diaries and Intelligence Summaries are contained in F.S. Regs., Part II. and the Staff Manual respectively. Title pages will be prepared in manuscript.

Hour, Date, Place	Summary of Events and Information	Remarks and references to Appendices
11.iv.16 No 9 Camp SUTTON VENY	routine as per appendix 2	WD-2
	2 men (allocated from 2S. B.L.R.) transferred to 3 B. Reserve Bde. R.F.A. EXETER.	WD-2 auth. W.O. L.9/Artillery/1356 23.iii.16 W.O. L.9/Artillery/471 23.iii.16
12.iv.16	routine as per appendix 2	WD-2
	Closing Board. Pres. MAJOR HOPKINS members. Capt E RIVINGTON. 2/Lt STOCKWELL	WD-2 WD-2
	6 signalling course of 3th. undermentioned commenced at 9.30. a.m. WESLEYAN INSTITUTE No.5 Camp SUTTON VENY.	WD-2
	Pte WHARTON " MAY " LANSDEN " WILLS	
	5 men discharged : unfit for G. Service.	WD-2 auth. T.F. Rec. L. 13/1106 10.iv.16
13.iv.16	routine as per appendix 2	WD-2 WD-2
	Capt. COLLIER ceases to be Bde. Bombing Officer and attached 2 B.C. for duty	WD-2
	Pte COOK returns L.75 of B.L. for duty	WD-2
14.iv.16	routine as per appendix 2	WD-2
	3 men transferred to 10th Reserve B.C. : recommended by	WD-2 auth: T.F. Rec. L. - 13/1076 7.iv.16

(4)

(73989) W4141—463. 400,000. 9/14. H.&J.Ltd. Forms/C. 2118/10.

Army Form C. 2118.

WAR DIARY
or
INTELLIGENCE SUMMARY.

(Erase heading not required.)

2/13 Bn LONDON REGIMENT

Instructions regarding War Diaries and Intelligence Summaries are contained in F. S. Regs., Part II. and the Staff Manual respectively. Title pages will be prepared in manuscript.

Hour, Date, Place	Summary of Events and Information	Remarks and references to Appendices
14.iv.16 No 6 Camp SUTTON VENY	2E HART transferred to 1/17 (3rd Bn) vice W. P. Rose	WD-D T.F Rec L 13/952 30iii.16
	4 men transferred from 105" Prov. Bn to 13th	WD-D auth: Div L. A/2349/35 11.iv.16
15.iv.16	routine as per appendix 2	WD-D
16.iv.16	reveille	WD-D
	Church Parade	WD-D
17.iv.16	routine as per appendix 3	WD-D
	Capt. C.T. HANKS (RAMC) signed E.624	WD-D
	Practice alarm sounded	WD-D auth: R.O. appendix 2?
	13th moved into First line transport and work 2/14 Bn LR	WD-D
	Wire entanglements erected by L' Thompson and 5 NCOs commenced at 9.30a	WD-D
	RE guard room.	
18.iv.16	routine as per appendix 3	WD-D

(5)

Army Form C. 2118.

WAR DIARY
or
INTELLIGENCE SUMMARY.
(Erase heading not required.)

2/13th Bn London Regiment

Hour, Date, Place	Summary of Events and Information	Remarks and references to Appendices
R.W.C. Camp SUTTON VENY	The undermentioned officers attended a Snipers' course commencing at 10.0 a.m. CAPT PLAYSTONE - FOSTER R. L.ts BOSEVEAR - TRANTER	WTD-A
18.iv.16	2 N.C.O.s and 2 men transferred from 105 Bn (Prov) to 13th	W.D.D. Auth 60(Lond)Div L. A/2349/35 11.iv.16
	routine as per appendix 3	WTD-A
19.iv.16	Lecture by Lt ROSEVEAR - RANGE	WTD-A
20.iv.16	routine as per appendix 3	WTD-A
	Lecture by G.O.C. Div. MAJOR GEN BULFIN 5 P.M. Lt W A F DREW admitted to SUTTON VENY military hospital	WTD-A
a.m. 21.iv.16	General	WTD-A
	Church Parade	WTD-A
22.iv.16	routine as per appendix 3	WTD-A
23.iv.16	reveille	WTD-A
5.45	Church Parade	WTD-A

(6)

Army Form C. 2118.

WAR DIARY
or
INTELLIGENCE SUMMARY.
(Erase heading not required.)

2/13- (Cᵒ London Regiment.

Instructions regarding War Diaries and Intelligence Summaries are contained in F. S. Regs., Part II. and the Staff Manual respectively. Title pages will be prepared in manuscript.

Hour, Date, Place	Summary of Events and Information	Remarks and references to Appendices
24.iv.16 M&Y Camp Sutton Veny	Routine as per appendix 4	W.D.S.O
	Wire entanglement lecture Sec Lts SHUTE and SHAVE	W.D.S.O
	PE WILLS (attached from HAC) having been granted a commission in R.F.C. ceases to attached	W.D.S.O auth. W.O.L. 48/7447 School 440/S.O.L.
25.iv.16	Routine as per appendix 4.	W.D.S.O
	MAJOR E.H. MACKENZIE gazetted [Temp] Lt Colonel dated 2.iv.16	W.D.S.O
5-	Sec Lt (temp) J. SHGREEN promoted to [Temp] CAPTAIN " " "	W.D.S.O
26.iv.16	Routine as per appendix 4	W.D.S.O
27.iv.16	Routine as per appendix 4	W.D.S.O
5-	Conference at Bd Cd. and with re emergency men	W.D.S.O
3 p.m.	2 men transferred to 107 Prov Bn immediate ay.	W.D.S.O T.F. Res. L. 17/1247 22.iv.16
	Sergt BENSON (26 (Cᵒ LR)) ceases to be attached having joined prior No. 5	W.D.S.O auth. W.O. telegm Nᵒ 2665. S.D. 3 ℆ 24.iv.16
	Office cases Bᶜ	

(7)

Army Form C. 2118.

WAR DIARY
or
INTELLIGENCE SUMMARY.
(Erase heading not required.)

2/13 Bn LONDON REGIMENT.

Instructions regarding War Diaries and Intelligence Summaries are contained in F. S. Regs., Part II. and the Staff Manual respectively. Title pages will be prepared in manuscript.

Hour, Date, Place	Summary of Events and Information	Remarks and references to Appendices
28.iv.16 N°8 Camp SUTTON VENY		
5 am	Routine as per appendix 4	WD-D
	77 H.A.C. N.Cos and men proceeded on 1 month's leave as per army Council Instruction	WD-D
P.M. 28.iv.16	Emergency alarm sounded	WD-D appendix 5
am 29.iv.16	A and B Coys under MAJOR THOMPSON – HOPKINS CAPTAIN BROCK – HORST 1st T+HOPSON – ROSEVEAR and 250. O.R move into first house of Warminster to Warminster Station to entrain for NEVLAND	WD-D appendix 5
.55 – WARMINSTER STATION	The above part entrained for NEVLAND Train due to start 3.20.am detailed at 3.35.am 45 minutes to entrain General's wagon. 14 wagon – 2 coats. 30 minutes to entrain 54 horses (including A.S.C & 13 Bde horses) 10 to entrain troops	WD-D WD-D (6)

WAR DIARY
to
Bn on Trek in IRELAND

WAR DIARY
or
INTELLIGENCE SUMMARY.
(Erase heading not required.)

Army Form C. 2118.

2/13 B² L.R.

Hour, Date, Place	Summary of Events and Information	Remarks and references to Appendices
29/11/16 N° 4 Camp, SUTTON VENY	C¹ to Capt Lindo A¹ Coy. C H Mackenzie, acting M.O. QM to CAPTAIN COLLIER. GLADSTONE. SLADE. FOSTER SPEEN L¹ RANGE - Sgt¹ LANCASTER. READ - SATES - RIVINGTON - SHUTE - The Chaplain and 313 O.R. move to WARMINSTER STATION Jt ealudin fr NEYLAND.	W220
WARMINSTER STATION	Advance pty arrivd at WARMINSTER STATION. and ſecond portion of transport.	W2X=A
	25 minutes trailowin 13 wagons and 3 carts	
	23 " " 69 hnes (including A.S.C. + Bd details)	W220
	8 " " hoops.	
	Train starts 4.53. a.m. due to start 5. a.m.	W220
NEYLAND.	A + B Coy reached field 1500 yds W. of NEYLAND STATION (and transport)	W220
	C + D Coy with transport ours Bn H.Q... "	W220
	tents pitched	W220

(9)

Army Form C. 2118.

WAR DIARY
or
INTELLIGENCE SUMMARY.   2/13th London Regiment

(Erase heading not required.)

Instructions regarding War Diaries and Intelligence Summaries are contained in F.S. Regs., Part II and the Staff Manual respectively. Title pages will be prepared in manuscript.

Hour, Date, Place	Summary of Events and Information	Remarks and references to Appendices
	WAR DIARY OF REAR PARTY	
28.iv.16 N° & Coy. SUTTON VENY	Rear Party consisting of CAPTAIN HERNE, Lt CALDBECK (act. Adjt) BAKER — Sect. STOCKWELL — SHAVE — DUFFY-ALLEN TEMPLE and 236 O.R. (including 12 NCOs and men on leave)	W.D.8—D
29.iv.16	reveil — general fatigue	W.D.8—D W.D.8—D
30.iv.16	reveil Church Parade	W.D.8—D W.D.8—D
	Pte WHIDDON transferred to 107 Prov. Bⁿ. enlist of P. Service.	W.D.8—D T. F. Res L 13/1232 27.iv.16
	S.M. EGDON 2/Lt discharged from Hospital.	W.D.8—D

Longridge Averill
15th May 1916

Geo Thompson
Major 2nd Bn Ldn Regt
Commanding 2/13 Bn Ldn Regt

WAR DIARY
or
INTELLIGENCE SUMMARY

Army Form C. 2118.

2/13th Bn LONDON REGIMENT

(Erase heading not required.)

Instructions regarding War Diaries and Intelligence Summaries are contained in F.S. Regs., Part II. and the Staff Manual respectively. Title pages will be prepared in manuscript.

Hour, Date, Place	Summary of Events and Information	Remarks and references to Appendices
30.iv.16 NEYLAND 5 am	Arrival	W2D2D
1.30	Church Parade	W2D2D
2.5 P.M.	Men arriving of transport & contents	W2D2D Appendix 5
4.15	2nd half with Bn HQ. 12 officers and 330. O.R. (horses)	W2D2D
	L. NEYLAND embarkation port.	W2D2D
4.30	S.S. SNOWDON left NEYLAND with 342 all ranks and 13 Bdo.	W2D2D
	details, — 34 A.S.C. and The whole 1st line transport	
	Anchored midstream	
S.S. SNOWDON	practice alarm	W2D2D

(10)

WAR DIARY

APPENDIX

Confidendial

From 1st APRIL ———— to 30th APRIL. 1916

SUTTON VENY
No 8 CAMP.

2/13th BATTALION
LONDON REGIMENT.

Appendix
Nº 1.

Programme of Training for Week commencing 3rd April 1916
2/13th Battn London Regt.

Coy.	Monday	Tuesday	Wednesday	Thursday	Friday	Saturday
A	Physical Training. Bayonet Fighting. Musketry Instruction Extended Order Drill. Digging 50 Other Rnks.Digging 11 a.m.- 12 noon Night Work	Day Out Post Scheme. 50 other ranks digging 7.30pm - 8.30 p.m.	Physical Training Bayonet Fighting Musketry Instruc. Close Order Drill 50 other ranks digging 11 a.m.- 12 noon.	Phys. Training Bayonet Fighting Btn.Close Order Drill. 50 other ranks digging 7.30p.m.- 8.30p.m.	Route March	Kit Inspection etc.
B	ditto.	ditto.	ditto.	ditto.	ditto.	ditto.
C	ditto.	ditto.	ditto.	ditto.	ditto.	ditto.
D	ditto.	ditto.	ditto.	ditto.	ditto.	ditto.

Specialists.

Signallers. Company Signallers will train with Signalling Section for the week, except Tuesday and Friday.

Machine & Lewis Course of Instruction for the week.
Gun Section.

Grenadiers. Brigade School of Instruction.

Scouts. With Companies.

W P David-Davis
Capt.& Adjutant.
2/13th Battn. London Regt.

179th Infantry Brigade.

Programme of Training for Week Ending 8th April, 1916.

UNIT.	MONDAY, 3rd.	TUESDAY, 4th.	WEDNESDAY, 5th.	THURSDAY, 6th.	FRIDAY, 7th.	SATURDAY, 8th.	REMARKS.
2/13th Bn. L.R.	200 All Ranks Digging. 11 a.m. - 12 noon 200 All Ranks Digging. 7.30-8.30 p.m. Night Work.	Day Outpost Scheme. 11 a.m. - 12 noon 200 All Ranks Digging. 7.30 - 8.30 p.m.	200 All Ranks Digging. 11 a.m. - 12 noon. 200 All Ranks Digging. 7.30 - 8.30 p.m.	Drill. 200 All Ranks Digging. 7.30-8.30 p.m.	Route March.	K I T I N S P E C T I O N, E T C.	All training is to be carried out in accordance with Divisional Syllabus issued herewith. Lewis Gun and Grenadier Training will be carried out in accordance with instructions already issued.
2/14th Bn. L.R.	Drill. 200 All Ranks Digging. 7.30-8.30 p.m.	200 All Ranks Digging. 11 a.m. - 12 noon 200 All Ranks Digging. 7.30 - 8.30 p.m.	Day Outpost Scheme. 200 All Ranks Digging. 7.30 - 8.30 p.m.	200 All Ranks Digging. 11 a.m. - 12 noon Night Work.	Route March.		
2/15th Bn. L.R.	2 Companies G.M.C. 100 All Ranks Digging. 9.30-10.30 a.m.	2 Companies G.M.C. 100 All Ranks Digging 7.30 - 8.30 p.m.	2 Companies G.M.C. 100 All Ranks Digging. 9.30-10.30 a.m.	2 Companies G.M.C. 100 All Ranks Digging 7.30 p.m.-8.30 p.m.	2 Companies G.M.C.	2 Companies G.M.C.	
2/16th Bn. L.R.	2 Companies G.M.C. 100 All Ranks Digging. 7.30 - 8.30 p.m.	2 Companies G.M.C. 100 All Ranks Digging. 9.30 - 10.30 a.m.	2 Companies G.M.C. 100 All Ranks Digging. 7.30 - 8.30 p.m.	2 Companies G.M.C. 100 All Ranks Digging. 9.30 - 10.30 a.m.	2 Companies G.M.C.	2 Companies G.M.C.	
BRIGADE.			C.O's and 2 Senr. Officers ALLEZ ALLEZ Scheme Brigade H.Q. 5.0 p.m.				

W.H. HERBERT.
Major, Brigade Major.
179th Infantry Brigade.

179th Infantry Brigade.

WEEKLY PROGRAMME OF TRAINING FOR MACHINE GUN SECTIONS.

(April 3rd, 1916 - April 8th, 1916).

The further training of the Lewis Gun detachments which have recently fired Part I, Machine Gun Course, including the 8 numbers who attended the examination held at these Headquarters on March 24th and 25th, will be continued during the fortnight commencing April 3rd, 1916.

1. The following programme is to be adhered to.

2. If it is wet section officers will arrange for lectures on the subjects laid down for the day.

3. N.C.O's are to be given suitable opportunities for instructing.

4. Lewis Gun detachments to accompany Battalions when a route march is the order of the day.

5. Section officers will inform their respective Orderly Rooms of their training area for the day.

MONDAY. April 3rd. — Physical Training, Judging Distance, Section Drill, Selection and Occupation of Positions, Description and Recognition of Targets, Immediate Action.

TUESDAY. April 4th. — Physical Training, Visual Training, Drill on Rough Ground, Duties of Numbers, Passing of Orders, Range Card for the Attack, Immediate Action.

WEDNESDAY, April 5th. — Physical Training, Fire Orders, Section Drill, Practise taking up Positions unseen, Use of Ground and Cover, Range Card for Defence, Immediate Action.

THURSDAY, April 6th. — Physical Training, Description and Recognition in Natural Country, Care and Cleaning, Points Before, During and After Firing, Night Firing, How to set up by day with Tripod, Immediate Action blindfold.

FRIDAY. April 7th. — Physical Training, Take up a position in Natural Country for:-
    (a) Overhead Fire - gun on tripod.
    (b) Indirect fire - guns on tripod and explain graticules, luminous stones method, spirit level method.
Immediate Action blindfold. Range Finding, Barr & Stroud.

SATURDAY. April 8th. — Section Officers will go over any of the Past week's work and conform to Brigade Orders No. 71 of 23.3.16. para. 3.

H. Wilson Young
B.M. f.o

"A" Form.
Army Form C. 2121
MESSAGES AND SIGNALS.   No. of Message _____

Prefix	Code	m.	Words	Charge		This message is on a/c of :	Recd. at _____ m.
Office of Origin and Service Instructions.			Sent				Date _____
			At _____ m.		_____ Service.	From _____
			To			
			By		(Signature of "Franking Officer.")	By _____

TO   2/13th   2/14th   2/15th   2/16th
     Battalions, London Regiment.

                                              AAA

B.M.1.   8th

Practice Alarm in accordance with 60th Divisional
Orders 180 dated 9th March for fourth week AAA
2/14th Battalion will move when ready via LONGBRIDGE
DEVERILL - EAST KNOYLE road AAA 2/13th will follow
2/14th when ready AAA 2/16th and 2/15th will follow
in above order, but will not debouch on to SUTTON
VENY - LONGBRIDGE DEVERILL Road until 2/13th have
passed AAA 1st Line transport Echelon A and B will
follow units AAA The trained Machine Gun Section
will parade as such with 2 Lewis Guns per Battalion
AAA All isolated men will parade one hour after the
battalions and will march in detachments to point 426
where they will come under the Command of Captain
A.J.GRAY, 10th Bn. Royal Scots. AAA This party will
carry 5 rounds of blank per man.

From 179th I B
Place
Time 8.0 a.m.

Appendix
N.º 2.

PROGRAMME OF TRAINING FOR WEEK COMMENCING 10th April 1916.

2/13th Battalion London Regiment.

Company.	MONDAY.	TUESDAY.	WEDNESDAY.	THURSDAY.	FRIDAY.	SATURDAY.	Remarks.
A.	C & D Coys. G.M.C...... 200 all ranks digging.... 10.30 to 12 noon Phys. Dl. Bay. Ftg...... Musketry Inst. Extended order & Close order drill. Attached men under R.S.M.	C & D Coys G.M.C. Phys. Drill Bay. Ftg. Musk. Inst. Extended order drill. Close order drill. Attached men under R.S.M.	C & D Coys G.M.C. Phys. Drill Bay. Ftg. Musk. Inst. Extended order drill. Close order drill. Attached men under R.S.M.	C & D Coys G.M.C. Route March.	C & D Coys G.M.C. Phys. Drill Bay. Ftg. Extended order drill. Close Order drill. Attached men under R.S.M.	Kit Insp. Phys. Drill. Bay. Ftg.	Route of Route March. Longbridge-Deverill - Point 559 on Longbridge Deverill-Maiden Bradley Road-Road Junction immediately EAST of M in Horningsham Reformatory School-Point 477 - Warminster Common - Longbridge Deverill. Advance & Rear Guards will be practiced.
B.	ditto.	ditto.	ditto.	ditto.	ditto.	ditto.	
C.	ditto.	ditto.	ditto.	ditto.	ditto.	ditto.	
D.	ditto.	ditto.	ditto.	ditto.	ditto.	ditto.	

SPECIALISTS.

Machine Gun Section. Brigade Programme under B.M/Gun Officer.
Signalling Section. Range & Telephonic duties.
Bombers. Divisional Programme under B. Bombing Officer.

H P Davis
Captain & Adjutant.
2/13th Battalion London Regiment.

179th Infantry Brigade.

Programme of Training for week ending 15th April 1916.

UNIT.	MONDAY, 10th.	TUESDAY, 11th.	WEDNESDAY, 12th.	THURSDAY, 13th.	FRIDAY, 14th.	SATURDAY, 15th.
2/13th Battn. L.R.	1 Company G.M.C. Drill. 200 All Ranks Digging. 10.30 - 12 noon.	1 Company G.M.C. Drill. Night Work.	1 Company G.M.C. 200 All Ranks Digging. 10.30 a.m. - 12 noon.	1 Company G.M.C. Route March.	1 Company G.M.C. Drill.	1 Company G.M.C.
2/14th Battn. L.R.	1 Company G.M.C. Drill. 200 All Ranks Digging. 10.30 a.m. - 12 noon.	1 Company G.M.C. Drill. Night Work.	1 Company G.M.C. 200 All Ranks Digging. 10.30 a.m. - 12 noon.	1 Company G.M.C. Route March.	1 Company G.M.C. Drill.	1 Company G.M.C.
2/15th Battn. L.R.	1 Company G.M.C. Drill. Night Work.	1 Company G.M.C. 200 All Ranks Digging. 10.30 a.m. - 12 noon.	1 Company G.M.C. Route March.	1 Company G.M.C. 200 All Ranks Digging. 10.30 a.m. - 12 noon.	1 Company G.M.C. Drill.	1 Company G.M.C.
2/16th Battn. L.R.	1 Company G.M.C. Drill. Night Work.	1 Company G.M.C. 200 All Ranks Digging. 10.30 a.m. - 12 noon.	1 Company G.M.C. Route March.	1 Company G.M.C. 200 All Ranks Digging. 10.30 a.m. - 12 noon.	1 Company G.M.C. Drill.	1 Company G.M.C.

KIT INSPECTION ETC.

REMARKS:

DIGGING. 50% Shovels and 50% Picks will be taken by Digging Parties. Digging will be under same arrangements as last week.

BOMBING. A fifth Bombing Party will commence training on Monday, 10th April under same arrangements as previous parties.

LEWIS GUN. Lewis Gun Training will continue in accordance with programme issued by B.M.G.Officer.

W.N.HERBERT.
Major,
BRIGADE MAJOR,
179th Infantry Brigade.

Appendix

N° 3

2/15th Battalion London Regt.

PROGRAMME OF TRAINING FOR WEEK COMMENCING
17th April 1916.

Company.	Monday.	Tuesday.	Wednesday.	Thursday.	Friday.	Saturday.
A	C & D Cos. G.M.C. Physical Drill; Baynt. Fighting; Muskty. Instrucns; Close Order Drill; 200 all ranks digging; 11 a.m. Night Work. 7 p.m. Attached men under R.S.M.	C & D Cos. G.M.C. Route March. Lecture on Sniping; 10 a.m.	C & D Cos. G.M.C. Physical Drill; Baynt. Fighting; Musketry Instructions; Extended Order Drill, Attached men under R.S.M. 200 all ranks digging; 8 p.m.	C & D Cos. G.M.C. Phys. Drill; Baynt. Fightg.; Musketry Instructions; Close Order Drill; En.Close Order Drill; Lecture by C.O.'s 5 p.m.	Church Parade.	C & D Cos. G.M.C. Kit Inspection; Physical Drill Bayonet Fighting.
B						
C						
D						

W. Davidson

Captain & Adjutant,
2/15th Battalion London Regt.

179th Infantry Brigade.

Programme of Training for week ending April 22nd 1916.

UNIT.	MONDAY, 17th.	TUESDAY, 18th.	WEDNESDAY, 19th.	THURSDAY, 20th.	FRIDAY, 21st.	SATURDAY, 22nd.	REMARKS.
1/13th Battn. L.R.	1 Coy. G.M.C. 200 All Ranks Digging 11 a.m. Night Work.	1 Coy. G.M.C. Route March.	1 Coy. G.M.C. 200 All Ranks Digging 8 p.m.	1 Coy. G.M.C.	1 Coy. G.M.C.	1 Coy. G.M.C.	
1/14th Battn. L.R.	1 Coy. G.M.C. Night Work.	1 Coy. G.M.C. 200 All Ranks Digging 11 a.m.	1 Coy. G.M.C. Route March.	1 Coy. G.M.C. 200 All Ranks Digging 8 p.m.	1 Coy. G.M.C.	1 Coy. G.M.C.	KIT INSPECTION, ETC.
1/15th Battn. L.R.	1 Coy. G.M.C. Night Work.	1 Coy. G.M.C. 200 All Ranks Digging 11 a.m.	1 Coy. G.M.C. Route March.	1 Coy. G.M.C. 200 All Ranks Digging 8 p.m.	1 Coy. G.M.C.	1 Coy. G.M.C.	
1/16th Battn. L.R.	1 Coy. G.M.C. 200 All Ranks Digging 11 a.m. Night Work.	1 Coy. G.M.C. Route March.	1 Coy. G.M.C. 200 All Ranks Digging 8 p.m.	1 Coy. G.M.C.	1 Coy. G.M.C.	1 Coy. G.M.C.	
Brigade.		Lecture on Sniping 10 a.m. C.Recreation Room No.10 Camp. One selected Officer per Co. to attend.		Lecture by G.O.C. Division at 5 p.m.			

MUSKETRY: A similar party to that now firing will be detailed from each Battalion to commence probably on Wednesday. This party will include all Machine Gunners and Instructors at Staff Divl. Bombing School.

BOMBING: Bombing will be suspended.

WIRE ENTANGLEMENTS: Each Bn. will detail 2 Officers & 10 N.C.Os. to report to R.E.Officer at 9.30 a.m. daily at Digging Ground. A different party should if possible be detailed each day. These Officers & N.C.Os. will instruct the remainder of the Battn. in construction of Wire Entanglements during the following week.

W. N. HERBERT.
Major,
BRIGADE MAJOR,
179th Infantry Brigade.

SUBJECT : Syllabus of Training.

G/404/42.

General Officer Commanding,
    180th Infantry Brigade.
    181st Infantry Brigade.
Officer Commanding,
    179th Infantry Brigade.

(1) During the 12th and 13th weeks commencing Monday, 17th April, the following training will be carried out.

(2) Musketry will be continued. All Machine Gunners and the Instructional Staff of the Divisional Bombing School will fire with the next party to commence.

(3) Bombing will be suspended until further orders, except that those men who have already done a course, will carry out ½ hours bombing practice on three days a week under Brigade arrangements.

(4) Route marching will be carried out on similar lines and routes as last week.

(5) Digging. This will be carried out on the lines laid down in this office G/464/5 of 30th March, 1916.
Battalions will carry out this form of training once a week by day for one hour, and once a week by night for a similar period of time commencing at 8 p.m.
The essence of the digging by day is that it should be done as rapidly as possible. By night the greatest attention should be paid to the absence of noise and confusion. During the first week two companies per battalion at the most should dig by night at the same time. During the second week the whole battalion should dig at the same time. The C.R.E., in laying out the tasks, should have intervals between men of 6 ft. to commence with, reducing them to 5 ft. when he considers the men sufficiently proficient not to cause accidents.

(6) Brigade Commanders will arrange with the C.R.E. to give instruction to men of their Brigades in Wire Entanglements. This should be practised by night as well so soon as the men have shewn sufficient aptitude in their construction by day.

(7) There will be a Tactical Exercise under Divisional Scheme for the 180th Brigade on Wednesday, 19th April.

(8) The G.O.C. will give a lecture to Officers at 5 p.m. on 20th April. Subject : Trench Warfare. Further details will be issued.

(9) The remainder of the training, e.g., Drill, Running, Physical Training, etc., is to be carried out on the same general lines as before.

(10) The 181st Brigade will detail the next party for a course of Instruction in the Stokes Gun at Perham Down. The date this Course commences will be notified later.

Sutton Veny,

13th April, 1916.

for Lieut. Colonel,
General Staff,
60th (London) Division.

"A" Form.   Army Form C. 2121

MESSAGES AND SIGNALS.   No. of Message _____

Prefix ___ Code ___ m.	Words	Charge	This message is on a/c of:	Recd. at ___ m.
Office of Origin and Service Instructions.	Sent			Date
	At ___ m.		_____ Service.	From
	To			
	By		(Signature of "Franking Officer.")	By

TO { O.C., 2/13th Battalion, L.R.   7.45
     2/14th Battalion, L.R.

Sender's Number	Day of Month	In reply to Number	
B.M.1.	17th.		AAA

Practice Alarm in accordance with Divisional Order 180 dated 9th March for 5th week AAA

When both battalions are ready to move off they will march off under Lt.Col.E.Dunsmore, 2/13th Leading AAA Route as follows. Point 455, Cross Roads LONGBRIDGE DEVERILL, Road Junction N. of G in CROCKERTON GREEN, Track S. of G in GREENHILL to camps AAA

The whole of 1st line transport will accompany units AAA

MAJOR.
BRIGADE MAJOR.
179th Infantry Brigade.

From   179th Infantry Brigade.
Place
Time   7.30 p.m.

Appendix
Nº 4

2/13th Battalion London Regiment.

PROGRAMME OF TRAINING FOR WEEK COMMENCING MONDAY 24th APRIL. 1916.

COY.	MONDAY.	TUESDAY.	WEDNESDAY.	THURSDAY.	FRIDAY.	SATURDAY.	REMARKS.
"A" "B" "C" "D"	Casuals.- G.M.C. Phys. Tng.& B.Ftg. Musketry Instr. Extended order drill. Attached men under R.S.M. Night work. 7.30.p.m.	Casuals.G.M.C. Phys. Trng.& Bay. Fighting Musketry Instr Extended order drill. Bn. Close order drill.	Casuals.G.M.C. Phys. Trng & Bay. Ftg. Musketry Inst. Extended order drill. Attached men under R.S.M. 200 All Ranks digging. 11.am	Casuals G.M.C. Phys. Trng & Bay. Fighting. Musketry Inst. Close order drill. Attached men under R.S.M. Bn. Digging. 8.p.m.	Casuals.G.M.C. Route March. Conference of Commanding Officers.	Casuals.G.M.C. Kit Inspect. Phys. Trng & Bay. Ftg.	

Sutton Veny.
24.4.1916.

H Davids?

Captain & Adjutant.
2/13th Battalion London Regiment.

179th Infantry Brigade.

PROGRAMME OF TRAINING FOR WEEK ENDING, SATURDAY, 29TH APRIL, 1916.

UNIT.	MONDAY.	TUESDAY.	WEDNESDAY.	THURSDAY.	FRIDAY.	SATURDAY.	REMARKS.
2/13th Bn. L.R.	1 Company G.M.C. Night Work.	1 Company G.M.C.	1 Company G.M.C. 200 All Ranks Digging 11 a.m.	1 Company G.M.C. Battalion Digging 8.0 p.m.	1 Company G.M.C. Route March.	1 Company G.M.C.	WIRE ENTANGLEMENTS Arrangements for this instruction are the same as for week ending April 22nd 1916.
2/14th Bn. L.R.	1 Company G.M.C. Move to No. 15 Camp.	1 Company G.M.C. Move to No. 15 Camp. Night Work.	1 Company G.M.C. 200 All Ranks Digging 11 a.m.	1 Company G.M.C. Battalion Digging 8.0 p.m.	1 Company G.M.C. Route March.	1 Company G.M.C.	KIT INSPECTION, ETC.
2/15th Bn. L.R.	1 Company G.M.C. 200 All Ranks Digging 11 a.m.	1 Company G.M.C. Battalion Digging 8.0 p.m.	1 Company G.M.C. Route March.	1 Company G.M.C. Night Work.	1 Company G.M.C.	1 Company G.M.C.	
2/16th Bn. L.R.	1 Company G.M.C. 200 All Ranks Digging 11 a.m.	1 Company G.M.C. Battalion Digging 8.0 p.m.	1 Company G.M.C. Route March.	1 Company G.M.C. Night Work.	1 Company G.M.C.	1 Company G.M.C.	
BRIGADE					Conference of Commanding Officers.		

W.N.HERBERT.
MAJOR,
BRIGADE MAJOR,
179th Infantry Brigade.

2/13th. Battalion London Regiment.

LEWIS GUNS.

An oral examination on the Lewis Gun will be held at Brigade Headquarters on 10th. May 1916.

~~2~~-Lieut. A. Baker will lecture to all Subalterns on the following dates, in a empty hut.

Monday	at	3 p.m.
Tuesday	at	5 p.m.
Wednesday	at	5 p.m.
Thursday	at	3 p.m.
Friday	at	5 p.m.

All Subalterns must have a practical knowledge of this weapon and will receive instruction from the above-mentioned Officer on the following subjects:-

    Filling Magazines.
    Loading & Unloading.
    How to put on and take off return Spring tension.
    How to apply and remove safety catch.
    Stripping and assembling.
    Nomenclature of parts.
    Points before, during and after Firing.
    Stoppages and Immediate Action.
    Fair knowledge of action of Mechanism.

All Officers attending the lectures will sign A.B. 153 at the commencement of the lecture which book will be left at Regimental Headquarters at the end of each lecture.

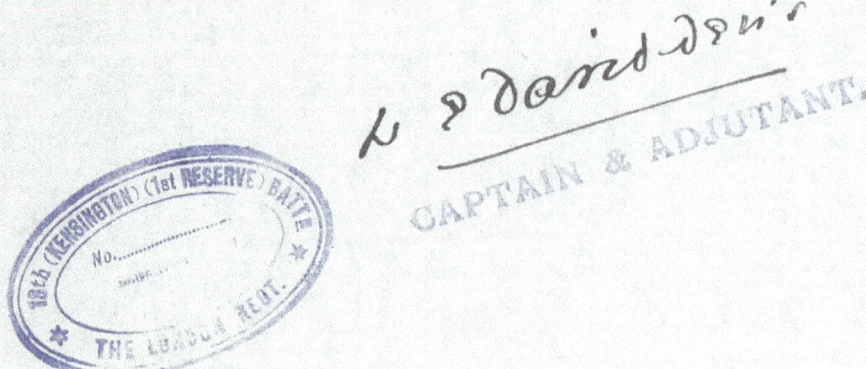

CAPTAIN & ADJUTANT.

179th Infantry Brigade.   No.102.

O R D E R S
by
COLONEL E. W. BAIRD, COMMANDING.

April 29th 1916.
LEYLAND.

1. **BOUNDS.**   No N.C.O. or man is allowed out of Bivouac Area after 7 p.m.

2. **WATER.**   All Water Carts will be filled when necessary at the Stand Pipe in the Supply Depot by the Railway Station. All Well Water in this neighbourhood is reported to be contaminated.

3. **MARCHING IN STATES** will be rendered to this Office by 7 p.m. today. Upon Embarkation States will be rendered in triplicate. In these States will be shown Nos. of Officers, ~~Vehicles~~ Other Ranks, Horses, Vehicles 4 wheeled, vehicles 2 wheeled and Bicycles.

4. **GUARD.**   The Battalion on duty will furnish a Brigade Headquarter Guard of 1 N.C.O. and 3 men upon arrival in Camp or billets. If stationary Guard will mount daily at 5 p.m. (Standing Order).

5. **ORDERLIES.**   Daily upon arrival in Camp or billets four Cyclist Orderlies from each Battalion and two Orderlies from A.S.C. will report to Brigade Headquarters. Two Battalion Cyclist Orderlies from each Battalion and ~~A.S.C. Orderlies~~ One A.S.C. Orderly will remain at Brigade Headquarters as permanent Orderlies. The remaining Orderlies will return to Units after reporting.

                       W. N. HERBERT.
                           Major,
                      BRIGADE MAJOR,
              179th Infantry Brigade.

Issued at 5.0 pm

O.C.,
2/13th Battalion L.R.
2/14th Battalion L.R.
2/15th Battalion L.R.
2/16th Battalion L.R.

    Leave may be given to men to leave Camp but Roll Calls must be held at stated intervals to ensure men not being too far away. Suggested hours for these Roll Calls:-
        1, 4, & 7 p.m.

Longbridge Deverill.
April 30th 1916.

                                Major,
                              BRIGADE MAJOR,
                            179th Infantry Brigade.

"A" Form.　　　　　　　　　Army Form C. 2121.
MESSAGES AND SIGNALS.

| Prefix | Code | m. | Words | Charge | This message is on a/c of: | Recd. at | m. |

Office of Origin and Service Instructions.

Sent At ... m.　　　　　　　　Date
　　　　　　　　　　　Service.　From
To
By　　　(Signature of "Franking Officer")　By

TO { O.C. 2/13 & 2/15

| Sender's Number | Day of Month | In rep'y to Number | AAA |
| BM. 11 | 31 | | |

No move troops are embarking to-night AAA my BM 9 to 2/13th and BM. 10 to 2/15th are cancelled

From 179th I.B.
Place
Time 6.10 p.m.　　　　W. J. Hutni Major

The above may be forwarded as now corrected.　(Z)

"A" Form.
Army Form C. 2121
MESSAGES AND SIGNALS.
No. of Message

TO	O.C., 2/13th Battalion. 2/14th Battalion. 2/15th Battalion.

Sender's Number	Day of Month	In rep'y to Number	
S.C.1.	28th.		A A A

Message received from Division.AAA. Remaining three Battalions of your Brigade will proceed to Ireland tomorrow.AAA. Entraining Station Warminster.AAA. Brigade Headquarters and 2/13th Bn.will travel by first trains.AAA. 2/15th Bn. will travel by second trains. 2/14th Bn.will travel by third trains. Times will be notified later.AAA. Battalions will move off two hours before departure of train.AAA. Transport will travel by the first train.AAA.
Following arrangements for rations will be observed No fresh meat is to be taken. One days preserved meat will be delivered to your Camp. This together with bread and groceries now in hand will be carried in Field Kitchens.AAA. One days iron ration will be delivered to your Camp in your baggage wagons. This will be issued by you immediately upon receipt.AAA. The remaining supplies, i.e. one days preserved ration will be loaded on Supply wagons which will meet you at Entraining Station.AAA. Wagons to carry xxx one Blanket per man are being sent to you.AAA.

From: STAFF CAPTAIN.
Place:
Time: 8.55 P.M.

MESSAGES AND SIGNALS. Army Form C. 2121

TO: O.C., 2/13th Battalion.
    2/14th Battalion.
    2/15th Battalion.

Sender's Number: SC.2. Day of Month: 28th. AAA

A.D.M.S. is now coming to your Camp to inspect all Isolated men and he will say who can go and who are to remain. AAA. Inform Brigade Headquarters as soon as possible number of Officers and men who are going with your Battalion. AAA.

Captain E.G. Monro, 2/14th Battalion, is appointed Brigade O.i/c Details.

Pay Books & acquittance Rolls will be issued.

From: STAFF CAPTAIN.
Time: 8.20 P.M.

STAFF CAPTAIN,
79th INF. BDE.

"A" Form.
Army Form C. 2121

MESSAGES AND SIGNALS.

TO	O.C.,	2/13th Battalion.
		2/14th Battalion.
		2/15th Battalion.

Sender's Number	Day of Month	In rep'y to Number	
SC.3.	28th.		AAA

The following reinforcements are ~~returned~~ Coming to you from the 181st Brigade.

2/13th Bn. Two spare horses and Two travelling Kitchens.

2/14th Bn. Two Travelling Kitchens.

2/15th Bn. Two Travelling Kitchens.

Brigade Headquarters: Three Mules.

From STAFF CAPTAIN.

Time 8-25 P.M.

STAFF CAPTAIN.
179th INF. BDE.

"A" Form.　　　　　　　　　　　　　　Army Form C. 2121
MESSAGES AND SIGNALS.　　No. of Message _____

| Prefix _____ Code _____ m. | Words | Charge | This message is on a/c of: | Rec'd. at _____ m. |
| Office of Origin and Service Instructions. | Sent At _____ m. To _____ By _____ | | _____ Service. (Signature of "Franking Officer.") | Date _____ From _____ By _____ |

TO { **O.C., 2/13th Bn.**

| Sender's Number | Day of Month | In rep'y to Number | AAA |
| **SC.4.** | | | |

Send seventeen Rifles and 550 Rounds of Mark VII Ammunition to Brigade Headquarters at once.

From **STAFF CAPTAIN.**
Place
Time **8.25 P.M.**

"A" Form. Army Form C. 2121.
MESSAGES AND SIGNALS. No. of Message _____

Prefix _____ Code _____ m.	Words	Charge	This message is on a/c of:	Recd. at _____ m.
Office of Origin and Service Instructions.				Date _____
	Sent		_____ Service.	From _____
	At _____ to _____			
	To _____			By _____
	By _____		(Signature of "Franking Officer.")	

TO { 2/13, 2/14, 2/15, 2/16th Bne Cdr Signalling Officer, Supply Officer

Sender's Number	Day of Month	In reply to Number	AAA
S.61			

The	Emergency	alarm	is	given
AAA	Carry	out	instructions	issued
_____	AAA	Acknowledge		

From 179th Inf Bde.
Place
Time 7.20 P.M.

Signature: [illegible]

STAFF CAPTAIN
179th INF. BDE.

"A" Form. Army Form C. 2121
MESSAGES AND SIGNALS. No. of Message _____

TO	O.C., 2/13th Battalion.
	2/14th Battalion.
	2/15th Battalion.

Sender's Number	Day of Month	In rep'y to Number	
S.C.6.	28th.		A A A

The following Chaplains of this Brigade will travel with their Units:-
    Captain Harding.
    Captain Reilly.
    Captain Anderson.
    Captain McPherson.

Ration Bags, Field Dressings, and Bicycles will be issued from these Headquarters to Captains Harding, Anderson, and McPherson upon application. AAA. ~~Please~~

From: STAFF CAPTAIN.
Place:
Time: 9.10.P.M.

STAFF CAPTAIN
INF. BDE.

"A" Form. Army Form C. 2121

MESSAGES AND SIGNALS

Prefix	Code	m.	Words	Charge	This message is on a/c of:	Rec'd. at	m.
Office of Origin and Service Instructions.			Sent At	m.	*No. Service.	Date 28 APR 1916	
			To By		(Signature of "Franking Officer.")	From By	

TO { O.C., 2/13th Battalion.

Sender's Number	Day of Month	In reply to Number	
S.C.10.	28th.	5	A A A

You will be receiving no more travelling kitchens.

From: STAFF CAPTAIN, 179th Infantry Brigade.
Place: LONGBRIDGE DEVERILL.
Time: 12.5 A.M

"A" Form.
MESSAGES AND SIGNALS.

TO: 2/13ᵈ Bn. L. R.

Sender's Number: SG 11
Day of Month: 30th

Send your transport Section less Travelling Kitchens and baggage wagons to Embarkation Pontoon immediately aaa. Report arrival and await orders aaa. you will detail necessary fatigue party. aaa

From: 179th Inf. Bde.
Time: 11.41 a.m.

"A" Form. Army Form C. 2121
MESSAGES AND SIGNALS. No. of Message _____

Prefix ___ Code ___ m.	Words	Charge	This message is on a/c of:	Recd. at ___ m.
Office of Origin and Service Instructions.				Date ___
	Sent		___ Service.	From ___
	At ___ m.			
	To ___			
	By ___		(Signature of "Franking Officer.")	By ___

TO { 2/15th Bn

| Sender's Number | Day of Month | In rep'y to Number | A A A |
| S.C. 13 | 30 | | |

Instead of numbers ordered of
Brigade Major to travel by
H.T. Lowndon substitute the following
Officers 12 other ranks 330
including Transport personnel

From 174 Inf Bde
Place
Time 1.5 P.M

The above may be forwarded as now corrected. (Z) [signature]
Censor. S.C.
Signature of Addressor or person authorised to telegraph in his name
* This line should be erased if not required.

Appendix

Nº 5.

WAR DIARY

APPENDIX

CONFIDENIAL

FROM 1ST MAY — TO 31ST MAY

LONGBRIDGE DEVERILL
No 12 CAMP

2/13TH BN
LONDON REGT

CONFIDENTIAL

WAR DIARY

From 1.5.16 To 31.5.16.

2/13th BATTALION LONDON REGIMENT.

WAR DIARY
or
INTELLIGENCE SUMMARY.

(Erase heading not required.) of Battalion on TREK in Ireland

Army Form C. 2118.

Instructions regarding War Diaries and Intelligence Summaries are contained in F. S. Regs., Part II. and the Staff Manual respectively. Title pages will be prepared in manuscript.

Hour, Date, Place	Summary of Events and Information	Remarks and references to Appendices
1.5.16. S.S. Snowdon	reveillé southern	12:00
	breakfast. Rifle inspection. issue field belts, men fall off t boats & raft	WED3
	S.S. Snowdon sailed f Queenstown 9.2	
2.5.16 Queenstown	S.S. Snowdon arrived.	WED3
	orders for disembarking received appendix 1	WED3 another Bn orders dated 2.5.16
	authorized disembarked	
	A + B Co with HQ disembarked	
Fota Park Camp	The whole Bt proceeded y moved front will commander of 15 Bn L.R. t Fota Park Camp.	WED3
	arrived at Fota Park Camp	
	southern. Tent pitched etc.	
3.5.16	reveillé	12:00
	southern 6-7 a estendes rifle drill y Platoon.	
	9-10 } training under Co arrangements 11-12 } 2-4 p	

(1)

(73989) W4141—463. 400,000. 9/14. H.&J.Ltd. Forms/C. 2118/10.

Army Form C. 2118.

WAR DIARY
or
INTELLIGENCE SUMMARY.
(Erase heading not required.)

Instructions regarding War Diaries and Intelligence Summaries are contained in F.S. Regs., Part II. and the Staff Manual respectively. Title pages will be prepared in manuscript.

Hour, Date, Place	Summary of Events and Information	Remarks and references to Appendices
4.5.16 TOTAPARRAM	Reveille	
	Antim. 6-7a Chinnaide d'uu Pettos	
	9-10 } Trainon und & overnments	Appx-D
	11-12	
	3-4	Appx-D
5.5.16	Reveille 6-7a Funeral fatigue	Appx-D
6am	a.m.	
6.5.16	Reveille. Coy.Ft. parade	Appx-D
	Capt. Powell & Major leave	Appx-D
30	B Coy leaves A.C. action. One Pack mule M.G. limber	Appx-D
20	Remainder B 1 N.C.O. & 13 men arriving at Camp pollent 2p.m. B Coy.	Appx-D
6.	B Coy moves out to BALLINROLLIG	Appx-D
6.	Orderly Room l Cpl C.O.R.L.	Appx-D
30	Draft at BALLINCOLLIG receive marks & activity record meditation.	Appx-D

Army Form C. 2118.

WAR DIARY
or
INTELLIGENCE SUMMARY.

(Erase heading not required.) 1ˢᵗ Battⁿ on TREK in IRELAND 2/13ᵗʰ B2 L R

Instructions regarding War Diaries and Intelligence Summaries are contained in F.S. Regs., Part II. and the Staff Manual respectively. Title pages will be prepared in manuscript.

Hour, Date, Place	Summary of Events and Information	Remarks and references to Appendices
7.5.16. BALLINCOLLIG BARRACKS	Reveille / Ins'bection	A→D
8.30	Battalion paraded & next march via Bdn E COACHFORD	B→D Bn Order
P.M.		
12.55 COACHFORD	arrival at COACHFORD	H→D
		H→D
2.55	in dew Field took	M→O
3.50	camp pitches in breadth	
4.20		L→D
8.5.16.	Reveille	
4.45	Bⁿ paraded & mead ready E MACROOM via CARRIGADROHID	H→D Bde Order 105 Bn 7.1.16.
P.M.		
1- MACROOM	Bn arrives at MACROOM CASTLE	K→D
1.35	order t field kits	L→D
2.50	Camp pitches	M→D

(3)

Army Form C. 2118.

2/13th Bn. L.R.

WAR DIARY
or
INTELLIGENCE SUMMARY.
(Erase heading not required.) { Batt⁰ & Tr⁵ R in IRELAND }

Instructions regarding War Diaries and Intelligence Summaries are contained in F.S. Regs., Part II. and the Staff Manual respectively. Title pages will be prepared in manuscript.

Hour, Date, Place	Summary of Events and Information	Remarks and references to Appendices
P.M. 1.— 8.5.16. MACROOM	Detachment under Major P. Morris Capt. Collier Lt. Thompson and 107 O.R. moves at 11 P.M. to rendezvous the R.I.C.	MCD
on 9.5.16. — 7.30	Detachment under Capt. Brockhurst–Foster v Rosevear proceeds at 12.30 a.m. to the purpose of making search in conjunction with the R.I.C.	MCD
30	Recall	MCD
30	Capt. Brockhurst column returns. 1 cask on arrest with meat.	MCD
20	H/M. P. Morris v column returns. 1 cask. No arrest. No arms.	

(4)

(73989) W4141–463. 400,000. 9/14. H.&J.Ltd. Forms/C. 2118/10.

WAR DIARY
or
INTELLIGENCE SUMMARY.

(Erase heading not required.) B⁰ @ TREK in IRELAND.

Army Form C. 2118.

2/13ᵗʰ Bⁿ L.R.

Hour, Date, Place	Summary of Events and Information	Remarks and references to Appendices
9.S.M. MACROOM	COLUMN under MAJ. R. THOMPSON - CAPT. GLADSTONE SLADE & LIEUT. KRASSEL 2ᵈ LIVINGSTON PATEL LANCASTER and 2ᵉ SELLS moved A.S.C. and 2/F. O.R. 16 Horses 2 P.S. WAGONS 1 MG Horse 1 H.Q. CART 1 F.O.O. Radio horses to HILLSTREET & naval route of transfer & making arrests in CORNOCK view to R.I.C.	
HILLSTREET	MAJOR THOMPSON'S Column arrived at HILLSTREET at 4.M. (carry forward)	
	(Returned under LT RANGEN 20 O.R. proceed to BALLY DALY & Caherbarnagh & arresting 2 men suspected an R.I.C. count were made 1 detachment under SM GATES and 20 O.R. proceed CAR to Cahirbernan & arrest, 1 man suspected in R.I.C. & arrests La mox	

5

Army Form C. 2118.

2/13ᵗʰ Bⁿ L.R.

WAR DIARY
or
INTELLIGENCE SUMMARY.

(Erase heading not required.) { Bⁿ in TRER in IRELAND. }

Instructions regarding War Diaries and Intelligence Summaries are contained in F. S. Regs., Part II. and the Staff Manual respectively. Title pages will be prepared in manuscript.

Hour, Date, Place	Summary of Events and Information	Remarks and references to Appendices
10.57K. HACROOM	Reveille	WEB
	Inspection C.O. A + B Cₒ	WEB
11.5/K	Rev Cille	WEB
3.	Ott Laffan leader	WEB
45.	BS len. 1 Platoon under Lt Thompson (?) posted to hospital prisoners & guard	WEB
	MILLSTREET via ARDNATRUSHY and CARRIGANIMMY	
2.35 (2.pm)	Halt during road with CARRIGANIMY	WEB
50 MILLSTREET	Arrived (levels breach)	
	Halt & hold parade for reading Orders	
–.15 p	Major R. Thompson's command for Bᵗ ~ piquet	WEBD
15 +	Asens & Cap Willes at Public Library	
	Rest of Cʰ Cap Willes in Col O'LEARY's empty mansion.	

(6)

(73989) W4141—463. 400,000. 9/14. H.&J.Ltd. Forms/C. 2118/10.

Army Form C. 2118.

2/13" Bn. L.R.

WAR DIARY
or
INTELLIGENCE SUMMARY.

(Erase heading not required.) of Bn. on TRER in IRELAND

Instructions regarding War Diaries and Intelligence Summaries are contained in F.S. Regs., Part II and the Staff Manual respectively. Title pages will be prepared in manuscript.

Hour, Date, Place	Summary of Events and Information	Remarks and references to Appendices
P.M. 5.10. HILLSTREET	Appearance of 10th placed under Canvas in field	A.S.P.B.
12.5.16	nivell	A.S.P.B.
4.45	Bn. paraded & billets & order	A.S.P.B.
1.30	I" Party under Br. Hvas consisted of 15. No officers and 475 P.? (including S. and z/18-20) were somewhere	A.S.P.B.
10.3.	Hen. will also look after of HILLSTREET & billeting	A.S.P.B.
P.M. 4.10. ROSSLARE	arrival at ROSSLARE HARBOUR	A.S.P.B.
10.30 HILLSTREET	II" Party with transport 6 officers & 120 O.R. were entraining	A.S.P.B.
P.M. 3.0	and left for ROSSLARE HARBOUR & HILLSTREET HARBOUR	W.S.P.B.
	II Party arrive at ROSSLARE HARBOUR	

(7)

Army Form C. 2118.

7/13 Bn L.R.

WAR DIARY
or
INTELLIGENCE SUMMARY.
(Erase heading not required.) of B⁲ @ TREK in IRELAND

Instructions regarding War Diaries and Intelligence Summaries are contained in F.S. Regs., Part II. and the Staff Manual respectively. Title pages will be prepared in manuscript.

Hour, Date, Place	Summary of Events and Information	Remarks and references to Appendices
12.5.16 ROSSLARE HARBOUR	B⁲ reste of through the train	WD A
13.5.16	Reveille	
	Transport and 2 officers and 46 O.R. entrained on S.S. SIPTAH and	WD A
	Sailed for FISHGUARD at 7 P.M.	
	B⁲ min B⁲ Head quarters even entrained on S.S. CONNAUGHT	WD B
	S.S. CONNAUGHT Sailed for FISHGUARD	
SS CONNAUGHT	all wl. bells Sound out + alarm post allotted Companies	WD D
FISHGUARD	S.S. CONNAUGHT arrives at FISHGUARD	WD A
	entrains & 11.45 P.M. for WARMINSTER less S⁵ SHUTE	WD B
	and 42 O.R.	

(8)

Army Form C. 2118.

2/13ᵗʰ Bⁿ L.R

WAR DIARY
or
INTELLIGENCE SUMMARY.

(Erase heading not required.) of Bⁿ on TREK to IRELAND

Instructions regarding War Diaries and Intelligence Summaries are contained in F. S. Regs., Part II. and the Staff Manual respectively. Title pages will be prepared in manuscript.

Hour, Date, Place	Summary of Events and Information	Remarks and references to Appendices
18.5.16 FISHGUARD	S.S. SIBIAH arriving at FISHGUARD	ALB-D
19.5.16 WARMINSTER	Bⁿ less transport and 30 officers and 68 OR arrive at WARMINSTER	ALB-D
	87 &2700R	
	detained	
	LONGBRIDGEDEVERALL Bⁿ arrived at Camp	ALB-D
No.11 Camp		
P.M. WARMINSTER	30 officers and 68 OR and transport arrive at WARMINSTER STATION	ALB-D
P.M. LONGBRIDGE DEVERILL No.11 Camp	hill transport arrive at Camp	ALB-D

(9)

2/13th L.R.
Army Form C. 2118.

WAR DIARY
or
INTELLIGENCE SUMMARY.
(Erase heading not required.) of Battalion on TREK in IRELAND

Instructions regarding War Diaries and Intelligence Summaries are contained in F. S. Regs., Part II and the Staff Manual respectively. Title pages will be prepared in manuscript.

Hour, Date, Place	Summary of Events and Information	Remarks and references to Appendices
15.V.16 No 12 Camp		
LONGBRIDGE DEVERILL	Reveille	W.O=D
	General fatigue	
16.V.16	Reveille	
	Routine as per appendix 2	W.O=D
	Pte JAY (attached M.T.) transferred to R.F.C	W.O. acct. W.O.L 543/74949 9dm/440 (MAIL)31.V.16
1.V.16	Reveille	W.O=D
	General fatigues	W.O=D
	Capt. F.W. ROSSELL (attached from Munster Fusiliers) ceases to attached	W.O=D
	Having joined R.L Balloon Training Sc for R.F.C.	W.O=D
2.V.16	Reveille	
	Brex.	W.O=D
30	S.N.Cos. attend a bombing course at M.S Camp. SUTTON VENY ⑩	W.O=D

WAR DIARY
of
REAR PARTY

Army Form C. 2118.

WAR DIARY
of REAR PARTY
INTELLIGENCE SUMMARY.
(Erase heading not required.)

2/13 Bn L R

Instructions regarding War Diaries and Intelligence Summaries are contained in F.S. Regs., Part II. and the Staff Manual respectively. Title pages will be prepared in manuscript.

Hour, Date, Place	Summary of Events and Information	Remarks and references to Appendices
N° 6 Camp SUTTON VENY		
3.v.16	Reveille	AT.D.D
	General fatigues	AT.D.D
	1 Sergeant and 4 men attached from 1st/5th S. Lanc't OTC	AT.D.D Authy. 60 (Home) Div. L A/1349/35 11.iv.16
4.v.16	Reveille	AT.D.D
	General fatigues	AT.D.D
5.v.16	Reveille	AT.D.D
	Parade	AT.D.D
6.v.16	Reveille	AT.D.D
	General fatigue	AT.D.D
	Inspection of cert. B O/'s & detach. 179 H/Bde. L'Col. de Putron	AT.D.D

(11)

WAR DIARY
or
INTELLIGENCE SUMMARY.
(Erase heading not required.)

Army Form C. 2118.

Instructions regarding War Diaries and Intelligence Summaries are contained in F.S. Regs., Part II. and the Staff Manual respectively. Title pages will be prepared in manuscript.

Hour, Date, Place	Summary of Events and Information	Remarks and references to Appendices
7.V.16 N°8 Camp SUTTON VENY	Reveille	
	Church Parade	
8.V.16	Reveille	
	General fatigues	
	G.H.C. "303"	
9.V.16	Reveille	
	General fatigues	
	S.H.C. "303"	
	4525 Pte MATTHEWS E.R. having been declared deserter from 15.IV.16	
	& having & saying kit at N°8 Camp SUTTON VENY on the 9.V.16	
	is struck off strength with effect from 15.IV.16	
	3 men attend Order/for a clean —	

(12)

Army Form C. 2118.

WAR DIARY
or
INTELLIGENCE SUMMARY.
(Erase heading not required.)

REAR PARTY

7/13th Bn LR

Hour, Date, Place	Summary of Events and Information	Remarks and references to Appendices
10.V.16 No 16 Camp SUTTON VENY	Reveille	WD 2
	General fatigue	WD 2
	P.H.C. 302	WD 2
11.V.16	Reveille	WD 2
	General fatigue	WD 2
	P.H.C. 303	WD 2
12.V.16	Reveille	WD 2
	General fatigue	WD 2
	P.H.C. 303	WD 2
	orders received to move to M.12 Camp LONGBRIDGE DEVERILL	WD 2

(13)

Army Form C. 2118.

WAR DIARY of REAR PARTY
INTELLIGENCE SUMMARY.

(Erase heading not required.)

2/13th Bn London Regiment

Instructions regarding War Diaries and Intelligence Summaries are contained in F.S. Regs., Part II and the Staff Manual respectively. Title pages will be prepared in manuscript.

Hour, Date, Place	Summary of Events and Information	Remarks and references to Appendices
13.v.16 No.2 Camp LONGBRIDGE DEVERILL	Reveille	WDB⊃
6.30	General fatigues & course	WDB⊃
P.M.	camp completed 4.10.P.M.	WDB⊃
	No 2 Camp SUTTON VENY vacated 4 4.P.M.	
14.v.16	Reveille	WDB⊃
	B.C. marched into camp from H. Return from RELAND	WDB⊃
	{ WAR DIARY of the whole of the Bn (B.C. continued) }	
15.v.16	Reveille	WDB⊃
	General fatigues	WDB⊃
16.v.16	Reveille	WDB⊃
	Routine as per appendix 2	WDB⊃
	Medical by M.O. of all available officers & other ranks	WDB⊃

(14)

Army Form C. 2118.

WAR DIARY
or
INTELLIGENCE SUMMARY.
(Erase heading not required.)

2/13ᵗʰ BATTALION L.R.

Hour, Date, Place	Summary of Events and Information	Remarks and references to Appendices
16.v.16 Nr. 12 Coy.	L/Corpl DUNFORD (attached for 11.B⁰ LR) and Pte Law (11 B⁰ LR) transferred	AM⁵⁰ auth. 60 (Low) Div. L.A/
LONGRIDGE SEVERAL	to 7/14 B⁰ LR	AM⁵⁰ 2349/35 C.
	R/m. MILLICHAMP (attached from 11 B⁰ L.R.) transferred to the B⁰.	WD⁵⁰
17.v.16	continue as per appendix 2	WD⁵⁰
	Sgt. SHAVE and 4 N.C.O. and 2 O.O.R. are tested to the Scales on Snipers	AM⁵⁰ auth = T.F. Rec. L. 17/13/9
	L/Bdwn CASSAN transferred to 107ᵗʰ Prov. B⁰ medically unfit for g. service	WD⁵⁰
	Pte MATTHEWS having been declared a deserter is apprehended and taken on the Strength	AM⁵⁰ auth. 6.0 (Low) Div. L. A/203042 13.v.16
	CADET LLOYD is transferred from 8 PADET B⁰.	AM⁵⁰ W⁷⁻¹ AD⁵⁰
18.v.16	continue as per appendix 2	
	Stretcher Bearers attend a Course of Instruction with 7/4 Field Ambulance	
	Sniping Section is formed	

(15)

WAR DIARY
INTELLIGENCE SUMMARY. 2/13" Bn LONDON REGIMENT

Army Form C. 2118.

(Erase heading not required.)

Hour, Date, Place	Summary of Events and Information	Remarks and references to Appendices
19.v.16 No 12 LONGBRIDGE DEVERELL		
6—	Routine as per appendix 2	W2B=D
7.30.	Bn Trench Scheme relieved by 2/14 Bn L.R. at 1.30.P.M. The Exercise took place in the Divisional Trenches at SUTTON VENY	W2B=D
20.v.16		
6—	Reveille	
	Routine as per appendix 2	W2B=D
	2nd Lt PHILLIPS appointed Assistant Adjutant for Musketry W2B=A auth. C.O.	
21.v.16		
6—	Reveille	W2B=D
0.30.	Church Parade	A2B=D
22.v.16		
—	Reveille	W2B=D
.30	Casuals R.M.C.	W2B=D
	Routine as per appendix 3	W2B=D
23.v.16		
—	Reveille	
	Routine as per appendix 2	W2B=D

(16)

Army Form C. 2118.

WAR DIARY
or
INTELLIGENCE SUMMARY.
(Erase heading not required.)

2/13ᵘ BATTALION L.R.

Hour, Date, Place	Summary of Events and Information	Remarks and references to Appendices
23.V.16 No.12 Coort. LINBRIDGE SEVERNE	4/Corporal Jones attached to 60(Lon) Div H.Q.	W22-2
24.V.16	Pencil. Routine as per appendix No 3. Corporal Butler - 2ⁿᵈ Hansv Headquarters (t 10) "Pov B" 1ˢᵗ Parad. Trench scheme 4 night trench exercises at 4.am. to be 9.10am.	A22-2 A22-2 T+ Rec. 2 13/15 '84 22.V.16 A22-2
25.V.16	Pencil. Routine as per appendix No 3 Corpᶫ Hopkins declared a deserter 4 Coros of enquiry assembled at No 12 Comp Long Bridge Severne on 23.V.16.	W22-2 W22-6
26.V.16	Pencil. Routine as per appendix No 3	W22-2
27.V.16	Pencil. Routine as per appendix No 3.	W22-2
28.V.16	Pencil. Church Parade	W22-2

(17)

Army Form C. 2118.

WAR DIARY
or
INTELLIGENCE SUMMARY.
(Erase heading not required.)

2/13 BATTALION. L.R

Hour, Date, Place	Summary of Events and Information	Remarks and references to Appendices
No 12 Camp LONGBRIDGE DEVERILL		
29.V.16	awaits continue Bn for appendix 4	WDd
	MAJOR PATHOPRIND proceed to FRANCE for attachment to the British Army (to the field until june 2nd)	
30.V.16	awaits	WDd
	Divisional rehearsal for H.M. The KING	WDd
	Pt TANNER attached to Bd. HQ as labman	WDd
	Pt BRACKELHURST discharged to commission E 8th QUEENS R.N. FUSILIERS. (2m. B=LR)	WDd SC L 1110162 A4
	Pt PEXTON (HAC) discharged for recruitment into RFC	WDd and W.O 9145 (AG. SR) A
31.V.16	awaits.	WDd
	Royal Inspection of 60 (LONDON) Division by H.M. The KING	WDd
	10 men transferred to 107 Prov Bn until fit for G Service and attached to "B" for ratios and pay and duty.	WDd Gweek T.F. Rec. L 13/1661 27.V.16
		WDd

Longbridge Deverill
5th June 1916

Geo Houghram
Commanding 2/13 Bn Lond Regt

Appendix

No 1.

179th Infantry Brigade.

DISEMBARKING ORDER.

by

COLONEL A.S. BAIRD, COMMANDING.

May 2nd 1915.

1. DISEMBARKATION.   Troops to disembark in the following order:-
　　2/13th Battalion L.R.
　　2/15th Battalion L.R.
　　Life Belts will be handed in, Kits drawn, Rifles issued, before 7 o'clock, at which hour Troops will be formed up on their Alarm Posts.
　　When the Ship has been cleared, troops will march to Rest Camp about 4 miles distant.

2. FATIGUES.   Each Battalion will tell off a Fatigue Party of 1 Officer and 20 Other Ranks who having disembarked will stack their Kits and Rifles on the Quay and return to the Ship to clean up.

3. TIME.   It is notified that the Time goes back 25 minutes to Irish Time. Disembarkation will take place according to this Time altered Time.

　　　　　　　　　　　　W. H. HERBERT.
　　　　　　　　　　　　Major,
　　　　　　　　　　　　BRIGADE MAJOR,
Issued at 4.50 Irish Time.　　179th Infantry Brigade.

2/13th Batt L R

179th Infantry Brigade.   **No. 103.**

ORDERS BY

COLONEL E. W. BAIRD, COMMANDING.
....
                                                Fota.
                                          May 2nd. 1916.

1. **DUTIES.**   The Battalion on Duty will detail a Brigade Orderly Officer who will visit the following Guard once by day and once by Night:-
   1. The Guard on Driscoll's Gate.
   2. The Guard at Fota Station.
   3. The Guard found by the Connaught Rangers at Slatty Bridge.

   The Orders for these Guards will be issued shortly. The Orderly Officers visiting these Guards will be acquainted with the Orders.

2. **CARE OF ARMS.**   Every precaution is to be taken to ensure against theft of Arms and Ammunition. No Rifles will be left in the Tent without a Tent Orderly. By day Rifles should be piled outside the Tent with a Sentry on each line. When Troops are on the march or moving by rail every man should be made responsible for his own Rifle, and warned that any loss of Arms or Ammunition will be dealt with very severely.

3. **BOUNDS.**   No N.C.O. or man is allowed out of Camping Area. The private grounds and shrubberies in Park of FOTA HOUSE are at all times out of bounds. Until a proper issue of fuel is received from the A.S.C. any wood which may have to be collected locally for the purpose of cooking must be done by a large fatigue party under an Officer. Small parties of men are prohibited from wandering about gathering wood indiscriminately.

4. **POSTAL ARRANGEMENTS.**   These will be notified later.

5. **MEDICAL.**   The Medical Officer attached to the 2/15th Bn.L.R. is also responsible for the Medical arrangements of the following Units:-
   Headquarters, 179th Infantry Brigade.
   2/14th Battalion London Regiment.
   518th Co.H.T., A.S.C.
   O.C., 2/15th Battalion L.R. will notify the above Units of the hours of sick parade each day.

6. ~~REFILLING POINT~~ **CAMP ROUTINE.**
   Reveille 5 a.m.
   ~~Last Post   8.30 p.m.~~   Retreat 8 p.m.
   Lights Out 9 p.m.

- 2 -

7.	WATER.	All Animals to be watered at Brickfields. All Water for drinking and cooking to be taken from Standpipes.
8.	ORDNANCE SUPPLIES.	Ordnance Supplies may be drawn on Indent from Ordnance Officer, QUEENSTOWN.
9.	HOSPITAL.	There is a MILITARY HOSPITAL at Queenstown.
10.	RETURNS.	The following Returns to be sent in at ~~18xxxxx~~ ~~by telephone every~~ 8 a.m. daily:- (1) Fighting Strength (including A.S.C. & Signal Section). (2) Number of casualties during preceding 24 hours. (3) No. of Rounds of Ammunition expended during preceding 24 hours.

W. N. HERBERT.
Major,
BRIGADE MAJOR,
179th Infantry Brigade.

LOST. On Board H.T. "RATHMORE" Short Rifle No.88934. O.C., Units will report to this Office by 9 a.m. tomorrow, Wednesday, the 3rd May 1916, if this Rifle has been found. Nil Returns will be rendered.

Issued at 5.30 p.m.

2/13th Battalion London Regiment.

ORDERS FOR SLATTY BRIDGE GUARD.
Detachment 3rd Connaught Rangers.

1. Stop all Traffic proceeding over Bridge until the Sentry is satisfied that the vehicles contain no Arms, Ammunition or Explosives without proper authority.

2. To examine passes and see that they are duly signed by proper authority, i.e. Provost Marshal, Queenstown, O.C., Troops, Queenstown, or O.C. Troops, Fota.

3. To fire on any vessel that approaches the Bridge from the West Side.

4. One Sentry is to be posted by day on the N. side of bridge, in addition to one on the S. side between dusk and dawn.

5. To allow no one without a pass to enter the Lodge at the South end of the Bridge.

6. To turn out the Guard to the Orderly Officer when required and to all Armed Parties.

7. The Sentry is to pay proper compliments to all Officers.

8. In case of attack to send one man to inform O.C. Troops, Fota.

                                       W. N. HERBERT.
                                                Major,
                                   Brigade Major,
FOTA CAMP.   179th Infantry Brigade.
May 3rd 1916.

2/13th Battalion London Regiment.

Emergency Alarm.

Companies will hold in readiness one Platoon in charge of an officer, commencing with "A" Coy.
Kit, with rifles piled, will be placed outside the Guard Room.
No, N.C.O. or men of the Platoon on Duty will be allowed to leave the confines of the Camp.
On the bugle call of two G's. (not preceeded by the Regimental call) the Platoon will immediately fall in and await orders.

N J Davidson's

Captain & Adjutant,
2/13th Bn. London Regiment.

3.5.16

179th Infantry Brigade.

No. 104.

ORDERS
by
COLONEL S. W. BAIRD, COMMANDING.

FOTA Camp.
May 2nd 1916.

1. **DUTIES.** Whilst in Camp, Battalions will be on duty by the day instead of by the week. All duties will commence at 6 p.m.

2. **BUGLE CALLS.** No Bugle will be sounded in Camp except the alarm and the following routine Calls:-
    Reveille
    Retreat, and
    Lights Out.

3. **DISPOSAL OF MANURE.** Arrangements have been made for all manure from Horse Lines to be collected at 3. p.m. every day. All Manure will be stacked by Units in one place at the end of their respective Transport Lines at that hour.

4. **BATHING HOURS.** Owing to the limited accommodation for watering horses at the Brickfields, the following Roster will be adhered to:-
    Bde. H.Q.   7.30 a.m.   12 noon.   5.30 p.m.
    2/13th Bn.L.R. 7.45 a.m.   12.15 p.m.   5.45 p.m.
    2/14th Bn.L.R. 8.0 a.m.   12.30 p.m.   6.0 p.m.
    2/15th Bn.L.R. 8.15 a.m.   12.45 p.m.   6.15 p.m.
    A.S.C.   8.30 a.m.   1.0 p.m.   6.30 p.m.
    Each Unit will send down with the Water party an extra two men to do the pumping.

5. **POSTAL ARRANGEMENTS.** Whilst in Camp at Fota, the post will leave Brigade Headquarters daily at 6 p.m. Mail Bags will be brought to Brigade Headquarters by this hour. All letters must be stamped.

6. **CENSORSHIP.** Letters need not be censored and anything except sedition may be written.

W. H. HERBERT.
Major,
BRIGADE MAJOR,
179th Infantry Brigade.

Issued at 2.30 p.m.

No. 105.

179th Infantry Brigade.

ORDERS
by
COLONEL E. W. BAIRD, COMMANDING.

Fota Camp.
May 4th. 1916.

1. **MOVES.**   Brigade Headquarters, the 2/13th Bn.L.R. and the 2/15th Bn.L.R. and 518th H.T., A.S.C. Co. will be prepared to move at 9.0 a.m. on Saturday, 6th May.
The O.C., 2/14th Bn.L.R. will hand over the following Transport:-
    1 Travelling Kitchen)
       (Teams complete)) To O.C., 2/15th.
    1 Water Cart)
       (Teams complete))

    1 Travelling Kitchen   To O.C., 2/13th.

2. **ORDNANCE STORES AND CAMP EQUIPMENT.**   Battalions and 518th Coy.H.T., A.S.C., will hand in all surplus Stores and Equipment to the Ordnance Officer at FOTA STATION, tomorrow as under:-
    2/13th: 9 a.m.   2/15th: 1.30 p.m.
    A.S.C. 4.30 p.m. Bde.H.Q. 5.30 p.m.
A fatigue party will be sent to the Station to load Stores as they are handed in.

3. **TENTAGE.**   The following Tentage will be taken:-
2/13th:(60). 2/15th: (72). 518th H.T., A.S.C.(7) Bde.H.Q. (14).

4. **BLANKETS.**   One Blanket only per man will be taken.

5. **ENTRENCHING TOOLS.**   Half Mobilization Entrenching Tools will be handed in to Ordnance at same time and place as Camp Equipment. Separate vouchers will be passed for these.

6. **TRANSPORT.**   A 5 Ton Steam Lorry will be placed at the disposal of each O.C. Battalion for the transport of Tents, etc. A special Guard will be detailed by O.C., Bns. for these Lorries which will have to ride on the lorry.

7. **HARNESS.**   The O.C., 518th Co.H.T., A.S.C. will send a cart to the A.S.C. Officer tomorrow at 10 a.m. to draw 14 sets of lead Double Harness.

           W. N. HERBERT.
              Major,
           BRIGADE MAJOR,
        179th Infantry Brigade.

Issued at 4.30 p.m.

No. 107.

179th. Infantry Brigade.

ORDERS

by

Colonel E.W. Baird, Commanding.

Ballincollig.
6th. May, 1916.

1. The column will march to-morrow towards MACROOM via Road Junction N. of Pt 168 Pt 152 - FahA DRIPSEY COACHFORD - CARRIGADROHID.

2. STARTING POINT. Road junction N of W in WESTVILLAGE.

3. MARCH TABLE.

Unit.	Starting Point time.	
Steam Transport.	8.0.am.	
S.I.Horse.	(	)
One Platoon 2/13th.Bn.L.R.	(9.0.am.)	Advanced Guard.
Brigade Head Quarters.	9.5.am.	
2/13th.Bn.Less one Platoon.	9.10.am.	
Detachment R.F.A. with mounted escort.	9.15.am.	
2/15th.Bn. Less one Company.	9.25.am.	
Train & A.S.C.	9.30.am.	
One Company 2/15th. Bn.	9.40.am.	Rear Guard.

The Ambulance will march at the head of the Train. First Line Transport will accompany Units.
Os. Comdg. Bns. will detail similar Guards for Train and Steam Transport as for to-day's march.

4. MEDICAL.
Any sick men of attached Units will report to M.O. 2/13th.Bn. at 7.30.am. *at Married Quarters, E Block*

5. ROUTINE.
Reveille to-morrow will sound at 6.0.am.

6. SUPPLIES
There will be no issue of supplies to-morrow. A double issue will be made on Monday morning.

7. ATTACHMENTS.
Captain Allen and 6 other ranks R.E. are attached to Brigade Headquarters for rations.

8. BOUNDS.
There is a concealed Guard on the Powder Mills below the Drill Field N.of the Barracks. This Drill Field is out of BOUNDS to all ranks.

W.N. HERBERT.
Major,
BRIGADE MAJOR,
179th. Infantry Brigade.

Issued at 7.0.pm.

No. 109.

179th Infantry Brigade.

ORDERS
by
COLONEL E. W. BAIRD, COMMANDING.

Coachford.
May 7th 1916.

1. The Column will continue the march to MACROOM tomorrow, via Point 262 - CARRIGADROHID.

2. Starting Point Road Fork E. of CHURCH.

3. March Table.

Unit.	Starting Point Time.	
Steam Transport.	8.30 a.m.	
S. I. Horse.	9.30 a.m.)	Advanced Guard.
1 Platoon, 2/15th Bn. L.R.	9.30 a.m.)	
Brigade Headquarters.	9.30 a.m.	
2/15th Bn. Less 1 Platoon.	9.35 a.m.)	
Detachment R.F.A. and Escort.	9.40 a.m.)	Main Body.
2/13th Bn. Less 1 Company.	9.40 a.m.)	
Train.	9.45 a.m.)	
One Company 2/13th Bn.	9.55 a.m.	Rear Guard.

The usual Guards will be detailed for Steam Transport and Train. First Line Transport will accompany Units. The Ambulance will march at the head of the Train.

4. All Drivers of Transport Wagons will wear their chin-straps down.

5. More care must be taken in loading wagons. It is noticed that many tarpaulins are being damaged by being allowed to hang over the wheel.

W. H. HERBERT.
Major,
BRIGADE MAJOR,
179th Infantry Brigade.

Issued at 4.35 p.m.

ORDERS FOR MAIN GATE GUARD.

MACROOM.

1. The Sentry's Beat will extend from 5 yards outside the Gate to 10 yards inside the Gate.

2. He will see that no unauthorised person enters the Camp.

3. He will see that no Soldier leaves the Camp alone. Men are only allowed in pairs or larger parties and must be armed.

4. He will pay proper compliments to all Officers, Armed Parties, etc.

W. H. HERBERT.
Major,
BRIGADE MAJOR,
179th Infantry Brigade.

Macroom.
May 8th 1916.

Would you like
Major Thayer here
no?

No. 109.

179th Infantry Brigade.

O R D E R S
by
COLONEL H. W. BAIRD, COMMANDING.

Macroom.
May 8th 1916.

1. **DUTIES.** The following Guards will be found by the Battalion on duty:-
   (a) 1 N.C.O. and 3 men on Main Gate.
   (b) 1 N.C.O. and 3 men at the Railway Station MACROOM. over Supplies. This Guard will mount at 8.0 p.m. and be dismissed at 7 a.m.
   (c) An inlying picquet of 4 N.C.Os. and 8 men. This picquet will furnish patrols to walk round the whole Camping Area during the night. One Patrol should always be out on duty.

2. **BOUNDS.** No one is allowed to leave the Camp except on duty without a Pass signed by an Officer, and then only in parties of not less than two, both of whom must be armed.

3. **WATER.** The 2/15th Bn. L.R. and A.S.C. will fill their Water Carts at the tap behind the Castle.
   The 2/13th Bn.L.R. Carts will be filled at a pump in the Town.

4. **SUPPLIES.** Supplies will be drawn tomorrow at 9 a.m. All Supply Wagons to be at the Station at that hour.

5. **POSTAL ARRANGEMENTS.** Mail Bags with letters for posting should be sent to the Brigade Office by 5.30 p.m. daily whilst the Column is halted at MACROOM.

6. **ROUTINE.** Reveille tomorrow will be at 6. a.m.

W. B. HERBERT.
Major,
BRIGADE MAJOR,
179th Infantry Brigade.

Issued at 6.50 p.m.

No. 110.

179th Infantry Brigade.

O R D E R S

by

COLONEL H. W. BAIRD, COMMANDING.

Macroom.
May 9th. 1916.

1. **DUTIES.** The same Guards and lnlying Picquets will be found as were detailed in yesterday's orders.

2. **TRANSPORT.** Officers Commanding Units to which Remounts were issued today will ensure that the harness issued to them is properly fitted by noon tomorrow. They will also make a thorough inspection of all their Transport and report to Brigade Headquarters on its condition by 6.0 p.m. tomorrow.

3. **SUPPLIES.** Supplies will be issued at the Railway Station at 9 a.m. tomorrow.

4. **DISPOSAL OF MANURE.** All horse manure is to be placed at the end of lines nearest Park along the E. side of the Camp.

W. H. HERBERT.
Major,
BRIGADE MAJOR,
179th Infantry Brigade.

Issued at 5.30 p.m.

179th Infantry Brigade.   No. 111.

O R D E R S

by

COLONEL A. M. BAIRD, COMMANDING.

Warroom.
May 10th 1916.

1. **DUTIES.**   Duties will be the same as detailed in Brigade Orders of the 6th May 1916.

2. **COMPLIMENTARY.**   The following message was received from the C. in C. Southern Command, by the G.O.C., 60th London Division:-
   "I very much appreciate the rapidity with which
   "you got off the Battalions yesterday and this
   "morning."
   In forwarding a copy of this telegram to 179th Brigade, the A.A. & Q.M.G. 60th (London) Division sends the following message:-
   "The G.O.C., 60th (London) Division directs me
   "to forward copy of telegram, and to state
   "that he is gratified at the manner in which
   "the Units of the 179th Infantry Brigade left
   "this Divisional Area."

   The Brigadier wishes to congratulate Officers Commanding Units and considers that great credit is reflected on all concerned.

3. **WATERING HORSES.**   All Horses will be watered at the S.E. end of the Park and will be taken to water through the Gate at the back of the S.Irish Horse Lines and not by the waggon way at the entrance of Camp.

4. **SANITATION**   It has been noticed that men are in the habit of cleaning their mess tins and plates by wiping them with grass which is afterwards thrown down by the tent side. This is most insanitary. Proper arrangements should be made for the washing of all plates and canteens after each meal.

5. **ATTACHMENTS.**   The following are attached to Brigade Headquarters for rations dated 8th May 1916:-
   Lieut. Crehyn, Veterinary Officer.
   No.4009 Pte. G.Tanner, 2/15th Bn.L.R.
         (Capt. Allen's Batman).
   T. Oliver, Chauffeur.

                                           W. H. HERBERT.
                                                 Major,
                                           BRIGADE MAJOR,
                                           179th Infantry Brigade.

Issued at 5.30 p.m.

179th Infantry Brigade.   No.111a.

O R D E R S
by
COLONEL B. W. BAIRD, COMMANDING.

Macroom.
May 10th. 1916.

1. **MOVES.**   The Column will march tomorrow towards MILLSTREET
                 via AGHANAGRONEY - CARRIGANIMMY.

2. **STARTING** Road Junction N. of E in CURREENROE RD.
   POINT.

3. **ORDER**   Units.   Starting Point Time.
   OF MARCH. Detachment S.I.Horse   9.45 a.m.) Advanced
                 1 Platoon 2/15th Bn. L.R.   10 a.m.) Guard.

                 Brigade Headquarters   10.5 a.m.)
                 2/15th Bn.Less 1 Platoon   10.5 a.m.)
                 R.F.A.Detachment & Mounted
                              Escort   10.10a.m.) Main
) Body.
                 2/15th Bn.Less 1 Company   10.10a.m.)
                 Ambulance M.T.   10.10a.m.)
                 Train   10.15a.m.)

                 1 Coy.2/15th Bn.L.R.   10.20a.m. Rear Guard.

                 The Steam Transport will start independently with
                 usual escort at 9.45 a.m.

4. **ESCORT.**   The usual escort will be detailed to march with the
                 Train.

5. **CAMP EQUIPMENT** O.C. Units will be prepared to hand over all
   ETC.   Horses, Tents, Equipment, etc. drawn since arrival in
                 Ireland. Carefully prepared vouchers will be made out
                 for these horses and Stores to be handed over in order
                 to avoid subsequent trouble.
                       All Stores will have to be handed in before dark
                 tomorrow, and will be handed in following order:-
                       2/15th Bn. L.R.
                       Bde. Headquarters.
                       2/15th Bn. L.R.
                       A.S.C.
                 A Time Table will be issued later.

6. **SUPPLIES.** Supplies tomorrow will be drawn at

7. **BAGGAGE.** All Baggage for Steam Transport except that of the
                 S.Irish Horse, R.F.A. and A.S.C. will be loaded on drive
                 by the Castle.

8. **ROUTINE.** Reveille tomorrow will be at 6 a.m.

9. **FATIGUE.** Officer Commanding 2/15th Bn. will detail a Fatigue
                 party of 50 other ranks to load Sleepers on lorry. This
                 party will report to Captain Allen,R.E. at 6.30 a.m. by
                 Gate leading out of Camp.

                                    W. N. HERBERT.
                                         Major.
                                    BRIGADE MAJOR,
                                    179th Infantry Brigade.

Issued at 10.10 p.m.

Appendix

Nº 2.

2/13th. Battalion London Regiment.

No. 12 Sandhill Camp,
Longbridge Deverill.

PROGRAMME OF TRAINING FOR WEEK ENDING 20th. MAY 1916.

TUESDAY.
7–7.30.   9–12.   2–4.
Running Parade (A,B,C,D Cos)
Phys. Dl. & Bay. Ftg.(do.)
Lecture by Sgt. Cook.(A Co.)
Gas helmet drill (B,C,D Cos.)
Wire entanglements –
 (A Co. by day & night).
 (B & C Co. by day).
Bomb throwing by Platoons –
 (B & D Cos.)
Extended order Dl. by
 platoons (C & D Cos.)
Musketry (B & C Cos.)
Lecture by Platoon Commdrs.–
 (B,C,D Cos.)

WEDNESDAY.
7–7.30.   9–12.   2–4.
Running Pde. (A,B,C,D Cos)
Phys. Dl. & Bay. Ftg. (do.)
Lecture by Sgt. Cook.(B Co.)
Gas helmet drill (A,C,D Cos)
Wire entanglements –
 (B Co. by day & night).
 (A & D Cos. by day).
Bomb throwing by platoons –
 (A & D Cos.)
Extended order drill by
 platoons (A & D Cos.)
Musketry (A & C Cos.)
Lecture by Platoon Commdrs.–
 (A,C & D Cos.)

THURSDAY.
7–7.30.   9–12.   2–4.
Running Pde. (A,B,D Cos)
(bomb throwing by Platoons –
 C Co).
Phys. Dl & Bay. Ftg. –
 (A,B,C,D Cos.)
Lecture by Sgt. Cook (C Co).
Gas Helmet Drill(A,B,D Cos).
Wire entanglements –
 (C Co. by day & night).
 (B & D Cos. by day)
Bomb throwing by Platoons –
 (B & D Cos.)
Close Order Drill (A & B Cos.)
Musketry (A & D Cos.)
Lecture by Platoon Commdrs.–
 (A,B & D Cos.)

FRIDAY.
7–7.30.
Bomb throwing (A,B,C,D Cos).
Route March.

SATURDAY.
9–12.
Kit Inspection.
Phys. Drill.
Bayonet Ftg.
Training under Coy.
 arrangement.

REMARKS:
All specialists train under O. i/c Specialists in the afternoons.
32 Bombers attending Bombing Course.

Lecture by Sgt Cook (AC)

W S Arird? D Pa's?

CAPTAIN & ADJUTANT.

SUBJECT : Syllabus of Training.

G/404/50.

O.C., 1/1st Hampshire Yeomanry.
O.C., 60th (London) Divl. Cyclist Co.
C.R.A., 60th (London) Division.
C.R.E., 60th (London) Division.
O.C., 60th (London) Divl. Signal Co.
Headquarters,
    179th Infantry Brigade.
    180th Infantry Brigade.
    181st Infantry Brigade.
O.C., 60th (London) Divl. Train.
A.D.M.S., 60th (London) Division.
Divisional Grenade Officer.

(1). During the 16th and 17th weeks commencing Monday, May 15th, the following training will be carried out.

(2) Divisional days :
May 23rd, on which day the Division will carry out a Route March.
May 25th, on which day the Division will carry out an attack.
The orders for these two days will be issued later.

(3) Bombers : 32 men per Battalion will commence a Bombing Course on Monday, May 15th, and a further 32 men per Battalion on Monday, May 22nd.
    These men should be selected from those who have already carried out a Bombing Course and whom it is proposed to include in the Battalion Grenadier Platoons.
    The Divisional Grenade Officer will arrange to carry out the necessary tests at the conclusion of each course.
    The Cyclist Co. will detail a further 48 men to commence a Course on Monday, May 15th, and will detail 32 men, who have already done a course, to go through a further course, commencing Monday, May 22nd.

(4) On all days of this next fortnight, except those mentioned in para. (2), Battalions are placed at the disposal of Brigade Commanders, the majority of days being allotted to Battalions for training under their own Commanding Officers.

(5) On days when tactical exercises are being carried out by Infantry Brigade Commanders, application should be made to the C.R.A., C.R.E., and A.D.M.S. for the co-operation of those units affiliated to the Infantry Brigade.
    Should Infantry Brigade Commanders require the co-operation of any of the Divisional Mounted Troops, application should be made to this office, stating the number required.

(6) Physical Training, Bayonet Exercises and the throwing of dummy bombs by those men who have already done a Bombing Course, should be included in the training to be carried out.

(7) A certain amount of barbed wire has now been received and handed over to the C.R.E. Infantry Battalions should be trained in the construction of entanglements both by day and night.
    Infantry Brigade Commanders will call on the C.R.E. for any instructors required.

(8) The Officer Commanding Divisional Mounted Troops will arrange to hold combined exercises for the Divisional Squadron and Divisional Cyclist Co.

(9) Programmes of training are to be forwarded to this office by May 14th.

(10) Sniping will be carried out in accordance with the instructions issued herewith.

Sutton Veny,

11th May, 1916.

Lieut. Colonel,
General Staff,
60th (London) Division.

2/13th. Battalion London Regiment.

PROGRAMME OF TRAINING FOR WEEK COMMENCING 22nd. MAY 1916.

MONDAY.	TUESDAY.	WEDNESDAY.	THURSDAY.	FRIDAY.
Running Pde (A,B,C,D.Cos.) Ceremonial Dl. (A,B,C, Cos.) Lecture by Sgt. Cook (D Co) Anti-gas helmet drill (A Co) Bomb throwing (B,C,D Cos). Musketry. Instruction: Field Service Course. (A,B,C,D Cos).	Running Pde (A,B,C,D Cos). Ceremonial Dl. (do.) Anti gas helmet drill (B Coy). Bomb throwing (A,C,D Cos). Musketry. Instruction: Field Service Course (A,B,C,D Cos).	Running Parade. Divisional Route March. ———— Trench Exercise 11.30 p.m.	Running Pde. (A,B,C,D Cos) Ceremonial Dl. do. Anti gas helmet drill (C Coy). Bomb throwing (A,B,D). Musketry. Instruction: Field Service Course (A,B,C,D Cos).	Divisional Exercise.

SATURDAY.		REMARKS:-	G.M.C. for casuals and Lewis Gunners. 32 Bombers attending Bombing Course. Snipers, Signallers, Scouts, Stretcher Bearers attending courses of Instruction.
Kit Inspection etc.			

[signature]

Lt-Colonel, Commanding.
2/13th. Battn. London Regt.

[signature]
CAPTAIN & ADJUTANT.
2/13th. Battn. London Regt.

179th Infantry Brigade.

PROGRAMME OF TRAINING FOR WEEK ENDING, 27TH MAY, 1916.

UNIT.	MONDAY.	TUESDAY.	WEDNESDAY.	THURSDAY.	FRIDAY.	SATURDAY.	REMARKS.
2/15th Batt. L.R.			Divisional Route March. Trench exercise 11.30 p.m.				G.H.Q. Final Party of Casuals to commence 7.30 a.m., 22nd instant.
2/14th Batt. L.R.			Divisional Route March. Trench exercise 7.30 p.m.		D I V I S I O N A L E X E R C I S E	K I T I N S P E C T I O N, E T C.	Bombing. A further party of 32 Bombers per Bn. will commence a course on Monday, 22nd instant.
2/13th Batt. L.R.	Trench Exercise 11.30 p.m.		Divisional Route March.				Snipers. Sniper training will continue on the same lines as for week ending 20th May.
2/16th Batt. L.R.	Trench Exercise 7.30 p.m.		Divisional Route March.				Lewis Gun Course. Lewis Gunners who have not fired the course will fire on Monday and Tuesday commencing 7.30 a.m., on Ground West of G.'s H. Ranges.

W.N. HERBERT. MAJOR.
Brigade Major, 179th Infantry Brigade.

For the M.G.O.

O.C.,
    2/13th Battalion.
    2/14th Battalion.
    2/15th Battalion.
    2/16th Battalion.

LEWIS GUN COURSE.

Part I.

Fired on Monday, May 22nd.   On Machine Gun Miniature Range to the West of G. & H. Ranges.

PRACTICES.   1 and 3 and Swinging Traverse will be fired.

AMMUNITION.   The Machine Gun Officer of the 2/16th Battalion will draw from Brigade Supply 7,000 rounds, sufficient for the 4 sections firing.

NUMBERS.   The 8 men who did not fire the last course and the 16 men last trained, are to be detailed to fire.

M.G.O's REPORTING.   Machine Gun Officers, the N.C.O. Instructors and Section to report to the Brigade Machine Gun Officer at the 600 yards firing point on G. & H. Ranges at 7.30 a.m.

PICKS AND SHOVELS.   Each Battalion will bring two picks and two shovels.

GUNS.   Each Battalion will bring 4 guns and 36 magazines.

RETURN SPRING TENSION.   This will be put on only when on range.

MAGAZINE FILLING.   For Practices 1 and 3 these must be spaced in groups of six rounds with 2 spaces between each group.
For the swinging traverse in two groups of 22 rounds with 3 spaces between groups.

CONDUCTING PRACTICES.   Guns will number from the right. On the command "Unload" No. 1's will remove magazine, AIM at target and press trigger, then lower gun till butt stock is resting on ground and immediately reporting "Gun clear". Starting from the right of the line of guns. The Officer conducting must satisfy himself that all guns are clear before ordering target inspection.

INSTRUCTORS.   Each instructor will stand two paces behind his gun, and must not assist the firer to clear stoppages unless and until he sees the firer is unable to do so by himself or with the assistance of his No. 2.

PART II.

Fired on Tuesday, May 23rd.   On A & B. Ranges.

PRACTICES.   7 and 9 and 10 and 14 will be fired.

- 2 -

AMMUNITION. The 2/14th Battalion will draw 11,000 rounds from Brigade Supply (adjoining 2/16th Battalion Orderly Room) sufficient for the 4 sections firing.

NUMBERS. Same as for Part I.

N.C.O'S. REPORTING. Machine Gun Officers, the N.C.O. Instructors and section to report to the Brigade Machine Gun Officer at the 400 yards firing point on A. & B. Ranges at 8.0 a.m.

GUNS AND RETURN SPRING TENSION. As for Part I.

MAGAZINE FILLING. For Practice 7 these must be spaced in groups of 20 with 2 spaces between groups.
For Practice 9 these must be filled each magazine with 24 rounds.
For practice 10 these must be spaced in groups of 5 with 2 spaces between groups.
For practice 14 these must be spaced in groups of 10 with 2 spaces between groups.

CONDUCTING PRACTICES. As for Part I.

INSTRUCTORS. As for Part I.

BUTT PARTY. 2nd Lieut. Andrews, 2/15th Battalion will with the Service Section report to the Brigade Machine Gun Officer at the range warden's hut A. & B. Ranges at 7.30 a.m.

BUGLER. The 2/13th Battalion will detail one bugler to report with section.

LIMBER WAGONS. On Monday, May 22nd, these will return to fetch guns at 12 noon. On Tuesday, May 23rd, these will return at 4.30 p.m.

RATIONS. On Monday, May 22nd, none required.
On Tuesday, May 23rd, required.

NOTE. Machine Gun Officers will carefully explain the nature of the practices to be fired to their sections, and particularly point out that practices 9 and 10 of Part II are classification practices. Practice 14 will be fired at falling plates, erected by the Butt Party at a distance of 25 yards from the butts, as per last course arrangement.
Men not firing must observe fire result, and make their observations known by signals and not shout corrections to the gunner.

A. Wilson Young

LONGBRIDGE DEVERILL.
20th May, 1916.

Lieut.
Brigade Machine Gun Officer,
179th Infantry Brigade.

TRENCH SCHEME.

— By —

Lt: Colonel C.M. Mackenzie.,
Commanding,
2/13th Battalion Lond. Regt.

Longbridge Deverill.   24th May. 1916.

1. **BATTALION HEADQUARTERS** will be at North End Farm.

2. **BATTALION PARADE** will be at 10.75pm
   2nd in Command, Company Commanders, Machine Gun Officer, Signalling Officer, & Transport Officer will proceed to Trench Headquarters at least one hour before the arrival of the Battalion.

3. **RATIONS.** Stew will be served out to the Battalion at 9.15pm under Company arrangements. A Haversack Ration will be carried with waterbottle filled.

4. **WATER.** Four canvas water buckets per Company will be issued on parade. O.C. Companies will be responsible for the return of these to the Transport Officer on completion of the Scheme.

5. **SANITATION.** Only Latrine Buckets will be used.

6. **AID POST.** Situation near Battalion Headquarters. The Medical Orderly will make arrangements for four stretcher bearers to parade with each Company — the remainder will be at the Aid Post. The Medical Cart and Water Cart will remain at the Aid Post.

7. **PATROLS.** As soon as the two front line Companies take over their allotted fronts, the Officers Commanding will send out listening patrols, in order to guard against surprise.

8. **PERISCOPES.** No man must look over the top of a parapet during day time without the aid of a periscope.

9. **BOMB STORES & RESERVE AMMUNITION.** Every Officer and N.C.O. must know where the reserve bombs and ammunition would be kept.

10. **WORKING PARTIES.** Working patries for work in front line trenches will be found by the two Front Companies. Working patries for work in communication or support trenches, will be be found by the two Companies in support.

11. **FIELD OF FIRE.** Platoon Commanders will satisfy themselves that each man knows his position in case of attack and has a clear field of fire.

12. **EQUIPMENT.** Less packs will be worn. packs may be removed in Trenches ~~Bayonets will be fixed.~~

13. **STAND TO ARMS** – at 2.45.a.m. unless otherwise ordered.

14. **Work.** O.C. Companies will obtain information about work required from the O.C. Companies of the relieved Unit. O.C. Companies will also furnish a report of work accomplished on vacation of trenches. They will furnish Wind Report at 5.a.m. and Progress Report at 3.30.a.m. Any information as regards hostile movements of the enemy will be reported to Battalion Headquarters at once. O.C. Companies will forward to Battalion Headquarters immediately they have relieved the outgoing Battalion, ~~and~~ report as to how their Company is distributed along its allotted area.

15. **SIGNALLERS.** The Signal Office will be at Battalion Headquarters.

TRENCH SCHEME: CONTD.

24th May, 1916.

16. **BATTALION DUMP**, is at Battalion Headquarters, and will be in charge of the Pioneer Sergeant, and the Pioneers.

17. **ORDERLIES**. O.C. Companies will send two Orderlies to Battalion Headquarters.

18. **ATTACK**. O.C's Support Companies will confer with O.C's Front Line Companies as to the disposition of any Platoon which may be ordered up in support in case of attack. No Supportd will be sent up unless orders have been received from Battalion Headquarters.

19. **DISPOSITION OF COMPANIES**.

    Right Front Line Company ---------" A " Coy.
    Left   -do-   -do- ---------" B " Coy.
    Right Support Company ------------" C " Coy.
    Left   -do-   -do- ------------" D " Coy.

(Signed) W.E.David-Devis.

CAPTAIN & ADJUTANT.

SUTTON VENY TRENCHES

F 50 + 100
S 50 + 65
R 1½ 60 = 150

F = FEATHER
D = DUG OUT
L = LATRINE

Scale of Front (approx.)
Scale: 0 — 100 — 200 — 300 — 400 — 500 — 600 — 1000 feet

Streets/features labelled on map:
- REGENT STREET
- ARCHER'S BEAT
- STRAND
- CHALK R
- SMITH ST.
- ANGEL LANE
- ST. JAMES ALLEY
- CASTLE ST.
- STEEN'S ST. R
- LONDON ROAD
- FAIR VIEW
- H.Q.
- KINGSWAY
- PARSON'S WALK
- YOUNG STREET
- OLD STREET
- FOOLS PARADISE
- HERBERT LANE
- KENSINGTON LANE
- BAIRD ST.
- THE BROADWAY (GRASS TRACK)

MG, OP markers throughout.

SUTTON VENY TRENCHES

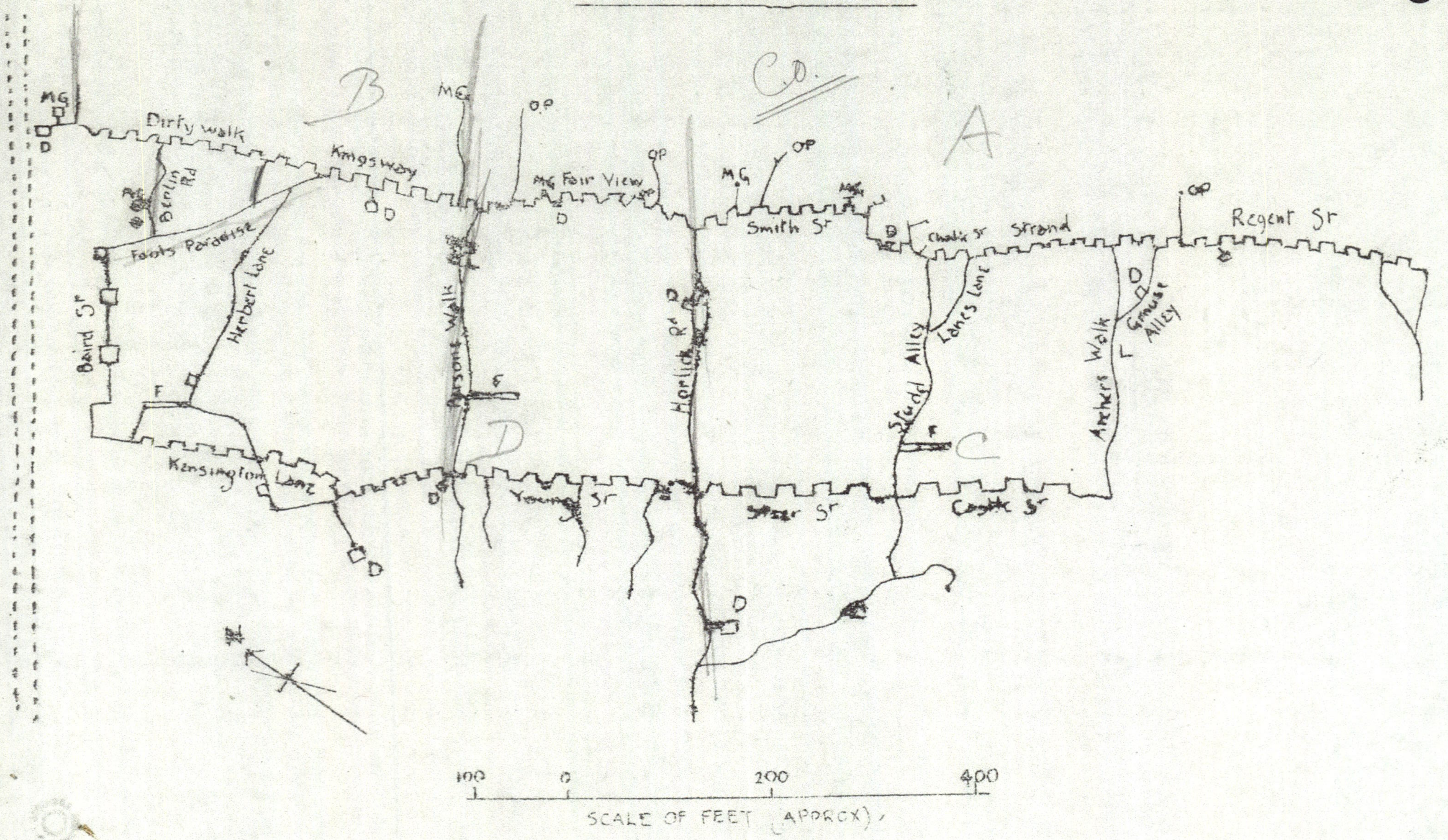

Labels visible on trench map (approximate reading):

- MG, O.P., Dirty Walk
- Kingsway
- Fair View
- Smith St
- Chalk St / Strand
- Regent St
- Grouse Alley
- Archers Walk
- Lancs Lane
- Studd Alley
- Coolie St
- Sezar St
- Horlick Rd
- Young St
- Parsons Walk
- Herbert Lane
- Fools Paradise
- Berlin Rd
- Kensington Lane
- Baird St

A, B, C, D markings on map.

SCALE OF FEET (APPROX).
0   100   200   400

"A" Form.   Army Form C. 2121.
                    MESSAGES AND SIGNALS.   No. of Message_____

Prefix____ Code____ m. | Words | Charge | This message is on a/c of | Recd. at____ m.
Office of Origin and Service Instructions. | | | | Date____
                         | Sent | | | From____
                         | At____ m. | | _____Service. |
                         | To____ | | (Signature of "Franking Officer.") | By
                         | By____ | |

TO { ~~____~~ LOM D }

Sender's Number. | Day of Month | In reply to Number |
* LOM 1 | 25th | H B 2 | A A A

| * By Cav | fatigue | party | ats | water |
| | if | required | | |

From L O M
Place
Time   1.8 am
     The above may be forwarded as now corrected.   (Z) Mackenzie Lt.Col.
                                        Censor. Signature of Addressor or person authorised to telegraph in his name.
                          * This line should be erased if not required.

"A" Form. Army Form C. 2121.
MESSAGES AND SIGNALS. No. of Message _____

Prefix • Code m.	Words	Charge	This message is on a/c of	Recd. at _____ m.
Office of Origin and Service Instructions.				Date _____
	Sent At _____ m. To _____ By _____		_____ Service. (Signature of "Franking Officer.")	From _____ By _____

TO | LOM A & B | | |

| Sender's Number. | Day of Month | In reply to Number | | A A A |
| LOM 2 | 25th | | | |

If	you	want	support	send
to	LOM C	and	LOM D	direct
me	but	let	me	know

From LOM
Place
Time 1.18

The above may be forwarded as now corrected.   (Z) Mackenzie
Censor. Signature of Addressor or person authorised to telegraph in his name.
* This line should be erased if not required.

"A" Form. Army Form C. 2121.
MESSAGES AND SIGNALS.

TO: LOM C & D

Sender's Number: LOM 3
Day of Month: 25th

AAA

LOM A and B will communicate with you direct if support is needed

From: LOM
Time: 1.19 am

"A" Form. Army Form C. 2121.
MESSAGES AND SIGNALS.   No. of Message_____

Prefix......Code.....m.	Words	Charge	This message is on a/c of	Recd. at......m.
Office of Origin and Service Instructions				Date
	Sent At...m. To By		...........Service............ (Signature of "Franking Officer.")	From By

TO { LOM B

Sender's Number.	Day of Month	In reply to Number	
* LOM 4	25th	AW 4	AAA

Send	to	LOM D	for	a
section	or	platoon	AAA	endeavour
to	send	2	more	small
patrols	to	was give	warning	of
enemy	bombing	AAA	don't	know
what	specifies	gas	attack	

From LOM
Place
Time 1.32 am

The above may be forwarded as now corrected.   (Z) Chalking 2!Lt
Censor.   Signature of Addressor or person authorised to telegraph in his name.
* This line should be erased if not required.

"A" Form. Army Form C. 2121.

MESSAGES AND SIGNALS.

TO	LOM ABCD		

Sender's Number.	Day of Month	In reply to Number	
LOM 5	25th		AAA

| Postpone | stand | to | arms | till |
| 2.30 am | | | | |

From LOM
Place
Time 1.53 am

(Z) Chickens Lt Col:

"A" Form.	Army Form C. 2121.
MESSAGES AND SIGNALS.

Prefix	Code	m.	Words	Charge	This message is on a/c of.	Recd. at	m.
Office of Origin and Service Instructions.			Sent			Date	
			At	m.	Service.	From	
			To				
			By		(Signature of "Franking Officer.")	By	

TO **LOM ABCD**

| Sender's Number. | Day of Month | In reply to Number | A A A |
| *LOM 6 | 25th | | |

Companies will collect all stores on their charge and leave trenches in the following orders D C A B AAA 2nd Captains will be responsible for dumping all stores handed at Bn: HQ where they will hand in list of articles on company charge. AAA no rubbish must be left in trenches

From **LOM**
Place
Time **17**

(Z) Chackeya Lt. A.
Signature of Addressor or person authorised to telegraph in his name.

"A" Form. Army Form C. 2121
MESSAGES AND SIGNALS. No. of Message 52

Prefix	Code	m.	Words	Charge	This message is on a/c of:	Recd. at 4.55 a.m
Office of Origin and Service Instructions.			16			Date 25/10
LorD			Sent At m. To By		Service. (Signature of "Franking Officer.")	From 28/10 By Weatherly

TO { LoM

Sender's Number	Day of Month	In rep'y to Number	AAA
HQ 7	25/10	—	

Are filled sandbags to be left as improvement to trenches

From LorD
Place
Time 3.55 am

The above may be forwarded as now corrected.   (Z)
† Censor. Signature of Addressor or person authorised to telegraph in his name.

Appendix
No 4

2/13th Battalion London Regiment.

PROGRAMME OF TRAINING FOR WEEK COMMENCING 29th MAY 1916.

MONDAY	TUESDAY	WEDNESDAY	THURSDAY	FRIDAY
Field Firing (A & B Coys) Running Pde. (C & D Coys) Bomb Throwing. Musketry Instruction :- Field Service Course. Physical Training & Bayonet Fighting. Bde.Ceremonial Pde.(5pm)	Running Pde.(A.B.C.D Coys) Btn.Ceremonial Drill Physical Training & Bayonet Fighting. Extended Order Drill	REVIEW	Field Firing (C&D Coys) Running Pde. (A&B Coys) Bomb Throwing. Extended Order Drill Physical Training & Bayonet Fighting.	Running Pde.(A.B.C.D.Coys) Extended Order Drill Physical Training & Bayonet Fighting. Bomb Throwing. Musketry.

SATURDAY

Kit Inspection etc.

Remarks :- Signallers, Lewis Gunners, Scouts, Snipers and Stretcher Bearers will train under O.i/c Specialist Section.

W S Warden

Captain & Adjutant,
for Lt.Colonel, Commanding,
2/13th Battn. London Regt.

179th Infantry Brigade.

PROGRAMME OF TRAINING FOR WEEK ENDING 3RD JUNE, 1916.

UNIT.	MONDAY.	TUESDAY.	WEDNESDAY.	THURSDAY.	FRIDAY.	SATURDAY.	REMARKS.
2/13th Bn.	2 Companies Field Firing 7 a.m.		R E V I E W.	2 Companies Field Firing 2.0 p.m.		K I T I N S P E C T I O N, ETC.	Bombing. The Officers selected to attend Bombing course will report to Brigade headquarters at time stated. They should be officers who have not already attended a course of instruction. Ceremonial. Special Orders will be issued as regards Ceremonial Parade.
2/14th Bn.	2 Companies Field Firing 11 a.m.			2 Companies Field Firing 7.30 a.m.			
3/15th Bn.		2 Companies Field Firing 7.30 a.m.			2 Companies Field Firing 2.0 p.m.		
2/16th Bn.		2 Companies Field Firing 2.0 p.m.			2 Companies Field Firing 7.30 a.m.		
BRIGADE.	Brigade Ceremonial Parade 5.0 p.m.	1 Officer per Company Bombing 5.0 p.m.		1 Officer per Company Bombing 5.0 p.m.	1 Officer per Company Bombing 5.0 p.m.		

W.N.HERBERT.
Major.
Brigade Major.
179th Infantry Brigade.

60TH DIVISION
179TH INFY BDE

2-13TH. BN. LONDON REGT

~~JAN — NOV 1916.~~

1915 SEP — 1916 NOV

60TH DIVISION
179TH INFY BDE

SECRET

179/60

Vol 1

War Diary

2/13th Bn. London R.

From 1st June 1916 to 30th June 1916.

WAR DIARY or INTELLIGENCE SUMMARY

Army Form C. 2118.

Place	Hour, Date	Summary of Events and Information	Remarks and references to Appendices
LONGBRIDGE DEVERILL	1/6/16	6 am Reveille	R&R
	9 am Routine - Physical drill, Bayonet Fighting, Bomb Throwing, Extended Order, Field Firing	R&R
"	2/6/16 6 am	Reveille	R&R
	7 am	Firing Range	as Appendix A.
	9 am	Physical Drill, Bayonet Fighting, Bomb Throwing, Musketry, Field Firing	R&R
		Strength	Appendix A.
"	3/6/16 6 am	Reveille	R&R
	9 am	Routine - Kit inspection, Physical Training, Bayonet Fighting	R&R
		C.O.'s inspection	Appendix A.
		Strength	
"	4/6/16 4 am	Reveille	R&R
	10.30 am	Church Parade	R&R
		Strength	Appendix A.
"	5/6/16 6 am	Reveille	R&R
	7 am	Turning Parade	R&R
	9 am	Fitting of New Equipment, Bomb Throwing, Physical Drill & Bayonet Fighting	R&R
	11-30am	Inspection of 1st Line Transport by 2 M.G.S War office	Appendix A.
		Strength	
"	6/6/16 6 am	Reveille	R&R
	9 am	Field Firing, Buying Section report that Officers	R&R
	11 am	M.O. for residents who have not fired above	R&R
		Strength	Appendix A

WAR DIARY
or
INTELLIGENCE SUMMARY.

(Erase heading not required.)

Army Form C. 2118.

Instructions regarding War Diaries and Intelligence Summaries are contained in F.S. Regs., Part II. and the Staff Manual respectively. Title pages will be prepared in manuscript.

Hour, Date, Place	Summary of Events and Information	Remarks and references to Appendices
Imphrey Barracks 7/6/16 6am	Reveille	RS
9 a.m.	Fatigue, [?] our't equipment; Extended Order Drill, for Mask Drill	RS
11.30 am	Relaxion	RS
	Bayonet fighting	RS
2 p.m.	Rapid fire, Bomb throwing, Physical drill & Bayonet fighting	RS
	NB: C. contained ?Inspire report ?Supplied at the Majority	Appendix A.
	Strength?	
" 8/6/16 6am	Reveille	RS
7 am	Running Parade	RS
9 am	Extended Order Drill, Rapid Fire, Bomb throwing & for drill etc.	RS
2 p.m.	Physical drill & Bayonet fighting	RS
	NB: C. ? officer; officers & others.	
	Strength – Draft of ? C.O. ? 102 men from 2/23 W. L. taken on	as Appendix A
	Strength.	
" 9/6/16 6am	Reveille	RS
7am	Running Parade	RS
9am	Physical Drill, Bomb throwing, Rifle Drill etc., Musketry Instruction	RS
	?C. ? infantry; Inspection of ?	RS
9.30 am	Inspection of draft by Commanding Officer.	RS
	Strength – 15 Officers & Hughes Band attached	RS
11.15 am	Inspection of Ladies Baggage Wagons by O.C. 80.5 Divisional Train	RS
10.0 am	Board of Enquiry on loss of Property by Lieut. Butcher ordered in	
	Brigade ? Member Capt. A.R. ? President	Appendix A
	Strength	

WAR DIARY or INTELLIGENCE SUMMARY

Army Form C. 2118.

(Erase heading not required.)

Instructions regarding War Diaries and Intelligence Summaries are contained in F.S. Regs., Part II. and the Staff Manual respectively. Title pages will be prepared in manuscript.

Hour, Date, Place	Summary of Events and Information	Remarks and references to Appendices
Inghuy Avories 10/6/16 6am Reveillé		
9 am	Played Tournay Respecting fighting. Inspection of Lines by C.O. M.O. & Field Party Parade when a Lecture was given before attempt. Draft of 10th O.B. 92 from 3/5 Bn L.R. (P.&L.) taken on strength	RPS RPS Appendix A
11/6/16 6am Reveillé		RPS
10.30am Church Parade	Strength	RPS Appendix A
12/6/16 6am Reveillé		RPS
7 am Morning Parade		RPS
9 am	Played Tournay Respecting fighting. New Intended Orders Until further will be most Thursday. Musketry Instruction given to Troops.	RPS RPS
5-30 pm Evening classes on Lewis Gun for all available Officers & Sergeants as Appendix A		RPS as Appendix A
13/6/16 6am Reveillé		RPS
9 am	Notice as on 12/6/16. Everything Lewis Gun. all clothing not to be taken away turned up to 2 Quarter Ag Abunts Property of Officers W.O. & suppressed to	RPS RPS
9 am	Board of general Kist of clothing & equipment to other matters. Teur Things per Mr R. Schildt	RPS

(73989) W4141—463. 400,000. 9/14. H.&J.Ltd. Forms/C. 2118/10.

WAR DIARY or INTELLIGENCE SUMMARY.

(Erase heading not required.)

Army Form C. 2118.

Instructions regarding War Diaries and Intelligence Summaries are contained in F.S. Regs., Part II. and the Staff Manual respectively. Title pages will be prepared in manuscript.

Hour, Date, Place	Summary of Events and Information	Remarks and references to Appendices
Enguinegatte 14/6/16 6 am	Reveillé	
7 am	Running parade	
8 am	Kit inspection for clothing items from Ordnance to be on 15/6/16	
9 am	Parade for men who have not fired	
	Strength	Appendix A.
15/6/16 6 am	Reveillé	
9 am	Foot march for C. continued	
	Strength	Appendix A.
16/6/16 6 am	Reveillé	
9 am	Running parade	
9 am	C. continued: dry practice under dog arrangements	
	Strength	Appendix A.
17/6/16 6 am	Reveillé	
9.15 am	Route march. Specialists train as sections	
	Strength	Appendix A.
18/6/16 6 am	Reveillé	
9 am	Church parade	
11 am	Marching out Inspection of Bank by G.O.R.E.	

Army Form C. 2118.

WAR DIARY
or
INTELLIGENCE SUMMARY

(Erase heading not required.)

Instructions regarding War Diaries and Intelligence Summaries are contained in F.S.Regs., Part II. and the Staff Manual respectively. Title pages will be prepared in manuscript.

Hour, Date, Place	Summary of Events and Information	Remarks and references to Appendices
Fovant 19/6/16 6.0 a.m.	Reveille	
7.0. a.m.	Fanning Parade	
8.30 a.m – 9.15 a.m	Issue of service Gas Helmets	
	Routine fatigue party sent for new drafts	
	Return of Barrack stores	
	Strength	Appendix A
" 20/6/16 6 a.m.	Reveille	
7 a.m.	Fanning Parade	
9 a.m.	Routine. 120 rounds .303 per man drawn from 1st magazine	
	all remainder of Barrack stores returned to Stores	
3.30 p.m	Inspection by Commanding Officer of whole Battalion and huts	
	Strength	Appendix A
" 21/6/16 5 a.m.	Reveille	
7.15 a.m.	A & B Companies with ½ Bn gns and half transport proceeded by march route to WARMINSTER STATION under command of C.O.	
8.15 a.m.	C & D Companies and remainder of transport proceeded by march route to WARMINSTER STATION under command of Major S THOMPSON	
9.54 a.m	1st Train entrained	
10.10 a.m	2nd Train entrained	

Army Form C. 2118.

WAR DIARY
or
INTELLIGENCE SUMMARY.
(Erase heading not required.)

Instructions regarding War Diaries and Intelligence Summaries are contained in F. S. Regs., Part II. and the Staff Manual respectively. Title pages will be prepared in manuscript.

Hour, Date, Place		Summary of Events and Information	Remarks and references to Appendices
SOUTHAMPTON	21/6/16 11.30 p.m.	1st Party arrive & detrain	RRB
"	" 12.30 a.m.	2nd " arrive & detrain	RRB
"	" 4–0 a.m.	The Battalion under command Lieut-Colonel Colin N. Mackenzie embarked on board s/s "LA MARGUERITE"	RRB
"	" 4-30 a.m.	Battalion embarked. Rifles & equipment stacked, life belts served out	RRB
"	" 5-0 a.m.	s/s "COURTLANDS" with transport & personnel on board sailed	RRB
"	" 6-30 a.m.	s/s "LA MARGUERITE" sailed	RRB
LE HAVRE	22/6/16 3.30 p.m.	" arrived	RRB
"	" 5-0 p.m.	s/s "COURTLANDS" arrived	RRB
"	" 5-30 p.m.	Battalion disembarked & proceeded by march route to Rest Camp at LE HAVRE	RRB
"	23/6/16 3 a.m.	Reveille for A. & B. Coys. & H'qrs.	RRB
"	" 4 a.m.	1st Party proceeded by march route to RAILWAY	RRB
"	"	Reveille C. & D. Coys.	RRB
"	" 5 a.m.	2nd Party proceeded by march route to RAILWAY	RRB
STATION	" 8 a.m.	Battalion entrained	RRB

WAR DIARY
or
INTELLIGENCE SUMMARY.

(Erase heading not required.)

Army Form C. 2118.

Instructions regarding War Diaries and Intelligence Summaries are contained in F. S. Regs., Part II. and the Staff Manual respectively. Title pages will be prepared in manuscript.

Place	Hour, Date	Summary of Events and Information	Remarks and references to Appendices
HOUVIN	23/6/16 10.15 p.m.	Battalion entrained & proceeded less A Coy. left as Rear Party) and fuel transport to MONT-ST-ENTOURNOIS. Night very bright.	Strength Appendix A. RB
MONT-ST-ENTOURNOIS	24/6/16 2 a.m.	Battalion billeted in town.	RB
"	9.30 a.m.	47 RIVINGTON & following party proceeded to PENIN.	Strength Appendix A. RB
"	11 a.m.	Battalion proceeded by march route to PENIN. Raining heavily.	RB
PENIN	" 2 p.m.	Battalion billeted. Officers billeted in the Chateau.	RB
"	25/6/16 10 a.m.	Battalion with transport proceeded by march route to ECOIVRES.	Strength Appendix A. RB
ECOIVRES	" 4 p.m.	Battalion arrived & billeted in rest huts. Reinforcements 36 o.r. taken on strength.	RB Strength Appendix A. RB
"	26/6/16 12.30 p.m.	Battalion proceeded by Company to MONT-ST-ELOY.	RB
"	" 3.30 p.m.	Billeted in rest huts.	Strength Appendix A. RB
"	27/6/16 7 a.m.	Reveille.	RB
"	" 10 a.m.	After this hour, the Battalion proceeded to NEUVILLE-ST-VAASTE in small working parties to assist the R.E.s in many fatigue work.	RB
NEUVILLE-ST-VAASTE	27/6/16 4 p.m.	Battalion Hd.qrs. established at WINCHESTER HOUSE. R.A. Stores & transport section remain at ECOIVRES.	RB
"	28/6/16	Battalion continue to assist R.E. in many fatigue work.	RB

WAR DIARY
or
INTELLIGENCE SUMMARY.

(Erase heading not required.)

Army Form C. 2118.

Hour, Date, Place	Summary of Events and Information	Remarks and references to Appendices
NEUILLE ST VAASTE 29/6/16	Battalion continue mining fatigues. 2nd Lt Ebdon W.A., 2nd Lt Gear L.E.W., 2nd Lt Phillips E.W., & 2nd Lt Bates L.C. and 8 N.C.O.'s sent to France of instruction in Bombing	Rfs strength Appendix A R&F
" 30/6/16	Battalion continue mining fatigues. 2nd Lt H. Williams and 10 other ranks attached to 179th L.I. Trench Mortar Battery	Offrs strength Appendix A R&F

C.A. Mackenzie Lieut Cn.
Cont 2/13th London Regiment.

2/13th. Battalion London Regiment
Appendix A

Strength Date	Officers	Other Ranks	Casualty affecting Strength
June 1	28	782	----------
" 2	28	782	----------
" 3	28	779	2390 L/C Stiles, 2057 Pte Leopold, 3660 Pte Webb - To 107th.Prov.Bn.Auth Records letter 13/1724 1/6/16
" 4	28	779	Commissioned Auth:-
" 5	28	775	2761 Pte Newham R. W.O.L.9/L.R/7302 3036 Pte Miskin C.L. " S.D.601,S.D.3 2414 L/c Bedells B " 9/Art/1738 3798 Pte Hemsley Discharged under para 392 K.R.
" 6	28	775	
" 7	28	775	
" 8	28	776	L/c Culverwell attested.
" 9	28	787	11 men of Brigade Band attached.
" 10	28	892	104 O.R. transferred from 2/28th.Bn.L.R. Cadet Walker taken on strength from Cadet Coy. Auth.43/S.M.E./789
" 11	28	993	101 men transferred from 3/5th.Bn.Ldn.Regt.
" 12	28	989	5 men trans. to 107th.Prov.Bn.(Med.Unfit) Auth.Records letter 13/1843 2 men trans. 101 Prov.Bn.(Med.Unfit) 2996 Pte Snelgrove trans.from 107th.Prov.B
" 13	28	989	
" 14	28	989	
" 15	28	987	3162 Pte Selfe ,3841 Pte Roberts. Trans. 107th.Prov Bn.. Auth.Records letter13/1854
" 16	30	987	Lieut.E.R.Kisch, Sec-Lt A.W.Tosland taken on strength from 3/13th.Bn.London Regt.
" 17	30	986	C.Q.M.S.Chapman commissioned Auth. W.O.L.137081(Q.M.G.8)
" 18	30	986	
" 19	30	986	
" 20	30	986	
" 21	29	946	16 men transferred 107th.Provisional Bn. (Auth:- 13/2843 & 13/1956) 25 O.R.transferred to 3/13th.Bn.L.R. (Auth.T.F.records 13/1768) Sec-Lt S.W.Caldbeck left as O i/c Details. 5696 Pte Rawlins S.G.,5710 Pte Baylis granted commissions Auth.W.O.L.(T.F.3) 9/London R./7440 and 7546. 574 Pte St Vincent trans. 3/1 Signal Coy Auth.Records letter 2/28/1064 4 A.S.C. Drivers attached
" 22	29	957	11 men of 2/14th.Bn.London R. attached.
" 23	29	957	
" 24	29	957	
" 25	29	957	Draft of 36 men from 3/13th.Bn.Ldn.Regt.
" 26	29	993	
" 27	29	993	
" 28	29	993	
" 29	29	993	
" 30	29	993	

Vol 2

CONFIDENTIAL

WAR DIARY

2/13th BATTALION LONDON REGIMENT
B.E.F. FRANCE

July 1. 1916 to July 31. 1916

Army Form C. 2118.

WAR DIARY
or
INTELLIGENCE SUMMARY.
(Erase heading not required.)

2/13 Bn L.R.
B.E.F. FRANCE

Hour, Date, Place	Summary of Events and Information	Remarks and references to Appendices
17/6 NEUVILLE S' VAAST	All quiet. Good weather. Coys furnished work parties for R.E.	WD S-O
2.7.16	5 men killed. Pte Smith E.C. 2361 — Thompson E.W. 3018 — Smith J.R. 4595 A Coy — Rogers G. 4606 — Mayhew S.V. 4697	WDS-O
	1 man missing whole killed. Pte Caro. H 5662 C. Coy.	WDS-O
	2 N.C.Os and 1 man wounded. 4 Sergt Williams.W. 1979 4 Cpl Mason A.E. 2982 C. Coy Pte Dickens T. 3985	WDS-O
	Sergt Meyer 5359 A.Cov. proceeded to attend an advance course at St Pol excellent results	WDS-O

(1)

Army Form C. 2118.

WAR DIARY
or
INTELLIGENCE SUMMARY.
(Erase heading not required.)

2/13 Bn L.R.
B.E.F. FRANCE

Instructions regarding War Diaries and Intelligence Summaries are contained in F.S. Regs., Part II and the Staff Manual respectively. Title pages will be prepared in manuscript.

Hour, Date, Place	Summary of Events and Information	Remarks and references to Appendices
2.7.16 NEUVILLE ST VAAST	Sect H.7 GAYNOR and 4 men attend Lewis Gun Course at CAMIERS	WD=D
am 3.7.16	Pt LESSITER g.w. 4256 wounded C.Coy	WD=D
1.30	H.Qrs Trench shelled by enemy	WD=D
	Quiet during day	
4.7.16	Quiet during night. Slight rain	WD=D
P.m	H.Q. Trench shelled by enemy	WD=D
1.55	Pt WAREHAM H.S. 3573 D. Coy. Killed by Sniper.	WD=D
4.7.16	Sect So SHAVE and Sarj HOLLIER attend 2 days' Sniping Course	WD=D
	at ACQ.	
	rain.	
5.7.16	Relieved by 2/15 Bn L.R.	
	A and B Coys and H.Q. to proceed to BRAY HUTS } move as per	WD=D
	C Coy moves to MAISON BLANCHE } appendix No.1	authority as per
	D Coy " " RHINE SHELTERS }	appendix No.1

(2)

WAR DIARY
or
INTELLIGENCE SUMMARY

Army Form C. 2118.

2/13 Bn L.R.
B.E.F. FRANCE

(Erase heading not required.)

Instructions regarding War Diaries and Intelligence Summaries are contained in F.S. Regs., Part II and the Staff Manual respectively. Title pages will be prepared in manuscript.

Hour, Date, Place	Summary of Events and Information	Remarks and references to Appendices
P.M. 6.7.16. BRAY HUTS.	HQr and A and C Coys. leave BRAY } appendix No 1. + Up moved to MAISON BLANCHE much rain after 7 P.M. Pt. MURRAY 3480 B.Coy. wounded.	WEOD appendix No 1. WEOD WEOD
7.7.16. MAISON BLANCHE	fine weather. Quiet.	
8.7.16 – 9.7.16	Pt. WAY C. 6757 A Coy killed 4 TH 4 CPL SCANTLEBURY C.W.C. 6567 Pt. WALLIS. A.H. 6786 – ROWSON W. 3379 Quiet. } A Co. wounded aerial torpedo	WEOD
9.7.16.	Training as in Appendix 2 Quiet. 100 weather. CAPt C.T. FOSTER + Sergt ATKINSON 570. attend III Army School of Instruction	WEOD appendix No 2 WEOD
10.7.16.	Training as per appendix 3	WEOD appendix No 3
11.7.16.	Training as per appendix 4	WEOD appendix No 4.

(3)

Army Form C. 2118.

WAR DIARY
or
INTELLIGENCE SUMMARY.
(Erase heading not required.)

2/13 B'LR
BEF FRANCE

Hour, Date, Place	Summary of Events and Information	Remarks and references to Appendices
12.7.16. MAISON BLANCHE	Move from MAISON BLANCHE. Appendix No 4	NCOs → Appendix No 4
	No 2 Sub Sector Taken over from 1/6 GORDONS	NCOs
	Pt STEPHENS A.J. 3074. D Coy. wounded.	NCOs
	CAPT SH PREEN - 208 Coy. S.M. MURRAY - 1635 CPL MAJOR proceeds to HAVRE for	
	New 60 Lond. Div. DETAILS	
13.7.16 BOYAU BLANC	Pt NICKS G.S. 5784 D Coy. wounded	NCOs
O.P. ABRIS	Bombing raid by 1/5 GORDONS.	NCOs
	1 enemy Killed rifle and equipment taken	
	Quiet.	
14.7.16.	Quiet	
	Relief orders received to proceed on 15/7/16 to rest billets BRAY. Appendix 5	NCOs Appendix No 5
15.7.16	Relieved 7/16 B²LR.	NCOs
	Relief commenced at 2 P.M.	
	Quiet. 100 hearty	
	C. Coy. moved from Centre B (front line) to B RHINE SHELTERS	NCOs
	Pt SMITH. R.P. 5743. D Coy. wounded.	NCOs
	Lt DAVID. G.S. and Sgt HAWKES L.B. (taken on strength from 3/13 B²LR	NCOs

(4)

WAR DIARY or INTELLIGENCE SUMMARY.

2/13 Bn L.R.
BEF FRANCE

Army Form C. 2118.

(Erase heading not required.)

Hour, Date, Place	Summary of Events and Information	Remarks and references to Appendices
K.3.K BRAY HUTS	Rest.	
16.7.16	Voluntary Church Parade	
17.7.16	Training: Bombing & Bayonet fighting. Meeting 2 Captains F.W.READ and Sergt SOSHAVE and 50 O.R. proceeded to Trench Mortar School at ABBEVILLE.	
18.7.16	Training. Bombing & Bayonet fighting. (4th Coy. March). Inspection by C.O.	
P.19.7.16	Quiet. 2/Lt RAWTOSLAND - 2/Lt CAR attend Bn Training School at HERMAVILLE. Moved to No 2 Sub Sector.	
13a.	Relieved 2/L R.F. L.R.	
	Orders as per appendix No 6.	Appendix No 6.
	Major S THOMPSON appointed president & Capt GURDSTON & members of a C.M. at Rear H.Q.	
	Sub REAR and 7 men proceed to ETAPLES. Followed seven for Crews.	
7.31 24.7.16 BONAU DIEU ABRIS	HON EASTMENT 5616 Killed	
	Sergt STURBRIDGE L.T. 2551 wounded	
	4 Sergt KING. J.B. 1516 "	B.Coy.
	Pte PHILLIPS. R. 4640 "	
	Pte INGLETON A. 3700 "	D.Coy.
	Shellfire returned.	

(5)

WAR DIARY
or
INTELLIGENCE SUMMARY.
(Erase heading not required.)

Army Form C. 2118.

2/13 B∴L∴R BEF FRANCE

Hour, Date, Place	Summary of Events and Information	Remarks and references to Appendices
21.7.16. BOYAU DES ABRIS	Situation normal. During afternoon a few heavy shells were fired by enemy on our left front. Sgt T.R. STOCKWELL proceeded to Trench Mortar School with Hd.Qrs of 3rd S.O. SHAVE Jr. was slightly wounded.	WEO
22.7.16	Situation normal. Pte SMITH. T. 3664 Taken on strength from 1/13th B∴L∴R. reinforcements. 21.7.16	AEO, 10 QO-r
23.7.16	Situation normal.	WEO
24.7.16	Situation normal. Sgt HAWKES L.B and 4 N.Co. alters. 0rdrs./Course at TREVIN CAPELLE wef 27.7.16. Sgt LUMLEY C.G. 2450 and 3 men attached to 178th M.Gun Cor.	WEO, WEO, WEO
25.7.16	Pte HILES Q.S. 05 0639 attached from M.T.S.C. for 2 months training. 2 men struck off strength owing to normal OR. 5767 PM P.J. LONG }sick wounded T.M 5755 — E. APPLETON }	WEO, WEO, WEO

(6)

Army Form C. 2118.

WAR DIARY
or
INTELLIGENCE SUMMARY. 2/13th Bn L.R.

(Erase heading not required.)

Instructions regarding War Diaries and Intelligence Summaries are contained in F.S. Regs., Part II. and the Staff Manual respectively. Title pages will be prepared in manuscript.

Hour, Date, Place	Summary of Events and Information	Remarks and references to Appendices
26.7.16. BOYAU DES ABRIS	Situation normal 7/S	WD=S
27.7.16	Lt DAVID R.E. and two men attend sniping course at ACQ from 27-29 July 1916.	WD=0
	Battalion moves from firing line in accordance with appendix N°7	WD=R appendix
	4ept MELHUISH A.D 2351 } killed. Pte CHAPPNESS B. 5525 } — SHARPE C.J. 2626 } — STONE W.H 2775 } Shell A.19. — HANN T. 2761 } — PARSONS T. 5144 } Sgt PODFREY H.S. 2788. hand (un leste)	WD=R
28.7.16 MAISON BLANCHE	Situation normal	WD=S
	MAJOR PATTERSON } CAPT R.D. GLADSTONE } attached Heather Group R.A. for relief. Lt I. RANDE } and Instruction for 4 days from 30. July 1916. Self E.W PHILLIPS }	WD=S

(7)

Army Form C. 2118.

WAR DIARY
or
INTELLIGENCE SUMMARY. 2/13" B" L.R.
(Erase heading not required.)

Instructions regarding War Diaries and Intelligence Summaries are contained in F.S. Regs., Part II. and the Staff Manual respectively. Title pages will be prepared in manuscript.

Hour, Date, Place	Summary of Events and Information	Remarks and references to Appendices
29.7.16 MAISON BLANCHE	Situation normal	OTSO
30.7.16 —	Situation normal. L⁺ THOMPSON & V. } and 4 N.C.Os attend Physical Training Course at HERMA-VILLE from 31 Jul – 5 Aug.16. Sn. SATER L.C.	425D
31.7.16 —	Situation normal. Sgt COLEMAN + CORPORAL COCKSON and 4 O.R. proceed Lattoon a Trench Mortar Course commencing 1. Aug.1916.	15ZSD 15ZSD

C.M. MacKenzie Lieut : Col.
Comd⁰ 2/13ᵗʰ London Reg.ᵗ

CONFIDENTIAL

WAR DIARY

Vol III

of

2/13rd Battalion London Regiment

From 1st August 1916   To 31st August 1916

Army Form C. 2118.

WAR DIARY
or
INTELLIGENCE SUMMARY

(Erase heading not required.)

2/13th Battalion London Regiment

Place	Date	Hour	Summary of Events and Information	Remarks and references to Appendices
MAISON BLANCHE	1916 1 Aug		Situation normal	RPS
			Casualties. 3 Killed by Trench Mortar No 5776 Pte KENT C.G. No 5779 Pte SEARLE C.G. and No 4538 Pte WITTRICK J.F.	RPS Appendix A
			Strength 5558 Sergt VAUGHAN H.F Struck off Strength having been granted a Commission	RPS Appendix A
do	2 Aug		Situation normal	RPS
do	3 Aug		Situation normal	RPS
			Strength 5834 Pte THOMAS D.G. Returned from Casualty Clearing Station & taken on strength	RPS Appendix A
BOYAU DES ABRIS	4 Aug		Relieved 2/16th Battalion London Regiment in front line Trenches. Relief effected without casualties.	RPS
			Situation Usual artillery and Trench Mortar exchange of fire. Otherwise somewhat less activity.	RPS
			Casualties No 3674 Pte GURLEY A.L. Wounded in action	RPS Appendix A
			Strength Draft of 75 men taken on strength	RPS Appendix A
do	5 Aug		Situation Somewhat less activity except on reports Artillery & Trench Mortars	RPS
			Casualties 3656 Pte STOATT C.W. Killed 2220 L/Sergt EYLES.W. and 3957 Pte PRIVETT A.J. Wounded	RPS Appendix A
			Strength Struck off Strength owing to immature report No 3844 Pte DODIMEAD C. No 3516 Pte VERRALL A.H. and No 2475 Pte OULD. S.G. No 2938 Pte WEBSTER J.R. posted to Canteen Corps & struck off Strength	RPS Appendix A

Army Form C. 2118

WAR DIARY
or
INTELLIGENCE SUMMARY
(Erase heading not required.)

Instructions regarding War Diaries and Intelligence Summaries are contained in F.S. Regs., Part II. and the Staff Manual respectively. Title Pages will be prepared in manuscript.

Place	Date	Hour	Summary of Events and Information	Remarks and references to Appendices
BOYAU DES ABRIS	6 Aug		Situation Normal	RPS
		10 p.m.	OPERATION A Raid was carried out from A.4.d.2.2 upon A.4.d.4.1 (vide Reference G. MAP ROCLINCOURT Edition 2.B. Sheet 51 B.N.W.1.) by a party 2 Officers and 39 other Ranks under LIEUT. W. READ. Owing to the tape breaking the party failed to support to return and on daylight (7th Aug) there were 2 Officers and 12 men still missing. One prisoner was brought in by No 2538 Corp. WILLS.	RPS Appendix B
			Casualties No. 2870 L/Corp. WEBB E.G., No. 2487 H/Corp. SECKER N. No 2735 Pte APPLEBY C.H. and No. 4371 Pte PRATLEY. R.E. killed in action. No. 5752 Corp. COLLINS. E.G. No. 5242 Pte GILPIN. E.J. No. 3828 Pte FEAKES.G.H. No. 4027 Pte HAMILTON. H.T. No 3260 Sergt HUMPHREYS W. and No 2896 Pte CUNDY H.L. wounded in action. LIEUT. W. READ, No 3697 Pte LIQUORISH. C.W. and No 3354, Pte PICKARD. G. reported missing and believed wounded. SECOND LIEUT. STOCKWELL F.R., No 5758 Pte CRAIG. N.E. No 5770 Pte FIELD. E. No 5774 Pte HAWES H.V. No 3891 Pte LAMB W.A. No 4018 Pte PARFITT. W. No 3330 H/Corp. STEVENSON. L. No 4632 Pte BARHAM. H.R. No 2887 Pte SHARP.J.W. No 3527 Pte BROWN F.A. No 4894 Pte HARMER. C.E. reported missing No 5717 Pte GORMAN G.P. to Casualty Clearing Station, Nature of Wound No 5674 Pte GURLEY A.L. to 60th Divl Rest Station and taken on strength	RPS Appendix A
do do	7 Aug 7 Aug	3.15 a.m.	Strength Operation An enemy patrol was seen to be approaching the front of Sap 41.L (A.10.d.8697). They were fired on & retired. A dead German was brought in subsequently & mortally wounded one.	RPS Appendix A RPS

1375 Wt. W393/826 1,000,000 4/15 J.B.C. & A. A.D.S.S./Forms/C. 2118.

Army Form C. 2.

WAR DIARY
or
INTELLIGENCE SUMMARY
(Erase heading not required.)

Instructions regarding War Diaries and Intelligence Summaries are contained in F. S. Regs., Part II. and the Staff Manual respectively. Title Pages will be prepared in manuscript.

Place	Date	Hour	Summary of Events and Information	Remarks and references to Appendices
BOYAU DES ABRIS	7 Aug		Carnoy	No 5394 Pte REAVELL.G.N. and No 4763 Pte GREENBERG.S. wounded in action during bombing raid 6 Aug 1916 but not reported until later.	RPS Appendix A
do	8 Aug	1.15 am	Operation	LIEUT. W. READ, No 5770 Pte FIELD. F. No 4632 Pte BARHAM H.R. and No 2887 Pte SHARP.J.W. returned from Bombing raid of 6 Aug. after having spent day in shell hole.	RPS
			Casualties	LIEUT. W READ and No 2887 Pte SHARP.J.W. wounded on bombing raid. No 3354 Pte PICKARD. R. Killed in action in bombing raid but body not brought in.	RPS Appendix A
				No 5772 Pte GEESON.W.W. No 3731 Corp. WATTS.E. No 5118 Pte HATTON.S. and No 1606 Pte WILLIAMS.E. killed in action	RPS Appendix A
				No 3166 Pte BEST. H.C. wounded in action	RPS Appendix A RPS
				No 5714 Pte DICKENS. C.E. to 42 Cas Clearing Station & others W shrapnel	RPS Appendix A.
			Strength	Normal	RPS
do	9 Aug		Situation	Normal	RPS
			Casualties	No 5842 Pte OSWALD.N. No 5743 Pte PIPE. J.C. No 5772 Pte ADAMS. J.J. and No 3587 Pte COLEGATE. E.C. Killed in action.	RPS Appendix A
				No 5843 Pte GREEN. W.A. Wounded in action.	RPS Appendix A.
				No 5615 Corp KNOWLES. P.O. and 5565 Pte L/Corp SAMUEL.H.B. to Casualty Clearing Station & struck off strength	RPS
do	10 Aug		Situation	Normal	RPS

WAR DIARY or INTELLIGENCE SUMMARY

Army Form C. 2

Instructions regarding War Diaries and Intelligence Summaries are contained in F.S. Regs., Part II. and the Staff Manual respectively. Title Pages will be prepared in manuscript.

(Erase heading not required.)

Place	Date	Hour	Summary of Events and Information	Remarks and references to Appendices
BOYAU DES ABRIS	11 Aug	12:30 a.m.	Operation. Mine exploded at A.4.a.2½.2., South of Pulpit. The main crater was consolidated.	RPS Appendix C
			Casualties. LIEUT KILLINGBAK (Royal Engineers) and Pte Sapphire killed in action. No 3557 L/Cpl LAWRENCE W.T., No 5268 Pte GINGELL and No 2291 ST VINCENT G.E. wounded in action.	RPS RPS Appendix A RPS Appendix A
			Strength. No 113913 L/Cpl WYLIE attached from 1st Aux. Bus. Coy. & taken on strength.	RPS Appendix A
			No 5809 Pte STEBBING W.F. to 42 CCS Casualty Clearing Station & struck off strength.	RPS Appendix A
BRAY	12 Aug		Operation. Relieved by 2/16th Battalion London Regiment and went out to Rest. No casualties.	RPS
do	13 Aug		Strength. No 5794 Pte REAVELL G.N. and No 4783 Pte GREENBERG C.S. discharged to duty & taken on strength.	RPS Appendix A
do	14 Aug		Strength. No 3642 Pte PHILLIPS S.C. to CCS Casualty Clearing Station & struck off strength. No 1859 Pte COOK T.A. to CCS Casualty Clearing Section & struck off strength.	RPS Appendix A RPS Appendix A
do	15 Aug		Strength. No 6012 Pte SAYER A.E. to Base Depot, Immature Youth & struck off strength.	RPS Appendix A
do	16 Aug	10 am	Parade. The CORPS COMMANDER presented Sergt (acting Cook) WILLS R.D. with the Military Medal for Gallantry during the Bombing Raid of 6th Aug. 1916.	RPS

WAR DIARY
or
INTELLIGENCE SUMMARY

(Erase heading not required.)

Army Form C. 2

Instructions regarding War Diaries and Intelligence Summaries are contained in F.S. Regs., Part II. and the Staff Manual respectively. Title Pages will be prepared in manuscript.

Place	Date	Hour	Summary of Events and Information	Remarks and references to Appendices
BRAY	16 Aug		Strength	No 5898 Pte SKUCE. E.E. Invalided to ENGLAND and No 3650 Pte PERCIVAL J.R. to Base Depot, Emmatine Upont, took struck W strength.	RPS Appendix A
				No 5586 Pte LEA. W.E. nominated to a Commission, taken W strength.	RPS Appendix A
do	17 Aug		Strength	No 1859 Pte COOK. T.A. returned to duty & taken on strength	RPS Appendix A
do	18 Aug		Casualty	No 4470 Pte SCHUELER. C.E. accidentally wounded.	RPS Appendix A
			Strength	No 5714 Pte DICKENS. C.E. returned to duty & taken on strength. No 4367 Pte LOCK. W.J. and No 4268 Pte WILLETT. J. to Cas Clearing Station & struck off strength.	RPS Appendix A RPS Appendix A
BOYAU DES ABRIS	20 Aug		Relief	Relieved 2/16th Battalion London Regiment in Front line Trenches. No Casualties	RPS
			Strength	No 2470 L/Sergt PAGE. C.L. & Cas Clearing Station & No 3921 Pte ROGERS S. Immersion Upont, struck W strength	RPS Appendix A
			Casualties	No 5669 Pte ERNST W.A, No 5672 Pte FRANCIS. J.W and No 5813 Pte COOMBES. H.F.M. Wounded in action Killed in action	RPS Appendix A
do	21 Aug		Situation	Normal	RPS
			Casualties	No 4913 Pte CAMPBELL. G.J. No 5168 Pte DAVIS. S.D. No 4388 Pte HOGG. H.W. and No 5030 Pte EVANS. H. Killed in action.	RPS RPS Appendix A

Army Form C. 2

WAR DIARY
or
INTELLIGENCE SUMMARY
(Erase heading not required.)

Instructions regarding War Diaries and Intelligence Summaries are contained in F.S. Regs., Part II. and the Staff Manual respectively. Title Pages will be prepared in manuscript.

Place	Date	Hour	Summary of Events and Information	Remarks and references to Appendices
BOYAU DES ABRIS	21 Aug		Strength. Draft of 5 men arrived from No 7 Infantry Base Depot: No 3166 Pte BEST. H.C. to Convel. Camp in D. Aen. taken on strength	RPS RPS Appendix A.
do	22 Aug		Situation. Normal	RPS
			Strength. No 2423 Pte BIBBY. H.B. sent to Cas Clearing Station & struck off strength	RPS Appendix A.
do	23 Aug		Situation. Normal	RPS
			Casualty. No 2511, Corp. CLUBLEY W.R. wounded and at duty	RPS
			Strength. No 4009 Pte TANNER C, No 1585 Pte COLEMAN B.H. and No 4088 Pte GENTRY. G. taken on strength of Brigade & struck of strength	RPS Appendix A.
do	24 Aug		Situation. Normal	RPS
			Strength. LIEUT. M.C.K. BAMBER reported from 3rd Line & taken on strength No 1148 Pte JONES V.E.K. to Division & struck off strength	RPS RPS Appendix A
do	25 Aug		Casualties. No 3848 Pte CARTER. F.G. 4602 Pte CURTIS. W.J. wounded in action also 2930 R/Serjt TURTLE P.J. No 4585 Pte WATKINS. E.F. No 1578 Pte DICEY A.F. and No 5824 Pte GIBSON G.P. wounded in action	RPS Appendix A.
do	26 Aug		Situation. Normal	RPS

1375 Wt. W593/826 1,000,000 4/15 J.B.C. & A. A.D.S.S./Forms/C. 2118.

Army Form C. 2

WAR DIARY
or
INTELLIGENCE SUMMARY
(Erase heading not required.)

Instructions regarding War Diaries and Intelligence Summaries are contained in F. S. Regs., Part II. and the Staff Manual respectively. Title Pages will be prepared in manuscript.

Place	Date	Hour	Summary of Events and Information	Remarks and references to Appendices
BOYAU DES ABRIS	26 Aug		Relief	Relieved by 2/16th Battalion London Regiment and moved into Support. No casualties during relief.	RPS
			Strength	No 3545 Pte EDNEY H. returned to Duty & taken on strength	RPS Appendix A
			Casualty	No 4889 Pte HOWELL G. wounded in action	RPS Appendix A
MAISON BLANCHE	27 Aug		Strength	No 3383 Pte SCOTT A.J. No 3708 Pte HARPER F.G. No 6075 Pte COHEN L.W. and No 3364 Pte COY G. sent to Cas. Clearing Stations and struck off strength	RPS Appendix A
				No 5803 Pte COOMBES H.F.M. at Div Conval. Cop & taken on strength	RPS Appendix A
			COURT MARTIAL	Field General Court Martial on No 3368 L/Corp A.M. JOHNSON for neglect to the prejudice of good order & military discipline	RPS
	28 Aug		Strength	No 3992 Pte MIDDLETON. G. & No 5809 Pte STEBBING T.F. to Divi. Conval. Corp & taken on strength.	RPS Appendix A
					RPS Appendix A
do	29 Aug		Strength	No 5804 Pte WHITE P.G. and No 5379 Pte GOODYEAR W.E. to Convalescence and struck off strength	RPS Appendix A
do			Court Martial	Finding of Court confirmed & sentence 14 days F.P.N.2 and strength recommended to mercy	RPS

WAR DIARY or INTELLIGENCE SUMMARY

Army Form C. 2

Place	Date	Hour	Summary of Events and Information	Remarks and references to Appendices
MAISON BLANCHE	30 Aug		Strength No 2470 A/Sergt PAGE. C. G. to Div Conval Coy & taken on strength	RPS Appendix A
do	31 Aug		Strength No 3617 Pte STRETTON A.E. accidentally wounded & struck off strength	RPS Appendix A

C. M. Mackenzie
Lieut Col. Commanding
2/13th Battalion London Regiment

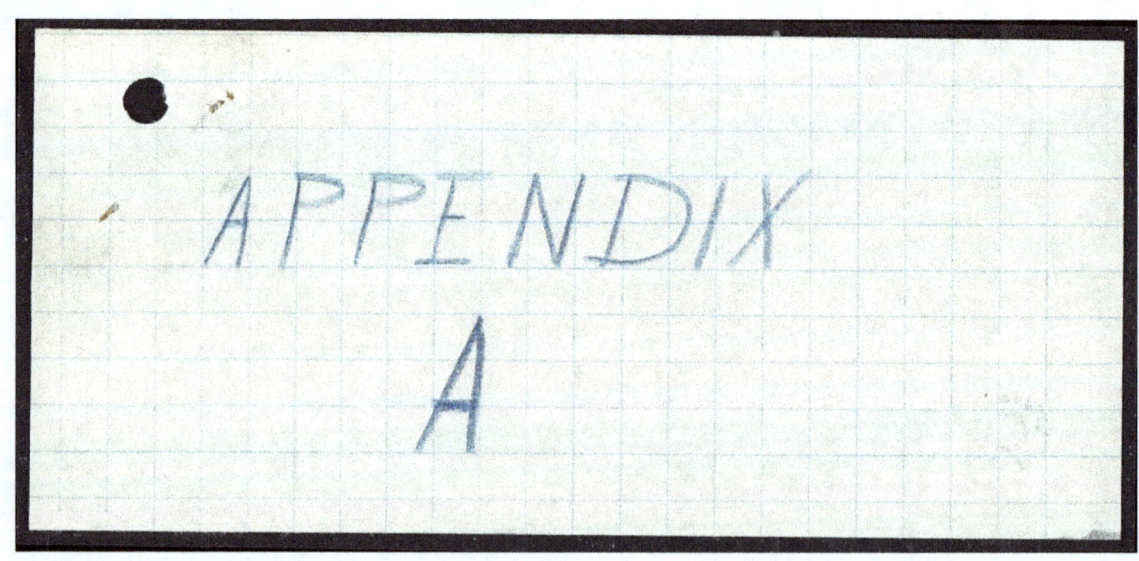

SECRET.

RAID BY .....2/13th London Regt.....
at......10.30......p.m. on......6th Aug: 1916......

UNDER LIEUT. W. READ and 2/LIEUT. F.R. STOCKWELL, 2nd in COMMAND.

NOTE: MAP REF:
ROCLINCOURT. Edition 2.B.
Sheet 51.B.N.W.1.

OBJECT:- To obtain identifications.

JUMPING OFF POINT:- A.4.d.2.2. (Point A. on Sketch Map.)

CENTRE OF OBJECTIVE:- A.4.d.4.1. (Point of entry and exit in Enemy Trenches). (Point C. on Sketch Map).

LIMITS OF OBJECTIVE:- North A.4.d.4.2.
South A.10.b.4.10.

POINT OF RETURN:- A.4.d.2.2. (Point A. on Sketch Map).

The party consists of five Groups:-
(1) COVERING PARTY: 2 N.C.Os.
1 Tape Man.
2 Lader men.
3 Blanket men.

(2) RIGHT BLOCKING PARTY:
2 N.C.Os. and 9 men divided into 2 Sections:-
(a) 1 N.C.O.
2 Bayonet men.
2 Bombers.

(b) 1 N.C.O.
1 Parados man.
2 Bayonet men.
2 Bombers.

(3) RIGHT RAIDING PARTY:
1 Officer.
1 N.C.O.
4 men.

(4) LEFT BLOCKING PARTY:
2 N.C.Os. and 9 men divided into 2 Sections:-
(a) 1 N.C.O.
2 Bayonet men.
2 Bombers.

(b) 1 N.C.O.
1 Parados man.
2 Bayonet men.
2 Bombers.

(5) LEFT RAIDING PARTY:
1 Officer.
1 N.C.O.
4 men.

SUMMARY:- 2 Officers.
8 N.C.Os.
32 men.
42.

SPECIAL ARRANGEMENTS.

1. The Officer in Command of party will remain at Point of Entry and will superintend the withdrawal.

2. The signal for withdrawal to be given by O.C. Raid will be several blasts on a Claxton horn.

3. A rocket signal (~~Red~~, Green, ~~Red~~) ALL will be fired from Coy.H.Q. and repeated from Bn.H.Q. as a Signal to the Artillery and T.Ms. that the party has returned.

4. An Officer will be on duty at the Starting Point to which a wire will be laid from Coy. Headquarters. This Officer will keep Battalion Headquarters informed of the progress of the raid and order Rocket Signal to be made when party has returned.

5. A party to be near starting point with a reserve supply of Bombs.

6. Arrangements made for Flanks support by Lewis ~~and Machine~~ Guns, Artillery and Trench Mortars.

7. **Pass Word.** Answered by and Vice versa. ADAM – EVE

8. **Code Word.** For withdrawal: WARMINSTER

9. All papers and documents to be left behind. Orders in case of being taken prisoner read over before starting.

10. Bayonets to be darkened.

11. Faces and hands to be blackened.

12. Jumping-off: Place prepared.

13. A Shelter ready for return. Extra rations before. A rum ration on return.

14. Medical Aid Posts prepared in Firing Line.

15. Extra Stretcher-bearers on duty.

16. Warn Sentry Posts.

STORES USED.

- 42 Body Shields.
- 2 8ft. Ladders.
- 6 prs. Hedging Gloves.
- 6 prs. Wire Cutters.
- 6 heavy Bill-hooks.
- 1 tape 200 yards long for guidance.
- 1 man pack for tape.
- 3 Sets of Blanket and Wire Bridges.
- 25 Knobkerries.
- 1 Claxton Horn for signal for withdrawal.
- 2 ½" Ropes.
- 50 Bomb Buckets.
- 6 Electric Torches.

BOMBS REQUIRED.

```
10 with 10 Bombs.  - 100.
32  "   5  "       - 160.
                     260.
```

Watches will be synchronised at 5.0 p.m. at Advanced Brigade Headquarters.

DUTIES OF GROUPS.

1. COVERING GROUP:

   (a) Tape Man. This man will follow after O.C. Raid, dropping a White Tape en route from Jumping Off Point "A" to point of Entry "C". He will carry Rifle and Bayonet, 10 rounds in Magazine and 4 extra clips; and five Bombs in bucket.

   (b) Blanket Men. These men will follow the Tape man, each carrying a Blanket wire Bridge which they will place over Enemy wire, to enable the rest of the party to get over quickly. They will be armed with Rifle & Bayonet, ten rounds in Magazine and four extra clips; and five Bombs in bucket.

   (c) Ladder Men. These men will follow Blanket men, and each carry an 8 ft. ladder, which they will place in Trench on either side of point of entry. They will not place the ladders in the Trench until after the Blocking and Raiding Groups have entered Enemy Lines. When they have placed ladders in Trench they will watch for Enemy endeavouring to come over parapet from Support to Front Line Trenches, and generally keep thin eyes opened for Enemy. They will be armed with Rifle and Bayonet, ten rounds in magazine and four spare clips; and five Bombs in bucket.

2. RIGHT BLOCKING PARTY:

   (a) 1st Section: This party will block the Right Communication Trench (H on Sketch.)

   (b) 2nd Section: This party will block Trench at T on sketch map. One man will get on parados at Point K. and prevent counter-Bombing from L.

   Arms:
   N.C.Os.   Rifle and Bayonet. 10 cartridges in magazine - 4 spare clips. 5 Bombs in buckets.

   Bayonetmen.   -do-   -do-

   Parados man. -do-   10 Bombs in bucket.

   Bombers. 10 Bombs in Buckets and Knobkerries.

3. LEFT BLOCKING PARTY:

   (a) 1st Section: This party will block Trench at M

   (b) 2nd Section: This party will block N   One man will get on parados at P and prevent counter-Bombing from O.

   Arms and Ammunition: Same as for R. Blocking Party.

4. RIGHT RAIDING PARTY:
   Officer in Charge (2nd in command).
   This party will work from point C. to Right Communication Trench, make a capture and bring along prisoner.

5. **LEFT RAIDING PARTY.**
    Officer in Charge (O.C. Raid).
    (Senior N.C.O. carries on with Party; O.C. Raid stopping at point of Entry.)

    This party will work from Point C. to Left Communication Trench, make a capture and bring back a prisoner.

GENERAL.

The duration of Raid will be limited to 15 minutes.

During the time the Raid is taking place, the Tape Man and Blanket men under the direction of the 2 N.C.Os. in Covering Party, will improve the communications and will each be provided with a pair of Hedge Gloves and Wire Cutters.

During the time of withdrawal the Covering Party will cover the retirement of the Blocking and Raiding Parties.

In the event of O.C. Raid being rendered "hors de combat" before the parties enter Trench, the second in command will take charge, but if he is rendered a casualty during the time the raid is taking place, the Senior N.C.O. of Covering Party will give the Signal for withdrawal.

It is absolutely essential that in the event of an Officer or N.C.O. in charge of a Group being rendered a Casualty, the next Senior will immediately take command.

Each N.C.O. in charge of a Group is responsible for his men and will see that all his men get out of Enemy Trench on receiving orders to withdraw.

In the event of one of the party being taken prisoner he will only give his name and rank. No other information under any circumstances is to be given.

No wounded or dead to be left in Enemy Trenches.

All Ranks are to take special note that the object of the Raid is to obtain a prisoner for identification purposes and immediately the Raiding Parties have made a capture, they will make for our own Lines. All Ranks will, however, should the opportunity occur, obtain any other identifications such as badges, papers, etc.

Enemy Bombs should be taken if possible. Machine Guns and T.Ms. also should be put out of action.

On return of Party they will proceed to previously arranged shelters and will await there until receipt of orders, and any prisoners should be securely fastened, and all documents removed from them, in order that they may not get an opportunity to destroy same.

The second in Command will be responsible for the safe-keeping of prisoners until the return of O.C. Raid.

No identification marks such as hats, badges, are to be removed by Raiding Party as souvenirs.

The indiscriminate use of Bombs is forbidden.

C. M. Mackenzie Lt.Col.
Comg: 2/13" London Regt.

ARTILLERY and T.M. PROGRAMME (PROVISIONAL).

- 2 minutes.   60x T.M.B.   Commence to cut wire.   [10.28]

  0.   ARTILLERY and
               179 L.T.M.B.   Open barrage on Front Line.   [10.30]

  0 + 3.   60x. T.M.   Cease Fire.   ) Infantry
               ARTILLERY.   Lift to back barrage.) Advance.
               179 L.T.M.B.   Barrage Flanks.   )

  SHOWER OF GREEN ROCKETS.   All Guns and Mortars cease Fire.

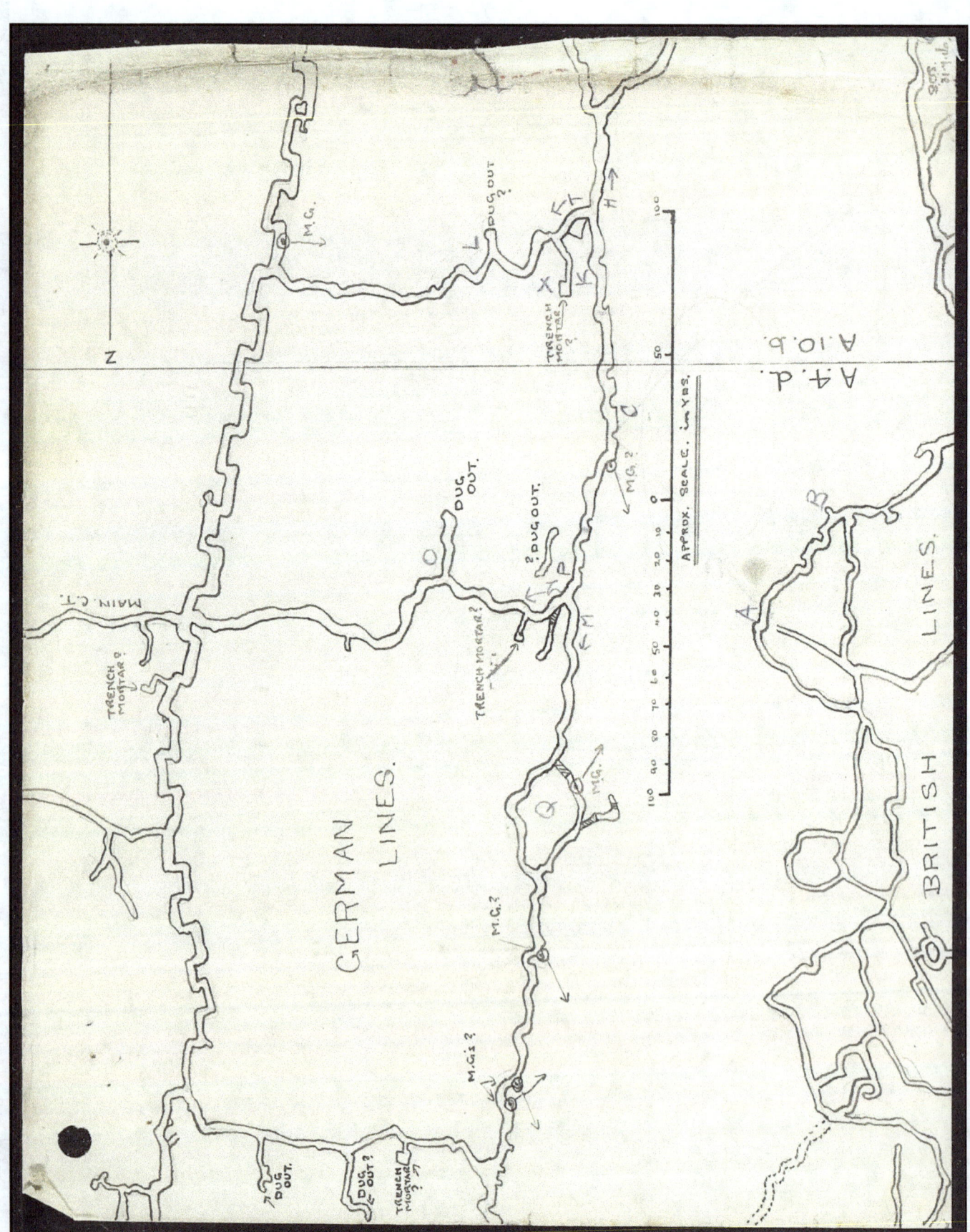

MAP Reference
Trench Map:
Roclincourt
51B. N.W.1.
Edition 2.c.
1/10,000.

Headquarters,
179th Infantry Brigade.

I beg to submit the following report on the Raid carried out by the 2/13th London Regiment on the 6th August 1916. The starting point was The PULPIT A.4.d.25.2. The objective was the FRONT LINE GERMAN TRENCH between A.4.d.35.2 and A.10.b.35.9. The point of entry was A.4.d.35.05.

The object was to obtain identification. Time limit 15 minutes.
Time for M.T.M. Wire Cutting x - 2.
" " Artillery bombardment and L.T.M. on Front Line x.
" " Artillery to lift and barrage Support Trenches and
   L.T.M. to barrage flanks: x + 3.
" " Infantry Advance: x + 3.   x - 10.30 p.m.

I had an Officer stationed in the PULPIT to telephone progress to me.

10.33 p.m. Message came "Raiders have started".
10.34 p.m.   "   "   "All Over".
10.37 p.m.   "   "   "Tape broken, party gone without".
10.39 p.m.   "   "   "No signs"
10.41 p.m.   "   "   "No signs"
10.45 p.m.   "   "   "No signs"
10.51 p.m.   "   "   "Mr. Shave gone on top to find out".
10.53 p.m. (one minute after time limit). I sent message "If possible send over and order party back". (This proved impossible owing to Enemy T.M. and Artillery barrage which was very heavy.)
10.55 p.m. Message received. Messenger sent over top, couldn't get through barrage.
10.57 p.m. Message received. Very Light at point of Entry (Three Very Lights were sent from point of Entry between 10.33 p.m. and 10.57 p.m.)
10.58 p.m. Message from CENTRE SUBSECTOR "3 men returned".
11.4 p.m. I sent 2/Lieut. Gates to 2/Lieut. Shave, who was in PULPIT. He reported Shells and Mortars dropping very close.
11.5 p.m. F.O.O. got message through to Artillery to "Add 50".
11.8 p.m. Sent Stretcher bearers attend wounded police. I subsequently heard that 4 Police were killed.
11.9 p.m. Message from RIGHT SUBSECTOR: "3 men returned with 1 prisoner". Immediately afterwards I heard one more raider had come in.
11.10 p.m. F.O.O. calling to Artillery to increase Range.
11.12 p.m. Message came "Very Light from point of entry".
11.14 p.m.
11.17 p.m. I sent an Officer to fire some of our own Very Lights to serve as some sort of a guide to Raiders.
11.25 p.m. Ordered RIGHT, LEFT and CENTRE SUBSECTORS to have Patrols ready to go out directly Artillery had ceased firing.
11.27 p.m. Message came "No signs of Raiders in NO MAN'S LAND".

After this I had no time to keep a record of sequence of events as the Raiders began to return and my time was occupied in checking names, receiving and sending many verbal messages, as there was no time for written orders.

About 11.45 p.m. a good number of Raiders had returned through CENTRE SUBSECTOR.

About 11.55 p.m. I had definite news of return of 23 Raiders.

I reported to Advance HORSE and sent up Signal to stop Artillery Fire at about 11.58 p.m.

I could not see my way to stop Artillery Fire before as it was only about 11.55 p.m. I heard that any considerable number of Raiders had returned.

7.8.16.
12.20 a.m.

I ordered RIGHT, LEFT and CENTRE SUB-SECTORS to thoroughly search their Trenches for returned Raiders and send out further Patrols.

About 1.30 a.m. I sent a written report to ADVANCED HORSE. I could not send frequent telephone messages to ADVANCED HORSE as I had only one phone by which I had to both send and receive messages. I thought it very important to keep in touch with my Companies and the PULPIT.

About 3.20 a.m. a final party of 3 came in.

TOTAL who came in: - Officers, 27 O.R.

I attribute the failure of the whole party to return as arranged entirely to the breaking of the guiding tape. Great care should be exercised in checking names of returned Raiders.

I should like to point out the difficulty of getting a connected narrative at the time, if anything goes wrong. The guiding tape should be paid out by hand.

The Enemy commenced a heavy barrage of Artillery and T.M's between 10.35 p.m. and 10.40 p.m.

I have interviewed several of the Raiding Party and they all say that when the order to withdraw came and they left the Trench, all sense of direction was lost owing to there being no tape and to the smoke and dust.

When the majority were out, 2/Lieut. Stockwell called out "To the Left". Most of the Raiders then went to the Left and struck the German Trenches at A.10.b.3.8. Many got in at this point and heard the Enemy talking, so they had to get out and make the best of their way home. I feel convinced that those men who are still missing got into the Trench at this point thinking they were in our Lines. They probably pushed far up and were taken.

The Objective Trench was blocked by wire Chevaux de frise at a point just short of A.4.b.35.2. It is doubtful if Objective Trench was blocked on Enemy Left.

2/Lieut. Stockwell and others were seen proceeding in a direction that must have been parallel to Enemy wire and would take them into German Trench at A.10.b.35.8.

The EDINBURGH CRATER seems to have stopped all the returning Raiders except 4, as all the others returned through CENTRE SUBSECTOR North of EDINBURGH CRATER.

The heavy barrage in NO MAN'S LAND must have been very disconcerting and would undoubtedly interfere with the sense of direction as many men were knocked down by explosions.

30 O.R. and 1 Officer have returned.
1 O.R. is known to have died of wounds.
1 O.R. (Name uncertain) is known to be killed.
MISSING: 7 O.R. 1 Officer.
1 Prisoner was taken.

I have already forwarded Lieut. Read's Report.

I should like to bring the following names, in connection with this Raid, to your notice:-

LIEUT. READ,W. who resolutely led his party to the Objective although the tape was broken. He was the last to leave the Objective Trench. He remained behind to assist a wounded man, although wounded himself, and had to take refuge in a shell hole. He crawled back to our lines about 1.30 a.m. (8/8/16) and with the assistance of Privates BARHAM and FIELD brought in Private SHARPE who was wounded. His own wrist was broken about 10.50 p. 6.8.16.

CAPTAIN HANKS,A.G.T., R.A.M.C. attended to the wounded in a most efficient manner under trying circumstances. He had to go from H.Q. LEFT SUB-SECTOR to H.Q. CENTRE SUB-SECTOR to attend 2 wounded, under a heavy fire of Enemy Mortars which did great damage to the Trench.

2/Lieut. SHAVE, S.O. Remained in an exposed position in PULPIT for 2 hours. For 1½ hours he was under heavy Fire from Enemy T.M's and Artillery. He went on top several times to see if he could obtain news. He performed his duty of keeping me posted with progress of events in a most efficient manner, thereby rendering me great assistance.

No.2538 Corporal WILLS R.O. took charge of 3 wounded men and brought them safely to the RIGHT SUB-SECTOR. Whilst doing this the party lost direction and CORPORAL WILLS crossing the THELUS ROAD East of EDINBURGH CRATER struck the GERMAN TRENCHES about A.10.b.35.35. Here he saw an Armed Enemy. Although his own Rifle had been blown out of his hand and he was only armed with Wire-cutters, he tackled the GERMAN and took him prisoner. Seizing his prisoner he guided his party of 3 wounded men with great skill to the RIGHT SUB-SECTOR.

No.4362 Private BARHAM H.R. and No. 5770 Private FIELD F. carried a wounded man, who subsequently died, into a Shell Hole. Here they were joined by Lieut. READ who brought in another wounded man. They refused to leave LIEUT. READ and make their own way back to our Lines. They returned with LIEUT. READ to our Lines about 1.30 a.m. 8/8/16.

(sd) C.M.MACKENZIE,
Lieut-Col.
Comdg. 2/13th London Regiment.

APPENDIX A

PARTICULARS

DATE	OFFICERS	INCREASE	DECREASE	OTHER RANKS	INCREASE	DECREASE	PARTICULARS
AUGUST							
1	31	–	–	923		1	1 Sgt. commissioned.
2	31	–	–	922	–	–	
3	31	–	–	922	1	–	1 man returned from Cas. Clearing Station.
4	31	–	–	923	75		Draft from 3rd Line.
5	31	–	–	998	–	8	1 evacuated to C.C.S. 3 men immature age: 1 man commissioned. 3 wounded
6	31	–	–	990	–	1	1 man wounded
7	31	–	2	989		19	1 Officer wounded, 1 missing: 8 men missing, 6 men killed, 5 wounded. (Bombing Raid)
8	29	–	–	970		3	2 men wounded (Bombing Raid) 1 man evac to C.C.S.
9	29	–	–	967		6	4 killed, 1 wounded, 1 evac. to C.C.S.
10	29	–	–	961		7	4 killed, 1 wounded, 2 commissioned.
11	29	–	–	954		4	3 wounded, 1 evacuated
12	29	–	–	950	2	–	2 returned from C.C.S.
13	29	–	–	952	–	–	
14	29	–	–	952	–	3	1 Commissioned, 1 Under Age, 1 Evac C.C.S.
15	29	–	–	949	–	3	2 Evac C.C.S., 1 Under Age
16	29	–	–	946	2	–	2 from C.C.S.
17	29	–	–	948	–		
18	29	–	–	948	–	4	3 Evac to C.C.S.; 1 Accidentally wounded
19	29	–	–	944	–	–	
20	29	–	–	944	–	5	1 Killed, 2 wounded, 2 evac to C.C.S.
21	29	–	–	939	6	1	5 draft from 3rd Line: 1 returned from C.C.S.
22	29	–	–	945		6	4 killed, 2 evac. to C.C.S.
23	29	–	–	939		3	3 on strength of 6ad Division for duty.
24	29	1	–	936		2	Lieut Bamber joins: 2 wounded
25	30	–	–	934	1	4	4 wounded: 1 returned from C.C.S.
26	30	–	–	931	2	5	1 Killed, 4 evacuated C.C.S.: 2 returned C.C.S.
27	30	–	–	928	1	1	1 evac. to C.C.S., 1 returned from C.C.S.
28	30	–	–	928		2	2 commissioned
29	30	–	–	926	–	–	
30	30	–	–	926	1	1	1 returned from C.C.S.: 1 Accidentally wounded
31	30	–	–	926			

REPORT BY LIEUT. W. READ, 2/13th LONDON REGIMENT, 8/8/16.

I beg to report that at 10.33 p.m. last night my party left the PULPIT to raid the GERMAN TRENCHES as per Scheme previously submitted. On the way over, the tape got into difficulties owing to the explosion of a Trench Mortar and this tape was not laid all the way to the Bosche Lines as previously arranged.

On arriving at the German Trenches I found that although the wire defences had been broken down by the Trench Mortars, the Trench itself was barricaded. Seeing the state of affairs, and also not having the necessary implements to break down these heavy barricades, I gave the order to withdraw. A few men got into the Right Trench by crawling underneath the barricade and found no Germans there.

I saw all the men out of the Trenches and then gave orders to the covering party to withdraw, when a Trench Mortar wounded several of them and also the last Bombers to leave the Trenches. A hail of Trench Mortars then came over.

I found 3354 Pte. Pickard, G. wounded. I got hold of him and got him back to a shell hole, where I came across No. 4362 Pte. Barham H.R. No. 5770 Pte. FIELD F. and 2887 Pte. SHARP. J.W. the latter slightly wounded.

Owing to the tape being destroyed, I was unable to find my way back and Ptes. Barham and Field reconnoitred for the purpose of finding the direction of our own Trenches. Ptes. Barham and Field took out the bolts of any Rifles they found. I came across one dead man whom I was unable to identify and bring along with me.

We then took refuge in a shell hole which turned out to be quite near EDINBURGH CRATER, and which I was unable to identify. We stayed there all day yesterday and regret to say that Pte. Pickard died about mid-day (7th). We were unable to bring him along, having already one wounded man and myself (broken wrist) so we left him there and have given particulars of his whereabouts to the Battalion.

We left the shell hole at approximately 9 p.m. yesterday to endeavour to find our own lines and we eventually met one of the Kensington Search parties at about 1.30 a.m. (8.8.16).

All men were counted out and I was the last to leave the German Lines.

I understand that No. 2538 Cpl. Wills, R.O. secured one prisoner. This man was very plucky throughout the whole raid and I should like to bring his name to your notice. I would also bring to your notice the names of No. 4362 Pte. Barham, H.R., No. 5770 Pte. Field. F. and No. 2887 Pte. Sharp, J.W. who, under very trying circumstances, were very plucky.

(sd) W. READ.
Lieut.

8th August 1916.

Advanced Headquarters,
179th Infantry Brigade.

   Reference your B.M.2 dated 1/3/1916. On the withdrawal of troops of the MHOW Cavalry Brigade my RIGHT SUPPORT was asked to provide a mining fatigue, and duly did this. No doubt by tomorrow other arrangements will have been made.

1/3/1916.

            Major.
       Comdng. 2/14th Bn. London Regiment.
          (London Scottish)

SECRET.   179th Infantry Brigade.   Copy No. 3

                    Operation Order No. 6.

REF: ROCLINCOURT.
     Sheet 51B. 1/10,000
     and attached sketch.

1. A Mine will be exploded at A.4.d.2½.2, at a time to be notified later.

2. The following parties will be detailed to sieze and consolidate the CRATER:-
(a) 1 officer 8 O.R.   Rifle & bayonet each 50 Rounds S.A.A.
    2/13th Btn. L.R.   10 bombs in bucket   "
    including 2 Lewis Gunners Slung Shovel   "
    Gunners with Gun   4 Empty Sandbags   "
    & 6 ~~bombing bombers~~ ~~and~~ Bombing Shield "
    Drums.

(b) 1 officer & 3 R.E.   Rifle & bayonet 50 Rounds S.A.A. each.
    12 O.R.   3 Picks remainder shovel.
    2/13th L.R.   6 loop-hole plates.
                          50 Sandbags empty.
                          2 pairs wire cutters.
                          2 pairs hedging gloves.

(b1) 1 officer, 8 O.R.   Rifle & bayonet 50 Rounds S.A.A. each.
    2/13th Bn.L.R.   Pick and shovel.
                                FRENCH
(c) 1 R.E. 10 O.R.   4 Rolls ~~German~~ wire.
    2/13th Bn. L.R.   2 half-rolls barbed wire.
                          12 Iron Picquets.
                          2 large Screw Picquets.
                          2 small mallets.
                          2 knife rests.
                          4 pairs hedging gloves.
                          6 pairs wire cutters.

(d) 8 O.R. 2/13th Bn.L.R. Rifle & bayonet 50 Rounds S.A.A. each.
                          1 Pick and 1 shovel.

(e) 1 R.E. & 10 O.R.   Same as (c) plus 12 pit props for
    2/13th Btn.L.R.   Bombing post.

(f) Reserve in Dug-outs. 1 officer & 20 O.R. 2/13th Bn.L.R.

3. Duties of Parties:-
   (a) Seizing Party.
         Starting Point: Point 4, on Sketch Map.
         Time: X.
         Objective: Far lip of Crater.
         General Instructions: The Officer Commanding this party
            will reconnoitre from Point 4 to a spot where the near
            lip of crater will probably be. He will lay a tape and
            mark the line with sticks with white tops.
                 Directly the Mine is blown he will lead his
            party to the far lip and distribute his men along it from
            Point 1 to Point 3, as shewn by dotted line where he
            will remain until he receives orders to retire from O.C.
            Consolidating Party.

   (b) & (b.1) Consolidating Party.
         Starting Point: Point 4.
         Time: Follow Party A.
         Objective: Near Lip of Crater.
         General Instructions:
              (b) will be divided into 3 parties of 4 each.
              Right party will construct Sniping Post at Point 3.
              Centre Party   ..   .. Bombing Post at Point 2.
              Left Party   ..   .. Sniping Post at Point 1.

(b.1) will construct communication trench between points 2 & 3 and will furnish two men to act as connecting files with party (a)

(c) Right Wiring Party.
This party will remain in dug-outs at top of Guillemot until ordered to move when they will proceed to point 4., and collect their stores. They will then proceed to a point 5 yards East of point 3 and erect an obstacle as shewn on sketch.

(d) Clearing Party.
Starting Point: Point 8.
Time. X.
Objective. WHITTAKERS CUTTING at Point 6.
General Instructions.
The party will divide into two parties of 4. Right Party will clear WHITTAKERS CUTTING between point 6 and 7 and afterwards to dig new trench from point 7 to point 2. Left party to clear trench from point 6 to Pulpit.

(e) Left Wiring Party.
This party will remain in dug-outs at top of STOKE STREET until ordered to move when they will proceed to left arm of WHITTAKERS CUTTING at point 5 and collect their stores. They will then proceed to a point 5 yards east of point 1 and erect an obstacle as shewn on sketch.

(f) RESERVE PARTY.
This party will be divided into two of 10 each. Right Reserve Party will remain in dug-outs at top of Guillemot and left Reserve Party in dug-outs at top of STOKE STREET where they will await orders.
50 bombs will be drawn by each party from their respective Company Bomb Stores.

4. The necessary stores will be dumped at STOKE STREET during daylight on 9th instant. When it is known at what date the mine is to be blown these stores will be taken up and placed in the positions from which they will have to be carried to crater. This will be done as soon as it is dark on the night on which it is arranged that the mine should be blown.
The stores for Right Wiring Party and A.4.d.1y.½ (near No.9 Post)
The Stores for Left Wiring Party in left arm of WHITTAKERS CUTTING A.4.d.2.2½.
Whilst the Right parties stores are being placed in position, a covering party of 6 O.R. will remain in observation and will not withdraw until they get orders from O.C., Siezing Party.

5. STRETCHER BEARERS. 8 Stretcher Bearers will be on duty at D.Coy.H.Q.

6. Artillery and Trench Mortars will co-operate Scheme attached.

7. Watches will be synchronized at 179th Brigade H.Q. at an hour which will be notified by wire numbered B.M.500.
The following will send representatives:-
O.C., Central Group R.A.
O.C., 2/13th L.R.
O.C., 2/4th Field Coy. R.E.
O.C., 175th Tunneling Coy. R.E.
O.C., 60th X.Medium Trench Mortar Battery.
O.C., 179th Light Trench Mortar Battery.

sd/ W.H.Herbert.
Major,
Brigade Major.
179th Infantry Brigade.

Copy Nos. 1 and 2 File.
3 & 4 2/13th Btn.L.R.
5 O.C., Central Group. R.A.
6. 175th Tunneling Coy. R.E.
7. 60x.M.T.M.Bty.
No.8 179th L.T.M.Battery.
9. 2/4th Field Coy.R.E.
10.

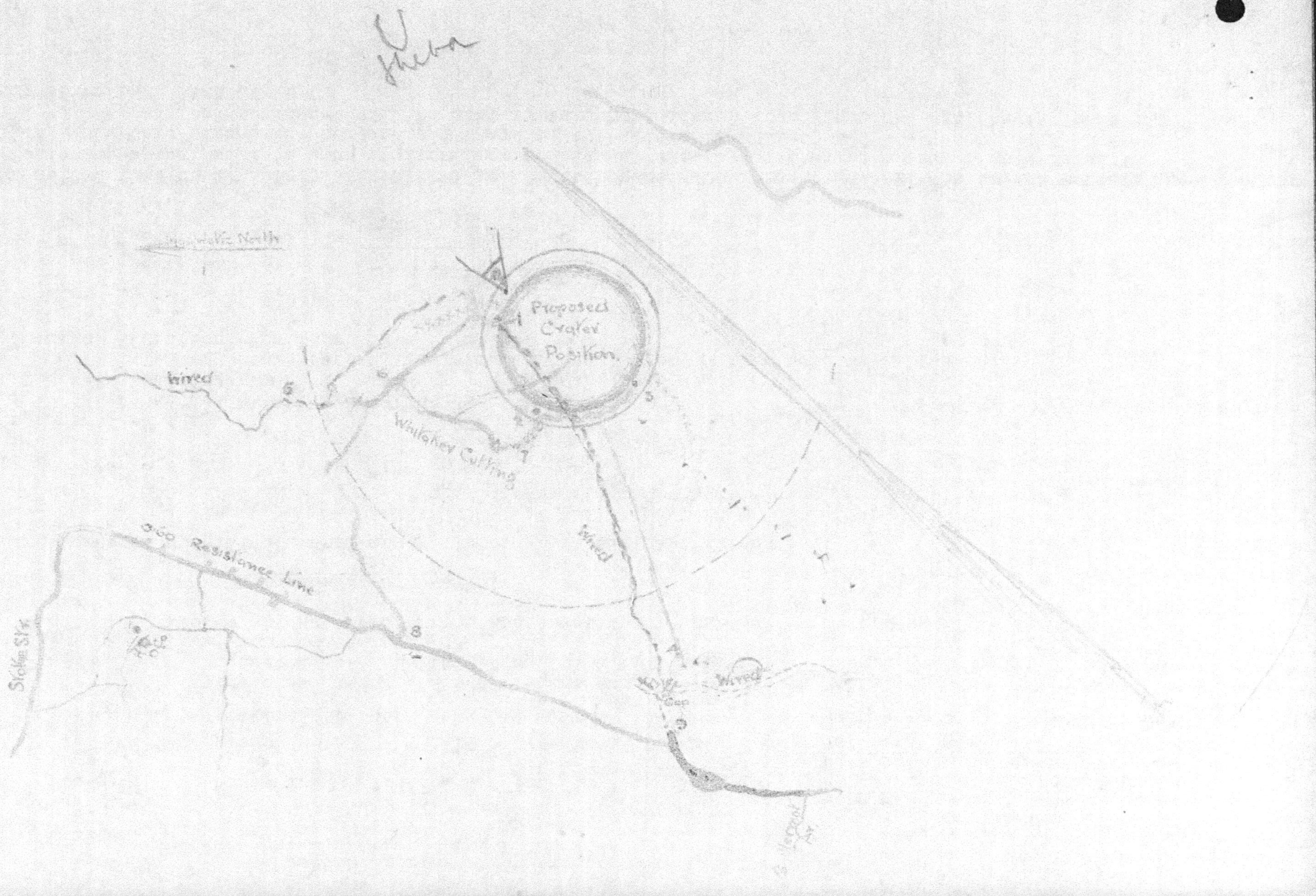
Proposed Crater Position.
Whitaker Cutting
Wired
Wired
Wired
Resistance Line
Stokes St.

Trench Mortar Programme.

	No. of guns.	Target.		Rate.	Time.
X.60 M.T.M.B.	2.	Enemy front line.	A 4 d 4.6 to A 4 d 1.9½	Rapid. Slow	X to X + 5. X+5 to X+30
	1.	Trenches	A 10 b 4.6 to A 10 b 3.½	Rapid. Slow	X to X + 5. X+5 to X+30
179 L.T.M.B.	2.	Trenches	A 4 d 5.5 and A 10 a 4.8)	Rapid.	X to X + 2.
	2.	Trenches	A 10 b 3.9½ to A 10 b 4.5 (	Slow.	X+2 to X+30

After X+30 T.M's will fire at any suitable target and endeavour to silence enemy T.M's.

ARTILLERY PROGRAMME.

Feint. The following bombardment will commence at X in order to distract attention.

X to X 5	Shrapnel	Section Fire	10 seconds	From A 10 C.9.9.1 to A 10 C.99.3.
X 5 to X 15	H.E.	"	20 "	" "
Howitzer	H.E.	"	20 "	" "

Mine. If called upon to fire only.

X to X 15	1 Section blocks Front line about A 4 d 4.5.
" "	1 Section " " " A 10 b 4.9.
" "	1 Battery searches 2nd line with shrapnell from A 10 b 6.95 to A 10 d 65.5.
X 15 onwards.	1 Section Howitzer A 4 d 35.65.
	" " A 10 b 68.70
	1 " 18 Pdrs. A 4 d 4.55.
	1 " " A 4 d 65.50 to A 4 d 65.36
	1 Battery " A 4 d 65.36 to A 4 d 65.07
	1 Section " A 4 d 65.07 to A 10b 60.95
	1 " " Block Front line A 10 b 35.95.

N.B. It has been decided that no artillery or Mortar Fire will be opened until required. If the trench mortars are required the following signal will be sent up from D coys Headquarters. A volley of 4 Very Lights fired in a westerly direction. On this signal the bombardment sheduled to begin at X will open.
If the Artillery are required a message will be sent by telephone direct from F.O.O. who will be in touch with O.C. 2/13th Battalion L.R. at D Coy H.Q.

Time Table of Operations.

11.th August, 1916.

12.30 a.m.	Mine went up.
12.34 a.m.	Messages sent to wiring parties to carry on.
12.49	Message received "The crater is taken and is being consolidated.
12.59	Report received that Lieut. Killingbak was killed.
1. 16	Right sniping post reported finished.
1. 23	R.E. with left wiring party reported wounded - shot through head.
1. 24	Party detailed for carrying pit props to bombing post reports back, having done job and been dismissed by Corporal R.E.
1. 28	Major R.E. sends another sapper to left wiring party.
1. 30	Corporal R.E. reports left bombing post finished.
1. 35	6 men from right reserve sent to complete trench.
1. 37	L/Cpl. Lawrance, C.Coy. is brought in wounded in the head.
1. 40	4 more men from right relief are sent for digging.
1. 42	Report received that left wiring party are being heavily sniped. Sapper sent in relief of wounded man has been killed by a trench mortar bomb.
1. 43	Order sent that left wiring party to come in.
1. 45	Report by Cpl. Ellis that right clearing party cannot get on as trench mortars have fallen and blown in all they have cleared.
1. 57	R.E. man brought in wounded in leg and dies. Left sniping post completed.
2. 10	Order sent for all left reserve to go and dig.
2. 14	Report received that all posts are occupied and that covering party are coming in.
2. 25	Cpl. David (Covering party) reports as above.
2. 30	Lack of diggers reported on all hands.
2. 40	Right wiring party is reported in. Orders sent to COLT B. for 10 men and 1 N.C.O. to report for digging at once.
2.55	Left wiring party reported all in.
4. 0	Orders given for all diggers to come in (getting light).
4.30	All D.Coy. men reported 'in' by Capt. Kisch.
4.50	All A.Coy. men reported 'in' by Major Hopkins.

C.M. Mackenzie Lt. Col.
Comdt 2/12th London Regt.

CONFIDENTIAL

Vol 4

WAR DIARY
of
2/13th London Regt.

From September 1st to September 30th 1916

VOLUME 9.

Army Form C. 2118

WAR DIARY
or
INTELLIGENCE SUMMARY
(Erase heading not required.)

Instructions regarding War Diaries and Intelligence Summaries are contained in F. S. Regs., Part II. and the Staff Manual respectively. Title Pages will be prepared in manuscript.

Place	Date	Hour	Summary of Events and Information	Remarks and references to Appendices
BOYAU DES ABRIS	Sept 1	4:30 a.m. to 7:30 a.m.	Operation. 2/13th Battalion London Regiment relieved 2/16th Battalion London Regiment in front line trenches. There were no casualties.	RPS
			Intermittent artillery & Trench Mortar fire all day. Gun superiority marked on both. Enemy many many Rifle Grenades. Machine guns unactive.	RPS
			Enemy Rifle Battalions up over THELUS. Our aircraft very active. Enemy aircraft unactive.	RPS
			Casualties. 3 wounded.	RPS
			Strength. Increase 1. Decrease 2.	RPS Appendix 1.
do	Sept 2		Operation. Intermittent Artillery and Trench Mortar fire all day. Gun superiority marked on both. Enemy many more M/Gun trumps but less Machine Gun activity. Fewer Flares used.	RPS
			Casualties. 1 wounded (slice show) removed at duty.	RPS
do	Sept 3		Operations. Never exchange. Enemy many more Stray shouts & Rifle Grenades. Our aircraft very active.	RPS RPS
do	Sept 4		Operations. Very quiet. Our aircraft very active.	RPS
			Casualties. 2 Wounded	RPS

WAR DIARY or INTELLIGENCE SUMMARY

(Erase heading not required.)

Army Form C. 2118

Instructions regarding War Diaries and Intelligence Summaries are contained in F.S. Regs., Part II. and the Staff Manual respectively. Title Pages will be prepared in manuscript.

Place	Date	Hour	Summary of Events and Information	Remarks and references to Appendices
BOYAU DES ABRIS	1916 Sept 4 (contd.)		Strength. 2 Decrease. 2 Increase.	R.P.S.
do	Sept 5		Operations. Fairly quiet. Enemy made a few 5.9" & 4" shells. Also a few aerial torpedoes.	Appendix 1. R.P.S.
do	Sept 6		Strength. 4 Decrease. 16 Increase. (1st Droop) Operations. Nothing to note. Casualties. 5 Wounded at return. 1 remained on Duty. Strength. 6 Decrease. 1 Increase.	R.P.S. Appendix 1. R.P.S. R.P.S. R.P.S.
BRAY	Sept 7	6 a.m. to 11 a.m.	Operation. Relieved by 2/16th Battalion London Regiment and proceeded to Rest Billets.	Appendix 1. R.P.S.
do	Sept 8		Strength. 6 Decrease. 4 Increase.	R.P.S.
do	Sept 9		Strength. 2nd Lieut W.A. DICKINSON joined the Battalion from HAVRE	Appendix 1. R.P.S.
do	Sept 11		Strength. 1 Decrease. 1 Increase.	Appendix 1. R.P.S.
BOYAU DES ABRIS	Sept 13	3 a.m. to 7 a.m.	Operation. Relieved the 2/16th Battalion London Regiment on 7 Northern Trenches. Enemy fired more heavy shells than usual. He increased our Rifle fire and checked enemy's sharpshooting.	Appendix 1. R.P.S. R.P.S.
do	Sept 14		Strength. 4 Decrease. 5 Increase. Casualty. 1 Wounded. Operations. Fairly quiet; more Machine Gun & rifle fire on our part; less enemy sharpshooting.	R.P.S. Appendix 1. R.P.S.

WAR DIARY
or
INTELLIGENCE SUMMARY
(Erase heading not required.)

Army Form C. 2

Instructions regarding War Diaries and Intelligence Summaries are contained in F. S. Regs., Part II. and the Staff Manual respectively. Title Pages will be prepared in manuscript.

Place	Date	Hour	Summary of Events and Information	Remarks and references to Appendices
BOYAU DES ABRIS	1916 Sept 14 (contd)		Casualties. 3 Wounded of whom 1 remained at Duty	RPS
			Strength. 1 Decrease	RPS appendix 1.
do	Sept 15		Operations. More activity in our Artillery & Trench Mortars. Our own Rifles have suppressed enemy sharpshooters	RPS
			Casualty. 1 Killed	RPS
			Strength. 1 Decrease	RPS appendix 1.
do	Sept 16		Operations. Nothing to report	RPS
			Casualties. 5 Wounded of whom 1 remained at Duty. 2nd Lieut. R.P. SHUTE reported for Duty from HAVRE	RPS
			Strength. 4 Decrease 1 Increase	RPS appendix 1.
do	Sept 17		Operations. Increased activity in all directions except enemy artillery which was quiet. Our aircraft active & flying very low	RPS
			Casualty. 1 Wounded	RPS
			Strength. 3 Decrease 1 Increase	RPS appendix 1.
do	Sept 18		Operations. Indented activity as yesterday	RPS
			Casualty. 1 Wounded	RPS
			Strength. 2 Decrease	RPS appendix 1.
MAISON BLANCHE	Sept 19	5 am & 7 am	Operations. Relieved by 2/16th Battalion London Regiment and went into Support	RPS
			Strength. 3 Increase	RPS appendix 1.

WAR DIARY or INTELLIGENCE SUMMARY

Army Form C. 2118

(Erase heading not required.)

Instructions regarding War Diaries and Intelligence Summaries are contained in F. S. Regs., Part II. and the Staff Manual respectively. Title Pages will be prepared in manuscript.

Place	Date	Hour	Summary of Events and Information	Remarks and references to Appendices
MAISON BLANCHE	1916 Sept 21st		Strength — 6 Officers reported (attached) as follows:- 2nd Lieut. C.M. WRIGHT from 3/22nd Battalion London Regiment 2nd Lieut. A.K. COBB " " " 2nd Lieut. F.R. FRANKLIN " " " 2nd Lieut. W.R. McQUEEN " 3/23rd " 2nd Lieut. J.A. SUTHERLAND " 3/24th " 2nd Lieut. O.K. HARDY " " " 2 Decrease	RPS RPS Appendix 1.
			Appointment. Capt R.P. GLADSTONE to be Adjutant vice Capt W.E. DAVID-DEVIS (to Regimental Duty) to date from Aug 4th 1916. (D.A.G. List No 99)	RPS
do.	Sept 22		Strength — 3 Officers reported as follows:- Posted 2nd Lieut. J.C.G. RAINGER from HAVRE 2nd Lieut. G.S. BLADON " " 2nd Lieut. L.J.C. YEO from 3/23rd Battalion London Regiment attached 7 Decrease 3 Increase 1 Decrease 1 Increase	RPS RPS Appendix 1. RPS
do.	Sept 23rd		Strength Operations Relieved 2/16th Battalion London Regiment in Front line Trenches	RPS Appendix 1.
BOYAU DES ABRIS	Sept 25	6 a.m. to 8.30 a.m.	Fairly general activity.	
			Strength 1 Decrease 1 Increase	RPS Appendix 1.

Army Form C. 2118

WAR DIARY
or
INTELLIGENCE SUMMARY
(Erase heading not required.)

Instructions regarding War Diaries and Intelligence Summaries are contained in F.S. Regs., Part II. and the Staff Manual respectively. Title Pages will be prepared in manuscript.

Place	Date	Hour	Summary of Events and Information	Remarks and references to Appendices
BOYAU DES ABRIS	Sept 26th 1916		Operations: Little activity, all on our side.	RPS
			Strength: 1 Increase	RPS / Appendix 1.
do	Sept 27th		Operations: Enemy used new heavy Trench Mortar. Otherwise fairly quiet.	RPS
			Casualties: 1 Killed 1 Wounded	RPS
			(2nd Lieut. M.C.K. BAMBER invalided to England sick (14th Sept 1916))	RPS
			Strength: 6 Decrease	RPS / Appendix 1.
do	Sept 28th		Operations: Generally quiet but commenced increase in our rifle fire at enemy working parties and patrols. Some enemy sharpshooting.	RPS
			Casualty: 1 Wounded	RPS
			2nd Lieut E.J. SMITH reported for duty from HAVRE	RPS
			Strength: 2 Decrease	RPS / Appendix 1.
do	Sept 29th		Operations: Generally quiet with a few intervals when new heavy Trench mortars came over from the enemy. Many flares up at night.	RPS
do	Sept 30th		Operations: Generally quiet. Three enemy aeroplanes flew low along our front but retired before our Lewis Gun Rifle fire. A few new heavy trench mortar shells came over.	RPS
			Strength: 1 Decrease. 5 Increase (Draft from 13th (Reserve Battalion))	RPS / Appendix 1.

C.H. MacCurrie
Lieut. Colonel,
Commanding 2/13 Bn London Regt.

Regimental No., Rank, and Name.	Sqdn., Batty., or Co.	APPENDIX I. Particulars of Casualties, etc., and Date.			
1/9/16					
5031 Private Howe E.	C	Shell Shock		1	2 925
5053 " Leymann W.H.	D	Wounded in Action			
2/9/16 3304 Cox	B	RETURNED FROM CCS			
5457 " Thrussell H.C.	C	Shell Shock (Remained at Duty)			925
3/9/16 Nil.					925
4/9/16					
4806 Pte. Slade R.	D	Wounded in Action			
5729 L/C Lane F.C.	D	" "		2	2 925
5268 Pte. Gingell H.C.	D	Returned from Cas. Clg. Stat.			
5031 " Howe E.	C	" "			
5/9/16					
Reinforcement of 16 men		Taken on strength		16	4 937
1495 L/C Reading L.A.	D	Sent 42nd. C.C.S.			
4393 Pte Chatham G.	A	" "			
3522 " Oxborrow W.A.	D	" "			
5079 " Lucas E.	D	Sent to 30th. "			
6/9/16					
5816 Pte. Gurnett N.A.	B	Wounded in action			
5812 " Pattison H.B.	B	" "			
5795 " Parish J.A.	B	" "			
4915 " Westlake R.	D	" "		1	6 932
5141 " Cornish T.F.	D	" " (Remained at Duty)			
5729 L/C Lane F.C.	D	Sent 30th. Cas. Clg. Stat.			
5819 Pte. Withall W.	B	" 42nd. " "			
3708 Pte Harper F.G.	C	Returned to duty from Cas. Clg. Stat.			
7/9/16 Nil.					932
8/9/16					
5819 Pte. Withall W.	B	Returned to duty from Cas. Clg. Stat.			
2896 " Cundy L.	A	" "			
3848 " Carter F.G.	A	" "			
4806 " Slade R.	D	" "		4	6 930
2327 L/Sgt. Bury E.J.	A	)Sent Base Depot. Medically Unfit. A.D.M.S			
2703 Dmr. Cohen S.	C	)letter M767 dated 6/9/16.			
4969 Pte. Trevethick J.B.	B	)			
2061 Cpl. Adkin A.W.	B	Commissioned(Posted to a Cadet School) Auth. 3rd. Echelon C.R. 35736/8/B, 6/9/16.			
3385 Pte. Whiting A.V.	D	)Sent Base Depot, Under age. Auth. D.A.G.			
2298 " StVincent C.	D	)Wires A.G. 466 and R.Y. 465, 7/9/16.			
9/9/16 Nil					930
10/9/16					
3824 Pte. Edwards	C	Sent Base Depot, Under Age. Auth. D.A.G. Wire A.2527		1	1 930
2423 " Bibby H.B.	C	Returned to duty from Cas. Clg. Stat.			
13/9/16					
2555 Sgt. Bowman H.McD.	D	Wounded in action			
4564 Pte. Newton	B	Sent to 42nd. C.C. Stat.			
3064 " Hyatt C.	D	Sent Base Depot, Underage. Auth. D.A.G. Wire		4	926
5957 " Walker B.	B	Transferred Field Survey Coy (A.G. 589) (Auth. 60th. London Div. Letter A/1086/3a			

Regimental No., Rank, and Name.	Sqdn., Batty., or Co.	Particulars of Casualties, etc., and Date.		
13/9/16 (Cont.)				
5812 Pte. Pattison H.B.	B	Returned to Div. Area from Cas. Clg. Stat.		
5079 " Lucas H.	D	"		
1495 L/Cl. Reading L.A.	D	"		
6075 Pte. Cohen L.W.	C	"	5	95
3586 " Scott A.J.	C	"		
14/9/16				
2453 Pte. Walden F.H.	C	Wounded in Action.		
5692 Pte. Pain T.W.H.	C	" "		
3833 Pte. Allen L.R.D.	D	" " (Remained at Duty)		
5681 L/C. Landless F.	C	Sent 30th. C.C. Stat.		
5141 Pte. Cornish F.F.	C	" 42nd. "		
5714 Pte. Dickens G.E.	D	" 30th. "	7	92
3166 Pte. Best H.C.	A	" " "		
3944 Pte. Crouch W.F.	D	Sent Base Depot, Under age. Auth. D.A.G. Wire A.G.837, 13/9/16.		
15/9/16				
5652 Pte. Aldous W.R.	C	Killed in action.	1	92
16/9/16.				
5240 Pte. Saunders A.C.	A	Wounded in Action		
5252 Pte. Freshwater G.	C	"		
4672 Pte Root J.F.	C	" (Since Died of Wounds)		
3778 " Cutting A.H.	A	"	1 4	92
5116 " Dammerill W.C.	C	" (Remained at Duty)		
1663 " Hollier F.W.	B	Reinforcement.		
17/9/16				
5777 Pte. Robinson F.E.	A	Wounded in Action.		
4872 " Munday R.E.	D	Sent 42nd. Cas. Clg. Stat.		
2423 " Bibby H.B.	C	" 30th. "	1 3	91
4064 " Newton F.S.	B	Returned to Div. Area from C.C. Stat.		
18/9/16				
5827 Pte. Sparks J.H.	D	Wounded in Action		
3554 Pte. Wright M.B.	C	Sent 42nd. Cas. Clg. Stat.	2	91
19/9/16				
4318 Pte. Taylor T.W.	B	Reinforcement		
1652 " Booth. P.C.	B	"	3	91
3522 " Oxborrow W.A.	B	Returned to Div. Area from C.C.S.		
20/9/16				
5160 Pte. Mockel E.	C	Sent Base Depot, German parentage.	2	91
3949 Pte Cook F.	C	" " " Under age.		
21/9/16				
Nil				
22/9/16				
3446 Pte. Ison E.	B	Sent 42nd. Cas. Clg. Stat.		
6 Other Ranks transferred to		179th. Machine Gun Coy.		
2555 Serg. Bowman H.McD.	D	Returned to Div. Area from Cas. Clg. Stat.	3 7	91
5714 Pte. Dickens G.E.	D	" "		
5141 " Cornish T.F.	C	" "		
23/9/16				
5564 Cpl. Gedge. E.E.	C	Sent to 30th. C.C. Stat.		
5784 Pte. Parsons T.	A	Returned to duty from Base Depot.	1 1	91
25/9/16				
5690 Pte. Norrish R.S.	B	Sent 42nd. C.C. Stat.		
3778 Pte. Cutting A.C.	A	Return to duty in Div Area from C.C. Stat	1 1	91

Regimental No., Rank, and Name.	Sqdn., Batty., or Co.	Particulars of Casualties, etc., and Date. (3)			
26/9/16					914
3837 Pte. Sparkes J.H.	D	Returned to duty in Div.Area from C.C.Stat.	1		
27/9/16					
3696 Pte. Sherwood G.	C	Killed in action			
3622 Pte. Gimber W.E.	B	Wounded in action.			
3096 Pte. Craggs J.W.	B	Invalided to England (Sick)			
3968 Pte. Knight E.	C	" " "			
5691 Pte. Ochs H.S.	C	Sent 30th.C.C.Stat	6		908
5733 " McCormack C.	D	" "			
28/9/16					
5156 Pte. Eady J.A.	C	Wounded in action.			
3926 Pte State F	D	Sent 42nd.C.C.Stat.	2		906
29/9/16					
Nil.					
30/9/16					
5563 L/C. Bull	A	Sent to C.C.Stat.	5	1	910

5 men sent as reinforcement from Havre.

Officer Commanding or Adjutant.

2/13th A.I.F Bn. E.E.F.

Vol 5

CONFIDENTIAL
WAR DIARY

From 1st to 31st October 1916

WAR DIARY
or
INTELLIGENCE SUMMARY
(Erase heading not required.)

Army Form C. 211

Instructions regarding War Diaries and Intelligence Summaries are contained in F. S. Regs., Part II. and the Staff Manual respectively. Title Pages will be prepared in manuscript.

Place	Date	Hour	Summary of Events and Information	Remarks and references to Appendices
BOYAU DES ABRIS	1916 Oct 1.	5 a.m. to 9 a.m.	Operation. The Battalion was relieved in Front line Trenches by the 2/1.5 Battalion London Regiment and proceeded to Rear Bivies at BRAY. 2nd Lieut. L.G. Carroll reported for duty from 13th (Reserve) Batt. Lond. Reg.	RPS RPS Appendix 1
BRAY	Oct 3		Strength. 1 Increase 2 Decrease	RPS Appendix 1
do	Oct 4		Strength. 1 Increase	RPS Appendix 1
do	Oct 5		Leave. Lt. Col. C.M. MacKenzie went on leave from Oct 5th to 12th inclusive and Major S. Thompson assumed command.	RPS
do	Oct 6		Operation. Inspection by Lieut-General Sir Charles Fergusson, Commanding XVIIth Corps.	RPS
			Strength. 2 Increase 4 Decrease	RPS Appendix 1
do	Oct 7	2.30pm & 7.30pm	Operations. The Battalion relieved the 2/15 Battalion London Regiment in the Front line Trenches, Centre II. No casualties during Relief. Our artillery quiet. Intermittent sweeping of T.M. fire.	RPS
			Strength. Second Lieut. M.S. Hoysack reported for duty from 13th (Reserve) Batt. London Regiment.	RPS Appendix 1
BOYAU DES ABRIS	Oct 8		Operations. Our artillery called upon for retaliation on several occasions owing to hostile enemy T.M. activity Trenchards. Enemy made considerable use of Stokes Mortars & Rifle Grenades	RPS

WAR DIARY
or
INTELLIGENCE SUMMARY
(Erase heading not required.)

Army Form C. 2118

Instructions regarding War Diaries and Intelligence Summaries are contained in F. S. Regs., Part II. and the Staff Manual respectively. Title Pages will be prepared in manuscript.

Place	Date	Hour		Summary of Events and Information	Remarks and references to Appendices
BOYAU DES ABRIS	1916 Oct 8		Casualties	3 Wounded of whom 1 remained at duty.	RPS Appendix 1.
			Strength	2 Increase 1 Decrease	
do	Oct 9		Operations	Our artillery materially active in futile efforts to check T.M. activity. Enemy bombardment 3 p.m. to 4 p.m. temporarily stopped this activity but it soon started again.	RPS
			Casualties	1 Wounded & missing believed killed, outside our wire on patrol. 1 Wounded remained at duty.	RPS Appendix 1.
			Strength	9 Decrease	
do	Oct 10		Operations	Our artillery bombarded enemy lines in conjunction with T.M.S. Enemy howr ascendant on T.M.S. Aerial Torpedos, Rifle Grenades & Stokey trench. Our retaliation was mostly ineffective. 2nd Lieut W.A. Etchells evacuated to European sick (29th Sept 1916)	RPS
			Strength	Increase 3 Decrease 2.	RPS
do	Oct 11	2 a.m 5 a.m	Operations	Enemy bombarded our lines South of Thelus Road for 45 minutes. Enemy raided our lines next to left company front. The raid was repulsed and one wounded and one wounded prisoner were taken.	RPS Appendix 2.
			Casualties	3 Killed 20 Wounded of whom 2 have since died of wounds + 2 remained at duty.	RPS

WAR DIARY or INTELLIGENCE SUMMARY

Army Form C. 2118

(Erase heading not required.)

Instructions regarding War Diaries and Intelligence Summaries are contained in F.S. Regs., Part II. and the Staff Manual respectively. Title Pages will be prepared in manuscript.

Place	Date	Hour	Summary of Events and Information	Remarks and references to Appendices
BOYAU DES ABRIS	1916 Oct 11th (cont)		Casualties (contd) Capt J. R. Rozelaar wounded. Lieut I. Range wounded and remained at duty.	RPS Appendix 1.
do	Oct 12th		Strength 2½ Decrease	RPS
			Operations Fairly quiet day	RPS Appendix 1.
			Casualties 1 Killed	
			Strength 1 Increase 1 Decrease	
do	Oct 13th	5 am 15 7.30 am	Operations The Battalion was relieved by the 2/16th Battalion London Regiment and moved into Support. There were no casualties on Relief.	RPS
MAISON BLANCHE	Oct 14th		Strength Increase 11. (8 men reported from No 7 Infantry Base Depot Havre)	RPS Appendix 1
do	Oct 15th		Casualties 1 Wounded	RPS Appendix 1
			Strength 2 Increase 6 Decrease	
do	Oct 16th		Strength Major P. A. Hopkins evacuated to England, sick. (18 Oct 1916) 2nd Lieut R. J. Benton and 2nd Lieut J. P. Savage taken on strength having been granted Commissions from the Ranks.	RPS Appendix 1.

1875 Wt. W593/826 1,000,000 4/15 J.B.C. & A. A.D.S.S./Forms/C. 2118.

Army Form C. 2118

WAR DIARY or INTELLIGENCE SUMMARY

(Erase heading not required.)

Instructions regarding War Diaries and Intelligence Summaries are contained in F.S. Regs., Part II. and the Staff Manual respectively. Title Pages will be prepared in manuscript.

Place	Date	Hour	Summary of Events and Information	Remarks and references to Appendices
MAISON BLANCHE (cont.)	1916 Oct 16th (cont.)		Strength (cont.) 94 Increase (Draft from 13th (Reserve) Battalion London Regiment) 2 Decrease	RPS Appendix 1.
do	Oct 17th		Strength 7 Decrease	RPS Appendix 1.
do	Oct 18th		Strength 2nd Lieut. K.S. Carroll joined for duty from 13th (Reserve) London Regiment. 1 Increase	RPS RPS Appendix 1.
do	Oct 19th	4.30 to 7 am	Operation The Battalion relieved the 21/6th Battalion London Regiment in front line trenches. No casualties occurred during relief. Casualties 3 Killed 1 Wounded Strength 4 Decrease 1 Increase	RPS RPS Appendix 1. RPS Appendix 1.
BOYAU DES ABRIS	Oct 20th		Operation Our artillery more active, enemy artillery very quiet. Enemy Medium Trench Mortars fairly active. 2" Trench Mortars & Stokes retaliated but were quite ineffective. Enemy aeroplane brought down in his own lines by Lewis gun fire. Considerable damage to our trenches done by Enemy Medium Trench Mortars. Casualties 1 Wounded Strength 1 Decrease 3 Increase	RPS RPS Appendix 1.

Army Form C. 2118

WAR DIARY
or
INTELLIGENCE SUMMARY
(Erase heading not required.)

Instructions regarding War Diaries and Intelligence Summaries are contained in F. S. Regs., Part II. and the Staff Manual respectively. Title Pages will be prepared in manuscript.

Place	Date	Hour	Summary of Events and Information	Remarks and references to Appendices
BOYAU DES ABRIS	1916 Oct 21st		Operations — Sniper activity on both sides by artillery. Enemy mainly active with medium trench mortars. Our Stokes & trench Mortar retaliation still ineffective. Enemy aeroplanes far more active than formerly.	RPS
			Casualties — 2 wounded	RPS Appendix 1.
			Strength — 3 Decrease	
do	Oct 22nd		Operations — Enemy artillery slightly more active, otherwise the normal artillery and trench mortar activity. More aeroplane activity on both sides.	RPS
			Casualties — 3 wounded	RPS
			Strength — 5 Decrease	RPS Appendix 1.
do	Oct 23rd		Operations — Usual intermittent artillery and trench Morton exchanges. Aircraft usually inactive.	RPS
			Casualties — 1 wounded and or duty	RPS Appendix 1.
			Strength — 2 Decrease	
do	Oct 24th	7.30 p.m.	Operations — The Battalion was relieved in front line Trenches by 43rd Battalion Canadian Infantry. No casualties occurred on relief. The Battalion proceeded on relief to BOIS DES ALLEUX	RPS
		10.15 p.m.		

Appendice n° I

Army Form C. 2118

WAR DIARY
or
INTELLIGENCE SUMMARY
(Erase heading not required.)

Instructions regarding War Diaries and Intelligence Summaries are contained in F. S. Regs., Part II. and the Staff Manual respectively. Title Pages will be prepared in manuscript.

Place	Date	Hour	Summary of Events and Information	Remarks and references to Appendices
BOIS DES ALLEUX	1916 Oct 26	9 a.m.	Operation. The Battalion moved to SAVY	R.P.S.
		1 p.m.	Strength 12 Increase	R.P.S. Appendix 1.
SAVY	Oct 27	9 a.m.	Operation. The Battalion moved to BUNEVILLE and PETIT HOUVIN.	R.P.S.
		2 p.m.		
BUNEVILLE	Oct 28	8.30 a.m.	Operation. The Battalion moved to BOFFLES and NOEUX	R.P.S.
		2.30 p.m.		
NOEUX	Oct 29	8 a.m.	Operation. The Battalion moved to PROUVILLE	R.P.S.
		12.30 p.m.		
PROUVILLE	Oct 30		Strength 1 Increase 2 Bcrews	R.P.S. Appendix 1.
PROUVILLE	Oct 31		Strength 2nd Lieut. E. MOONEY reported for duty from 13th (Reserve) Battalion London Regiment.	R.P.S. Appendix 1.

C. M. MacKenzie
Lieut. Col. Commanding
2/13 (Bn?) Lon Regt

Regimental No., Rank, and Name.	Sqdn., Batty., or Co.	Particulars of Casualties, etc., and Date	STRENGTH		
			Inc.	Dec.	Total
3/10/16					
208 C.S.Murray G.S.	A	Sent to Base Depot.Auth. 60th.Div.letter A/1413/2			
5846 Pte.Evans A.C.	D	Sent to 30t.Cas.Clg.Stat.		2	908
5156 Pte.Eady J.A.	C	Returned from Cas.Clg.Stat.	1		909
4/10/16					
4470 Pte.Schueler C.E.	C	Returned from Cas.Clg.Stat.	1		910
6/10/16					
5846 Pte.Evans A.C.	D	do			
5691 Pte.Ochs H.S.	C	do	2		
3814 Pte.Wallace R.	C	Sent 30th.Cas.Clg.Stat.			
3978 Pte.Barton C.W.	D	Sent Base Under Age.			
5573 Pte.Catling H.S.	A	To Cadet School(3rd.Army 775AMS)			
5628 Pte.Thorn H.L.	B	" (9/Ldn R/5736.T.F.3)		4	908
8/10/16					
5733 Pte.McCormick	D	Returned from Cas.Clg.Stat.			
5690 " Norrish R.S	C	do	2		
3566 L/Cpl.Shaw F.R.	C	Wounded in action			
5794 Pte.Wicks G.S	C	do			
5515 Pte.Hare A.M.	C	Sent 42nd.Cas.Clg.Stat.			
3813 Pte.Parrish J.H.	C	do		4	906
9/10/16					
3904 Cpl.Thompson R.	C	Wounded & Missing,beld.killed			
2634 L/Sgt.King G.	C	Sent to 30th.Cas.Clg.Stat.			
5699 L/C.Thom F.	C	do			
5627 Pte.Parfitt J.W.D.	B	do			
3571 Pte.Cook L.G.	B)	Sent to Base Depot,Medically			
3687 Pte.Austin A.E.	C)	Unfit for service in the			
5085 Pte.Williams A.	C)	Firing Line (Auth.A.D.M.S.60th.			
4886 Pte.Sparrow E.	D)	Division M.1022,5/10/16)		9	897
4537 Pte.Meacham C.G.	D)				
10/10/16					
3926 Pte.State F.	C	Returned to Divl.Area			
5699 L/C Thom F.G.	C	from Cas.Clg.Stats.			
3814 Pte Wallace R.	C	do	3		
5810 Pte.Elphick S.C.	C	To Cas.Clg.Stat.			
5594 Pte.Reavell G.E.	A	To a Cadet School(Auth.C.R. No.38357/1/3 dated 6/10/16)		2	898
11/11/16					
5839 Pte.Maggs E	B	Killed in Action			
4560 " DeBeaupre R.	A	"			
4456 L/C.Wilcockson A	A	"			
3028 L/Serg.Harper H.E.	B	Wounded in action			
5250 Pte.Leach H.	A	"			
5309 L/C. Clark E.W.	A	"			
3036 Sgt Simon J.B.	A	"			
2632 L/Serg.Barham R.H.	A	"			
2356 L/C.Roberts S.	A	"			
4394 Pte.Vannables	A	"			
5239 Pte.Tarbin E.G.	A	"			
5588 " Mathams S.M.	A	"			
4036 " Andrews W.F.	A	"			
5572 " Carr D.V.	A	"			
5934 " Harris F.G.	A	"			

Regimental No., Rank, and Name.	Sqdn., Batty., or Co.	Particulars of Casualties, etc., and Date.		
11/10/16 Continued:-				
5761 Pte. Landrey S.G.	A	Wounded in action.		
5775 Pte. Jackson W.E.	A	"		
5790 L/Cpl. Moore A.J.	B	"		
1390 Pte. Bull W.F.	B	"		
3523 Pte. Adey F.E.	B	"		
5789 Pte. Brook E.	A	"		
2818 Pte. Tynan W.D.	B	Sent to 30th Cas.Clng.Stn.		
3685 Pte. Cocks J.	B	"		
5727 Pte. Kyte N.D.	D	Transferred to 1st Artists Rifles Authority:- C.R.34869/a.	24	874
12/10/16.				
4972 Pte. Bevan F.	C	Killed in action.	1	
3813 Pte. Parish J.H.	C	Returned from Cas.Clng.Stn.	1	874
14/10/16.				
3642 Pte. Phillips S.	C	Returned from No.7 Inf.Base Depot.		
5809 Pte. Stebbing G.E.	B	"		
3992 Pte. Middleton G.	C	"		
5777 Pte. Robinson F.S.	A	"		
5564 Cpl. Gedge H.E.	C	"		
5845 Pte. Green W.U.	D	"		
4872 Pte. Munday E.A.	D	"		
5567 L/Cpl. Scantlebury C.W.	A	"		
2634 L/Segt. King G.	C	Returned from Cas.Clng.Stn.		
5627 Pte. Parfitt J.H.D.	D	"		
2818 Pte. Tynan W.D.	B	"	11	885
15/10/16.				
5027 Pte. Wicks T.G.	C	Returned from Cas.Clng.Stn.		
3685 Pte. Cocks H.	B	"	2	
5649 Pte. McClelland W.H.	B	To Cas.Clng.Stn.		
5670 Pte. Ernst R.S.	C	"		
4995 Pte. Wager G.	B	"		
5559 Segt. Meyer C.G.	A	"		
5811 Pte. Snowden G.N.	B	"		
5825 Pte. Neal G.N.	B	"	6	881
16/10/16.				
5556 Segt. Benbow L.J.	A	(Granted Commission.to this unit. (Authority - Adj.General A/18082		
5596 L/Cpl. Savage J.P.	A	(13.10.16 & G.H.Q.M.S.510/9462 of (2.10.16.		
Major P.A.Hopkins.	A	Invalided to England.	3	
Sec.Lieut.L.J.Benbow	D	Granted commission to this unit.		
Sec.Lieut.J.P.Savage	B	"		
Draft (See separate list)		From 3rd Line.	96	974
17/10/16.				
3816 Pte. Barnes J.W.	A	To Cas.Clng.Stn.		
5557 Segt. Cutmore H.E.	A	Sent to Cadet School.for Training.		

Officer Commanding *or* Adjutant.

Regimental No., Rank, and Name.	Sqdn., Batty., or Co.	Particulars of Casualties, etc., and Date.		
17/10/16. Continued.				
2038 Sgt. Hallam F J	C	Sent to Cadet School for Training.		
2385 Sgt. Swift A.	C	"		
4006 Sgt. Mortlock W.K.	D	Authority "Divl. Letter A.439 of 15.10.16.		
2538 Sgt. R.D. Wills	A			
5623 Cpl. Groom H.S.	B	"	7	967
18/10/16.				
Sec. Lieut. L.G. Carrol	B	Joined for duty.		
3992 Pte. Middleton G.	C	Returned from Cas.Clng.Stn.	2	969
19/10/16.				
5133 Pte. Cowland J.T.	A	Killed in action.		
5259 Pte. Hoddy A.	A	"		
5251 Pte. Hardwick J.A.	C	"		
3577 Pte. Nicholls J.	C	Wounded in action.	4	4
5934 Pte. Harris G.F.	A	Returned from Cas.Clng.Stn.	1	966
20/10/16.				
3307 L/Cpl Briggs	B	Reinforcements from Base Depot.		
5456 Pte. Billing W.E.	B	"		
4573 Pte. Price D.D.	B	"	3	
5978 Pte. Holder H.C.	B	Wounded in action.	1	968
21/10/16.				
3885 Pte. King L.	A	Sent to England Sick.		
3781 Pte. Frederick J.	C	Wounded in action.		
4310 L/Sgt. Prior S.A.	B	"	3	965
22/10/16.				
5682 Pte. Lavers A.E.	C	Wounded in action.		
2674 Sgt. Hardy W.J.	C	"		
5697 Pte. Shaw L.H.	C	"		
3456 Pte. Ross H.	B	To Cas. Clng. Stn.		
3553 Pte. Hopkins C.J.	C	"	5	960
23/10/16.				
1652 Pte. Booth H.C.	B	To Cas.Clng.Stn.		
5617 Pte. Nowell V.	B	"	2	958
28/10/16.				
5682 Pte. Lavers A.E.	C	Returned from Cas.Clng.Stn.		
5670 Pte. Ernst R.S.	C	"		
4995 Pte. Wager G.	B	"		
5564 Cpl. Gedge H.E.	C	"		
3992 Pte. Middleton G.	C	"		
3577 Pte. Nicholls J.	C	"		
3566 L/Cpl. Shaw F.L.	C	"		
4872 Pte. Munday R.	D	"		
5649 Pte. McClelland W H	B	"		
5559 Sgt. Meyer C.G.	B	"		
5811 Pte. Snowden G.N.	B	"		
1652 Pte. Booth H.C.	B	"	12	970

30/10/16.				
4310 L/Segt. Prior S.A.	B	Returned from Cas.Clng.Stn.	1	
4647 Pte. Brooks J.	A	Wounded accidental.		
5634 Pte. Cripps P.	B	Granted Commission Authority- W.O.Letter 9/Generl.No.4923/ S.D.3 C. dated 10.9.16.	2	969
31/10/16.				
Sec.Lieut. E.Mooney	C	Joined for duty from 3rd Line. Authority,- Divl.letter A/1034/ 71 dated 24.10.16.	1	970.

Captain & Adjutant,
2/13th Battn. London Regt.

Roll of Draft to be attached to ~~XXXX~~ Coy

5429	Pte	Andrews J.	5971	Pte.	Arpthorpe R.F.
5464	"	Brewer F.E.	6013	"	Burns D.
6008	"	Broad H.	5386	"	Croft W.W.
5499	"	Edgar D.J.	5435	"	Hall E.
5510	"	Jolliffe T.A.	5983	"	Last E.J.
5462	"	Rayson A.	6024	"	Tiplady F.S.
6033	"	Woods E.W.	2278	L/Sgt.	Alsop H.C.P.
5463	"	Bowles H.J.	5960	Pte.	Bacon J.T.
5961	"	Cadby E.T.	6006	"	Cowdray H.G.
6001	"	Ford F.G.	5414	"	Gilliver D.A.
5495	"	Hughes W.E.	4828	"	Hyams I.
5461	"	Jacobs L.	5503	"	Kemp R.
5937	"	De Keyser H.	5473	"	Lynch J.P.
5524	"	Ryall F.	5962	"	Stevens J.R.

5532 Pte. Vercoe E.D.

6014 Pte Connell J.   6019 Pte Clare W.W.

Roll of Draft to be attached to "B" Coy.

3967	L/cpl.	Tester A.E.	6005	Pte.	Gough C.H.
5511	Pte.	Harrison J.E.	5605	"	Knocker H.A.
5501	"	Lawrance S.	6011	"	McGregor J.
5484	"	Spittle W.J.	6000	"	Smith W.
5969	"	Whiteway L.H.	5977	"	Stroud C.V.
6016	"	Anderton W.C.	5402	"	Carlisle R.H.
6012	"	Hillier W.R.	5978	"	Holder H.C.
5996	"	Beachey G.H.	4897	"	Ramm H.J.
6018	"	Rees R.	5431	"	Tricker H.J.
5504	"	Wallace R.E.	5975	"	Weston A.J.

5974 Pte. Alston J.A.

Roll of Draft to be attached to "C" Coy.

24	Sgt.	Haynes R.H.	5397	Pte.	Flanders J.B.
5020	Pte.	French V.T.A.	4963	"	Garwood P.
5164	"	Hamserton C.J.	5390	"	Maguire C.
4030	"	Mowson W.	5538	"	Richmond P.
5380	"	Smith R.W.	5099	"	Style H.G.
5067	"	Tyson G.	5134	"	Armon P.H.A.
5131	"	Cloake H.	5537	"	Farrell M.J.
3546	"	Fletcher T.	3553	"	Hopkins C.J. x
3763	"	Smith W.H.	4911	"	Smith W.
4958	"	Stagg T.	5998	"	Watkins H.

2044 Pte. Watts L.A.

x This man's conduct sheet is not yet to hand.

Roll of draft to be attached to "D" Coy.

6021	Pte.	Chance W.J.	5144	Pte.	Dean A.
5103	"	Hamshere W.	4533	"	Johncock A.
4522	"	North A.	6015	"	Palmer F.B.
5991	"	Randall C.H.	5149	"	Spring G.F.
5685	"	Walker R.B.R.	5437	"	Wyatt L.
5151	"	Waring W.A.	1318	L/cpl.	Prior W.H.
5112	"	Clark H.G.	5127	Pte.	Double E.P.
5087	"	Lloyd W.	3897	"	Miles A.C.
3742	"	Moon W.J.	4497	"	Moran J.C. x
5114	"	Page H.V.	4956	"	Smith H.

5138 Pte. Whitehouse P.

x This man's conduct sheet is not yet to hand.

APPENDIX 2

From:- Officer Commanding.
2/13th Battn. London Regiment.

To :- 179th Infantry Brigade.
Advanced Headquarters.

11th October, 1916.
Ref:- T.D.2

11th Oct 1916

On receipt of your B.M.97 of the 10th instant, I ordered O.C., Companies in the Firing Line to send out listening posts and arrange for these posts to give immediate warning if there were any enemy movements towards our observation line. I ordered the garrisons at MOSCOP and IVY to be prepared to send up reinforcements immediately on receipt of messages from any one of the Companies in the Firing Line, and report at once to me what action (if any) had been taken. The LEWIS GUN OFFICER was warned to have his team on the alert and to co-operate with the Companies. He had Lewis Guns in position to bring cross fire on the enemy's side of the Pulpit Crater.

2.0 A.M.
At 2 a.m. the enemy opened with Heavy Trench Mortars and damaged the Firing Line of the Sub-Sector and the Support Line. This action continued until 2.45 a.m. No other enemy action was taken during this period.

4.15 A.M.
At 4.15 a.m. a party of about 12 Germans was seen west of SHEBA'S BREASTS and dispersed by the Lewis Gun in STOKE STREET.

5.0 A.M.
At 5 a.m. the enemy put up a barrage on our Firing Line and Support Line with 77 m.m.s. and 4.2 hows. and severely damaged them. Shortly after 5 a.m. two parties - estimated numbers, 15 each - came round the north side of the crater and over our near lip respectively and entered the saps, but were driven off, leaving 2 dead, 1 wounded prisoner and 1 unwounded prisoner. During their retirement, several of the enemy were wounded and <u>four or five</u> killed.

The following is the report from O.C., Company holding the crater :-

The post in the right arm was held by 2 men on the crater, two men half way down the sap and 4 men and an N.C.O. at the post near the firing line. The enemy (about 15 in number) was first seen by the half way post coming over the near lip and were fired at. One of the men at this post was wounded and the other man retired on the reserve party on observing 5 men entering the sap near his post. The enemy followed him up, but on being bombed by the men at the post, they retired up the sap and on being pursued, were found to have disappeared. The post in the PULPIT CRATER SAP near the mine shaft had two men posted on the crater above the mine shaft and the rest of the post just below the mine shaft. They saw a party of the enemy come from the direction of SHEBA'S BREASTS and cross the north edge of the crater. The sap guard fired, and some of the enemy made a detour and came round the left of the post. Two of the enemy were killed and eventually brought in. One wounded man and one unwounded man were captured. The guard in the short sap north of the PULPIT CRATER SAP saw Germans approach from the enemy wire and immediately afterwards our Lewis Gun in STOKE STREET opened fire. About a dozen Germans approached the post and bombed it. One of the Germans got into the sap and was killed. The rest of the party were driven off.

CONTD:-

-2-

Cont'd:-

6.10 A.M.	The enemy barrage lifted about 6.10 a.m. During the bombardment, our Hows., 18 prs. & Stokes Gun were active.

No other portion of our line was attacked, but the enemy Trench Mortar and Sling Bomb fire killed two men and wounded six in the Long Sap and Lichfield Sap. All our men are accounted for, and none were taken prisoners.

I regret to say that the O.C., Company (Captain F.R.Roseveur) holding the PULPIT was wounded. This officer had made careful and adequate arrangements on receipt of my orders and his Company successfully beat off the raiding party. The other casualties during the enemy's raid are as under :-

2/13th Battn. London Regt..Other ranks killed...2
                            Other ranks wounded.18
2/15th Battn. London Regt..Other ranks killed...1
                            Other ranks wounded..2

I wish to draw special attention to the coolness and efficiency of No.5596 Lance-Corporal Savage J.P., who was in charge of PULPIT GAP near the mine shaft. He handled his men with good judgment, killing two men, securing two prisoners, and causing the remainder to retire.

Major, Commanding.
2/13th Battn. (Kensington) London Regt.

From:- Officer Commanding,
         2/13th (Kensington) Battalion London Regiment.

To :- 179th Infantry Brigade,
         Advanced Headquarters.

                                        12th October, 1916
                                        Ref :- V.D.33

           SUBJECT: RAID ON PULPIT SAP.

           Since my report of the 11th instant, a third dead
German has been brought in from north of the PULPIT CRATER.
He was found near the end of the short sap (A.4.d.50.40).
His effects and arms have been forwarded to your Headquarters.

           It is hoped that another identification may be
obtained tonight.

           With regard to our casualties :-

           This Battalion lost 1 officer wounded, 2 other
ranks killed, and 18 other ranks wounded.

           The German raiders did not put more than 4 or 5
of our men out of action.

           From personal enquiries from the Medical Officer,
, from Company Officers and N.C.O's, I am satisfied that not
more than two of the above casualties were caused by rifle
or machine gun fire, and not more than 3 casualties by bombs.
The rest of the casualties (16) were caused by 77 mm's,
4.2 hows., T.M's and Sling Bombs sent over during the barrage.

                                        Major, Commanding,
                                   2/13th (Kensington) Battn. London Regiment.

CONFIDENTIAL

2/13th Battalion London Regt.

War Diary

for

November 1916

Army Form C. 2118

WAR DIARY
or
INTELLIGENCE SUMMARY
(Erase heading not required.)

Instructions regarding War Diaries and Intelligence Summaries are contained in F. S. Regs., Part II. and the Staff Manual respectively. Title Pages will be prepared in manuscript.

Place	Date	Hour	Summary of Events and Information	Remarks and references to Appendices
PROUVILLE	Nov 1.	2 p.m.	Operation	Inspection by Commander-in-Chief	RPS
do	Nov 3	8.30 a.m. to 3 p.m.	Strength Operation	2/13th Battalion London Regiment proceeded to VAUCHELLE-LES-QUESNOY	RPS
VAUCHELLE-LES-QUESNOY	Nov 4		Strength	5 Decrease	RPS
do	Nov 5		Strength	2 Increase 2 8 Decrease	Appendix 1. RPS appendix 1.
do	Nov 7		Strength	1 Increase	RPS appendix 1.
do	Nov 9		Strength	3 Increase	RPS appendix 1.
do	Nov 10		Strength	1 Decrease	RPS appendix 1.
do	Nov 11		Strength	1 Decrease	RPS appendix 1.
do	Nov 12		Strength	43 Increase (Draft 43 men)	RPS appendix 1.
do	Nov 14	9 a.m. to 3 p.m.	Operation	2/13th Battalion London Regiment moved to LONGPRE-LE-CORPS-SAINT entrained at	RPS
LONGPRE-LE-CORPS-SAINT	do	4.30 p.m. to 6.15 p.m.	Operation	2/13th Battalion London Regiment entrained and proceeded at 7.20 p.m. to MARSEILLES.	RPS
MARSEILLES	Nov 18	12.20 a.m.	Operation	2/13th Battalion London Regiment detrained and proceeded to CARCASSONNE Camp, the Transport Section going to FOURNIER Camp.	RPS

Army Form C. 2118

WAR DIARY
or
INTELLIGENCE SUMMARY
(Erase heading not required.)

Instructions regarding War Diaries and Intelligence Summaries are contained in F. S. Regs., Part II. and the Staff Manual respectively. Title Pages will be prepared in manuscript.

Place	Date	Hour	Summary of Events and Information	Remarks and references to Appendices
MARSEILLES	Nov 19	8 a.m	2/13th Battalion London Regiment (less Transport Section) left Camp and proceeded to Quay.	R.P.S.
do	do	9 a.m to 11 a.m	2/13th Battalion London Regiment (less Transport Section) embarked on S.S. TRANSYLVANIA.	R.P.S.
			2.1 Decrease	R.P.S. Appendix 1.
do	Nov 20	2 a.m	S.S. TRANSYLVANIA sailed.	R.P.S.
MALTA.	Nov 22	11 a.m	S.S. TRANSYLVANIA arrived and came to anchor in MASA SIROCCA BAY	R.P.S.
do	Nov 24	10 a.m to 12 noon	S.S. TRANSYLVANIA up-ran anchorage and proceeded to GRAND HARBOUR, VALETTA.	R.P.S.
do	Nov 27	10 a.m	S.S. TRANSYLVANIA left her moorings.	R.P.S.
SALONIKA	Nov 30	10 a.m	S.S. TRANSYLVANIA anchored in harbour	R.P.S.
do	do	11 a.m to 2.30 pm	S.S. TRANSYLVANIA made fast to Quay and 2/13 Battn. London Regt. disembarked (less Transport Section).	R.P.S.
do	do	4 pm	2/13th Battn. London Regt. (less Transport Section) arrived at No. 15 Standing Camp on the outskirts of SALONIKA - MONASTIR road.	R.P.S.

No. 7 Infantry Base Depot.

Nominal roll of draft proceeding to join 2/13th Bn. London Regt. on 10th November 1916.

```
No. 1507  L/Cpl.  Brown, W.F.
    4616    "     Pulley, W.
    6127  Pte.    Beer, H.E.
    6182    "     Wood, L.J.
    6067    "     Mortimer, C.C.
    6069    "     Mager, A.J.
    6071    "     Cotterill, A.D.
    6192    "     Davis, W.H.
    5910    "     Howell, W.R.
    5878    "     Killip, T.
    5905    "     Slatter, F.S.
    6073    "     Hickenbotham, J.R.
    6125    "     Clark, T.W.
    4935    "     Worss, R.H.
    6131    "     Babb, F.
    6134    "     Dickeson, A.W.
    6044    "     Dadswell, R.A.
    6052    "     Conyers, C.M.
    5347    "     Huggins, C.W.
    5381    "     Gooch, N.
    5882    "     Davis, T.E.
    5881    "     Osborne, S.J.
    6057    "     Craggs, C.J.
    5995    "     Cane, F.D.
    6038    "     Rhodes, H.B.
    6199    "     Butler, H.
    5470    "     Duncan, W.
    6092    "     Peck, F.S.
    6093    "     Keene, N.A.
    6078    "     Haselden, G.A.
    6162    "     Loader, G.P.
    6161    "     Phillimore, R.M.
    6153    "     Tapster, F.S.
    6172    "     Edwards, E.M.
    6134    "     Davis, F.G.
    6083    "     Ford, A.M.
    5498    "     Hopkins, T.F.
    6103    "     Head, W.T.
    5941    "     Harvey, F.
    6189    "     Williams, R.J.
    4959    "     Maynell, F.
    6027    "     Heasman, G.T.
    5401    "     Wilkenson, H.            Bootmaker
    6554    "     Caswell, H.S.              do.

    4931    "     House, A.P.
    5622    "     Gimber, W.E.H.


    6027    "     Heasman, G.T.
```

Regimental No., Rank, and Name.	Sqdn., Batty., or Co.	Particulars of Casualties, etc., and Date.	Inc.	Dec.	Strength
1/11/16					
Nil					952
2/11/16					
Nil.					952
3/11/16					
Nil.					952
4/11/16					
5784 Pte.Parsons T.	A	Sent to a Cas.Clg.Station from			
3438 Pte.Grew J.T.	B	Canadian Field Amb.		4	
4066 Cpl.Wood S.	A				
5962 Pte.Stevens H.H?	A				
3874 Pte.Ellis	A	Sent Base, Under Age.		1	957
5/11/16					
4647 Pte.Brooks C.F.	A)	Returned to duty from Cas.			
5697 Pte.Shaw L.H.	C)	Clg.Station.	2		959
5671 Pte.Fowler S.D.	C				
4243 Pte.Pincher W.J.	A				
4694 Pte.Dimes F.J.	C				
5712 Pte.Coley D.M.	D				
3258 Pte.Rivers G.W.	B				
5838 Pte.Overall G.E.	D.				
4050 Pte.Reeves W.H.	B				
4736 Pte.Dunkin A.L.	C				
5737 Pte.Hadley A	H				
4585 Pte.Allen S.M.	B				
3663 Pte.Orman A.E.V.	C				
3495 Pte.Evans W.	C				
570 Sgt.Atkinson W.D.	A				
4535 Pte.Seward A.	B				
3082 Pte.Pearce J.	C				
4260 Pte.Curtis A.R.	B				
5762 Pte.Lovell G.E.J.	A				
3445 Pte.Hurley A.C.	B				
3518 Pte.Fairer F.W.	D				
3397 Pte.Langdon C.R.	D	Sent to Cas.Clearing Stations			
4076 Pte.Derry S.H.	B				
5129 Pte.Tyler P.	D				
3621 Pte.Way F.C.	D				
4047 Pte.Hull J.	B				
2673 Sgt.Partridge D.W.	C				
4631 Pte.Bunney A.M.	C				
4310 Sgt Prior S.A.	B				
3538 Pte.Bissett A.	B			28	931
6/11/16					
Nil					931
7/11/16					
3737 Pte.Hadley A.	B	Returned by Cas.Clg.Stat.	1		932
8/11/16					
Nil					932
9/11/16					
3538 Pte.Bissett A.	B	Returned to duty from			
5838 Pte.Overall G.E.	D	Cas Clg.Stat	3		935
4243 Pte.Pincher W.J.	A				

Sub. No. of Order.	Subject.	Regimental No., Rank and Name.	Sqdn., Batty. or Co.	Particulars of Casualties, &c., and date.	Inc.	Dec.	Strength
	10/11/16	5584 Pte. Ingall C.H.L.	A.Coy.	Sent to England Comm.Auth.W.O.L. 9/75/703		1	934
	11/11/16	5554 Pte. Wright	C. "	To a. C.C.Stat		1	933
	12/11/16	4076 Pte. Derry	B.Coy.	Returned from C.C.S.	1		934
	13/11/16	4089 Sgt Wallis J	A	} Sent to Base as permanently unfit with 60th Divt A.D.M.S			
		5826 Pte Hopkins P	B				
		4022 " Watkins	B				
		5088 " Ellis G	C				930
	12/11/16	Draft of 42 men as per list attached from No 7 Inf Base Depot			42		972
	13/11/16	5129 Pte Tyler P	C Coy	Returned from Cas. Clg. Stat.	1		973
	19/11/16	4022 Pte Goodyer V	A	} Left behind Sick in Hospital in France when Battalion embarked		19	954
		2996 Pte Snelgrove V A	A				
		5784 " Parsons T	A				
		2067 A/Sgt Kemp J H	A				
		4243 Pte Fincher J H	A				
		5668 Sgt Brooke F L	B				
		3486 Pte Webb G A	B				
		5433 " Price D D	B				
		2791 " Moreton W A	B				
		4565 " Hempston J J	B				
		5687 " Marshall A L	C				
		4954 " Reed T M	C				
		5685 " Milne C	C				
		2764 " Clarke E A B	C				
		5831 " Salton V S	C				
		4392 " Parsons D A	D				
		2780 " Shingleton W H	D				
		4080 " Snead	D				
		3378 " Robins F C	D				
		5580 Pte Haines G K	A	} Left in France to be trans- ferred to Cadet Schools		2	952
		Sgt Reto C W S	D				
	34/11/16						952
							952

www.ingramcontent.com/pod-product-compliance
Lightning Source LLC
Chambersburg PA
CBHW080906230426
43664CB00016B/2739